Sir Hubert Wilkins

Among the Books by Lowell Thomas

SIR HUBERT WILKINS

His World of Adventure

A Biography by

LOWELL THOMAS

McGraw-Hill Book Company, Inc.
New York Toronto London

SIR HUBERT WILKINS

Library of Congress
  Catalog Card Number: 61-16533

64240

I would like to salute three people for the help they gave me on
this book:
    Colonel Edward P. F. Eagan, who cajoled and prodded me
into adding new material to the book-length manuscript I had
shelved some thirty years ago when I became involved in radio.
Colonel Eddie Eagan also was largely responsible for the ashes
of Sir Hubert being taken by nuclear submarine to the North
Pole.
    Winston Ross, who was most helpful in rounding up docu-
ments, photographs, and information about Sir Hubert's activi-
ties, both in his early and late years.
    Lady Suzanne Wilkins, who checked the manuscript and wrote
the final chapter.

                                                        L.T.

Contents

It was soon after World War I that I first heard of George Hubert Wilkins, and even then he already was a legend among those who knew him.

I was in London, at Covent Garden Royal Opera House, telling the story of T.E. Lawrence and the Desert War. Until then the world had heard little of the Arab revolt against the Turks, and nothing at all of Lawrence's feat of organizing the Bedouin and helping overthrow the Ottoman Empire. More than a million Britishers came to hear me tell about Lawrence and the Arabs as a part of my story of the Middle East campaign, General Allenby's capture of Jerusalem, and the sweep on to Damascus. One day before the end of my run, I received a cable from the Prime Minister of Australia. Many of the troops under Allenby's command were Anzacs, and Billy Hughes, the dynamic, informal Aussie P.M., invited me to come to the lands down under and tell their story to their compatriots.

In those days no airplanes flew to Australia, so this meant a sea voyage of more than a month. I accepted, and in the course of my visit I naturally met many men, both in Australia and New Zealand, who had been prominent in World War I. Among them was Sir John Monash, top general of the Australian forces, their commander in chief in Europe.

Sir John presided at a luncheon in honor of my wife and me, in Melbourne. Naturally we talked about Lawrence, since my story of the Arab part of the Palestine campaign had created a sensation. The role Lawrence played had been kept virtually a secret, and I had been the only civilian observer with him.

I asked Sir John whether Australia had any counterpart to Lawrence, any individual who stood out from the tens of thousands who had served under him.

Monash replied, "Yes, there was one. But when I mentioned him in the first edition of my war memoirs, it caused such an uproar I dropped the reference from the second edition." There had long been a tradition that a commander in chief seldom, if ever, praised any individual below the rank of a general, for if he mentioned one, he was under constant pressure to include a host of others and their deeds of valor. The name of the young officer who had caused him this embarrassment, he said, was Captain George Hubert Wilkins.

When I asked Sir John for a few details, he told me how in the period just prior to and during the first years of the war, Wilkins, a young chap from the "out-back" country of South Australia, had been in the Arctic with a Canadian expedition led by Vilhjalmur Stefansson. Somewhere up there in the Polar Sea, mail eventually reached them by ship, and in their letters they heard that the British Empire and her allies were locked in a great battle with the Kaiser's Germany. Wilkins, as soon as he could be spared, resigned from the expedition, made his way out over the ice, and eventually went to Ottawa to get his release. After that, because of red tape, he had to sail for Australia and there join the Australian Flying Corps. From Australia, at last, he was ordered to the fighting front in France.

What happened to him from then on is a story of epic proportions. Although Wilkins went into action some two years late, he made up for that in a hurry, by taking part in every major Australian engagement. He was a highly accomplished and absolutely fearless combat photographer. Wounded many times, and even buried by shellfire, he always came through. At times he brought in the wounded, at others he supplied vital intelligence of enemy activity he had observed in his work. At one point he even rallied troops as a combat officer. Said Sir John Monash, "His war record was unique."

Stefansson, under whom Wilkins had spent the years 1913 to 1915 in the Arctic, had high praise for his protégé. Years later, after Wilkins had been knighted, and had many more expeditions under his belt, Stefansson gave Sir Hubert the highest accolade of all. He said he was one of the foremost explorers of this or any era.

And others testified to Wilkins' qualities as colleague and leader. Bernard Grant, the journalist with whom Wilkins, as a motion-picture photographer, shared the alarms and risks of the Balkan War in 1912, wrote at the time: "I must pay a tribute to Wilkins of the cinematograph, one of the best companions in the world, because of his continual cheerfulness, his knowledge of handi-craft, of horses, and of all rough work and outdoor life. He has had many adventures in wild places of the world which have taught him valuable lessons, among them being the gift of leader-ship, instant decision in moments of peril, and a quick way of righting something that has gone wrong.... Personally, I do not know what I should have done without such an experienced fellow by my side, and I am glad here to give the praise that was his due." Wilkins, at the time Grant wrote this of him, was just twenty-four.

Sixteen years later, after Wilkins and Ben Eielson had electri-fied the world with their epic flight over the Arctic from Alaska to Spitsbergen, the British Minister of Colonies, L.S. Amery, told the Royal Geographical Society: "Not since Balboa stood on a peak in Darien and saw for the first time the broad Pacific, has so significant a new view of the world been spread before human eyes in one day as when Wilkins and Eielson flew in twenty-two hours across the unexplored Arctic Ocean from America to Eu-rope."

When General Monash told me about Wilkins, I of course real-ized that he must be an outstanding man with a great story to tell. But some years were to pass before I finally met Wilkins in New York. From then on we saw a good deal of each other—when he was between expeditions. Then we talked of Australia, of his experiences in two wars, of his explorations. He never ceased to astonish me with his knowledge. His memory seemed to hold every experience like a specimen in amber.

In all, he had been on more than a dozen expeditions, frequently as the leader. And then there had been numerous flights—around the world, to the Arctic, and to the Antarctic. The last time we were together was on a memorable flight to the North Pole in 1957, a project that happened to be my own idea. It included a look at the Dew Line, a visit to a camp of scientists on an ice floe in the Arctic Ocean, and the Ultimate North. In the party was my friend Admiral Donald MacMillan, last survivor of the Peary expedition that reached the Pole in 1909, and now a patriarch in his eighties. MacMillan himself had made some thirty journeys to the Arctic but actually had never gotten to the North Pole. I thought something should be done to fulfill this great desire of his life.

Eventually the idea broadened. Actually my son, Lowell Jr., had organized the expedition, and was the head of it. Since we were to fly north in a Globemaster, a huge plane with plenty of room, why not include a few more veterans of Arctic exploration? So along with MacMillan we invited Colonel Bernt Balchen, first man to pilot a plane over both poles, Peter Freuchen, Danish explorer and chronicler of Arctic adventures, and my old friend Sir Hubert Wilkins.

Early on our journey, shortly after arrival in Alaska, we were saddened by the sudden death of that colorful Viking, Peter Freuchen, whose ashes we carried on to the Pole and finally scattered over the American base at Thule in Greenland—Thule, where he had lived as a young explorer among the Eskimos, and to which Freuchen himself had given that name.

On this flight, as always, Sir Hubert Wilkins was quiet, efficient, humorous, and knowledgeable. I wish we had recorded the conversations between these Arctic giants during those days and nights in Alaska, in the plane, on the polar ice, at the North Pole, and in Greenland. Between them they had been nearly everywhere in the North. As for Sir Hubert, he regaled us with matchless stories of the expeditions he had been on, the flights he had made, and, of course, that first historic venture under the polar ice in 1931, when he was leader of the *Nautilus* expedition.

On our return to the States, Wilkins went back to his work as a cold-weather expert with the U.S. Quartermaster Corps. He was carrying on experiments at a laboratory in Natick, Massachusetts, when he suffered his fatal heart attack. Some months later, Commander James Calvert of the U.S. Navy carried his ashes north beneath the polar ice in the atomic submarine *Skate*. On the seventeenth of March, 1959, when the *Skate* was at the geographical North Pole, Calvert gave the order to surface. When the ship broke through the ice and her deck rose clear in the dim polar night, the submarine crew climbed from the hatch into an Arctic gale, with the thermometer at 20 degrees below zero. Amid falling snow Calvert read the traditional Navy burial service and then scattered to the Arctic winds the ashes of Sir Hubert Wilkins, one of the most brilliant explorers of all time.

That, in brief, is the outline. Now for the story of Sir Hubert Wilkins' life and world of adventure as he told it to me over the thirty-odd years I knew him.

1

Out-back Boyhood

Some people think I should have a family tree. A number of them have written to me to say they have gone to the trouble to trace my English ancestry back to Bishop John Wilkins of Chester, who lived through the turmoil of the English Revolution, married Oliver Cromwell's sister, and survived the Restoration of the Stuarts in 1660. They even claim that from an engraving of his face they can see a family resemblance between us.

Now, it is true that more than three hundred years ago the good bishop, startling as it may seem today, was advocating the use of a submarine. He called it "an Ark for submarine Navigations," to be propelled by oars projecting from its sides and maneuvered the way a fish moves its fins. Not only that, but in 1648 he wrote that a submarine would be the best method of transport to the North Pole. There would be no trouble from the cold, he asserted, because the submersible could be warmed by fires inside. Nor would there be danger from the ice because the adventurous voyager would be traveling beneath the ice. This was all just my ancestor's speculation at the time, of course. But what amazingly accurate speculation it was for 1648!

Actually, I know nothing about our family any farther back than my pioneer grandfather, who sailed out of England to Australia more than a hundred years ago when the continent was still unexplored. It had been supposed to be almost uninhabitable desert, and of course much of it still is. A handful of adventurers, my grandfather among them, landed on the coast of South Australia and made their way into the interior, where they found a beautiful, fertile plain. Compared to crowded England with its

7

tiny fields and its ugly factory towns spreading grimy coal smoke everywhere, this mild, sunny land of limitless horizons was an inviting paradise.

Returning to London, the explorers obtained a charter from the British Government, similar to the charter granted to the historic Hudson's Bay Company in Canada. This was the formation of the South Australia Company. Early in 1836 two ships started out to carry settlers to the new country, with my grandfather and grandmother sailing in the first ship. After a long voyage the pioneers reached the shore at a point that is now Glenelg, South Australia, where they landed and built a camp. The spot was beautifully situated on a natural harbor. In the weeks that followed my grandfather helped to survey the site and lay out the plan for a new town near Glenelg. That town is now the city of Adelaide, capital of South Australia. It was so named at the express wish of King William IV of England after his royal consort, Queen Adelaide.

The first child born in the Glenelg camp, in October of 1836, was my father, Harry Wilkins. Shortly after my father's birth, a fire swept through the camp, destroying most of it. All my grandfather's family papers were burned with his other property, leaving the Wilkinses in a new land with a new generation cut off from its English past, not only by thousands of miles of ocean but also by the loss of the family records.

In 1851 when gold was discovered at Ballarat, Victoria, three hundred miles southeast of Adelaide, my father joined the gold rush. This was a gigantic boom for the sparsely settled land; the rush even attracted disappointed "Forty-Niners" from far-off California. By 1853, when my father was seventeen, the gold fields near Ballarat had produced more than three million ounces of the precious metal, valued at more than twelve million pounds. But 1853 was the peak year and the inevitable slack set in. Failing to find his fortune, my father turned back to the wide open spaces to become a drover; he was one of the men who drove the first big herd of cattle into South Australia. These men were called "sundowners." They urged the animals along from horseback by their musical cries and cracking whips, assisted by trained dogs, and they camped wherever they were in that vast, unfenced country when the sun sank down below the horizon.

My father loved the outdoor life. He took up a big holding of land some 120 miles north of Adelaide, married, and settled down. His station, the Australian term for a big farm, spread out to the east of a wild mountain, Mount Bryan. It was in rolling terrain on the edge of the rain belt, part of it on the dry desert without trees, and part in the bush country where the gum trees, or eucalyptus, were in places dwarfed by poor soil and lack of water.

My parents spent nearly all their adult lives on that station. My father worked hard to raise sheep and cattle and to provide for my mother and his growing family. Life was not easy; my mother had twelve children before I was born on October 31, 1888, and most of them had died in infancy. During these years my parents saw Australia grow up about them. By the time my elder brothers Frank and Peter were born, the state to the east, New South Wales, had been partly settled. So had Victoria and part of Queensland. The cities of Sydney and Melbourne had already grown large, and along the coast, at least, Australia was no longer a pioneer country.

But in the interior it was different. Nameless when my parents settled there, it became Netfield—because my father was the first in those parts to fence the land. When wire fencing came on the market he realized its value for keeping out the pesky kangaroos and the wallabies, whom one might call first cousins to the kangaroo. Amusing to watch as they hop about wild, these animals are no help to the farmer trying to raise a crop. The same is true of the rabbits that had already overrun much of Australia by my father's time, even though they had been imported from England but a few years before. My father borrowed money from the government and enclosed roughly five or six thousand acres within wire net, a considerable feat in those days for a farmer in the Australia "back blocks," as our holdings in the interior were termed.

My earliest recollections are of this almost endless expanse of land stretching to the far horizon, of the great herds of sheep, and of the men on horseback chasing the leaping kangaroos, and the wild, yellow-dog "dingos" that would kill one of the flock when given half a chance.

I remember, too, as a small child going out with my father to carry food to the aborigines when they gathered by the hundreds for their tribal meetings, which they called "corroborees." These were the original people of Australia, who had been there when white men first arrived.

The Australian natives are of several different physical types and cultures. In our part of the Big Land Down Under, they were a small, swarthy people who looked something like the Neanderthal man I saw illustrated in science books. There were always a few families of them wandering about. They were nomads, shifting from place to place along the borders of settled land, living mainly from the small game which they tracked and killed with admirable skill and cunning.

For their tribal festivities they assembled in great numbers. At other times when game was scarce, they would come into the stations to ask for food. My father always fed them whenever there was need. I went out among them with my father, and came to learn some of their terms which they created from English words. They often asked us for "bullocky tucker," which meant anything so large or heavy that it must be transported in an ox-cart. When they wanted tea, sugar, or tobacco they asked for "nanto tucker," which meant anything that could be carried on a man's back or on a pack horse. "Nanto" meant horse.

They would cook the food we gave them in huge iron caldrons over their open fires. They might fill a caldron half full of milk and pour whole sacks of flour into it, stirring it up until it was firm. When this was cooked they called it "burgoo," a term, I learned long afterward, used for a kind of stew made in Kentucky. The natives ate this mixture quite neatly, with their fingers. As a little chap too small to see over the rim of the steaming caldrons I often wanted to taste "burgoo," but I was not allowed to.

When I grew older, I occasionally went camping and hunting with the "abos." Even as a youth I was struck by their intelligence and their highly developed principles of conduct, as contrasted with their primitive technical development. Their totem system was far more intricate than the European social structure in a comparable setting. It required some considerable intelligence, without the aid of writing, to understand it; yet many of these people seemed to know it thoroughly. At an early age the boys were well versed in their vast system of laws dealing with personal conduct, property, marriage, and intermarriage. They had what seemed to me an enormous knowledge of primitive natural science —botany, biology, geography, geology. Because they knew so much about the natural world around us, they were always explaining its laws to me. From this contact with them, my curiosity to know more was stimulated beyond measure.

These aboriginal people believed in a Supreme Controller of the universe, and they believed in spirits here on earth. While they were supposed by our most learned anthropologists to be mere savages, among the most primitive people on the face of the earth, it seemed to me that their moral standards were truly admirable. I always found them chaste, law-abiding, and kind. I still think that their behavior was superior to much of ours in our supposedly high state of civilization.

Although learning from these natives was an important part of my early education, I also had to attend school. My English schooling began at home because the school teacher lived in my father's house and drove his horse and wagon from there to the school. This was a stone building at Mount Bryan East, a small community about three miles from our door. With the teacher living right at hand, it is not surprising that lessons were laid out for me by the time I was three; I was reading and writing before I was five. At nine I had passed the state school examinations, which qualified me for entrance to high school.

Between my school work and the necessary tasks on the station, my boyhood was not burdened with idle hours. When I was nine I had my own horses, my own plot of land, my own hay, and my own flock of two hundred sheep to care for. I led an active outdoor life, helping my father and my grown-up brothers with the station work—riding boundaries to mend fences, killing rabbits and other pests, helping with the reaping and sheaving. In those days we reaped wheat by stripping the heads from the stalks in the fields. Then they were hauled to the winnower where the grain was separated from the chaff.

Because most of the farmers were too busy on the land to drive great distances to get supplies and sell fresh produce, hawkers drove through the country in horse-drawn traps, stopping at all the stations within twenty miles or more. They would buy all the surplus butter and chickens, fruit and almonds we had for sale, and take them into the towns. These travelers, or anyone who came by, would often stop for the night. It was the custom in that wide-open country to be hospitable to visitors. Through these passing people most of the news of the countryside was spread from one isolated station to another.

Once or twice a year our family drove twenty-five miles to Burra, the nearest town. We always went there for the sheep sales. When we made this long trip we drove two or four horses to the wagon, depending on the season and the condition of the roads. We always started before dawn so as to get there and back in a day.

In those days, as now, the busy season was shearing time, when expert shearers came and camped on the place. Most of these men were professional sheep-shearers who really knew their business and worked steadily. Some, however, were young fellows just wanting to make quick money. Still others were wanderers, not overanxious to work. We hired perhaps twenty-five shearers, plus a number of roustabouts whose job it was to go out after the flocks, perhaps for several miles, herd them together, drive them through the shearing sheds, then through pools of sheep-dip, and brand them.

A good man could shear 100 to 120 sheep between sunrise and sunset. My brothers could shear 200, and so could my father. It became a kind of family tradition that each son should shear his 200 sheep. I sheared 75 when I was fifteen. It was a job one had to learn by experience. You must hold the sheep still and slice the thick mat of wool neatly and quickly off its body without wasting wool or hurting the sheep. Before very long our skins absorbed the odor of mutton and wool, and our hands were soon soft and white from the lanolin in the fleece.

Nearly every evening, except in sheep-shearing time, we went out hunting. The quarry included bandicoots, a kind of large rodent with a long, pointed nose, and kangaroos, and wallabies. We used kangaroo dogs, a species of greyhound, to run the game. For sport on Saturday afternoons, we used to let down a few panels of fence so the game could come into the enclosure. Then we went after it on horseback. The point was to kill the running animals with a stirrup, which we would remove from the saddle and swing like a polo mallet. The animals would run, dodge, and turn in their tracks while we rode pell-mell after them, one foot in the remaining stirrup and one hanging free, our only weapon the empty stirrup held at the ready.

The horses seemed as keen for the hunt as we were. When the quarry would suddenly jump the fence, the horse would leap too, hot after it. Many men were killed at this sport. My uncle was killed when a hare ran under the fence. His horse jumped the fence sideways, fell, and crushed him. I was pretty well cut up myself once when my foot caught in the stirrup and I was dragged head down by a horse galloping after a kangaroo. A kangaroo can outrun a horse for a few hundred yards, then the horse will begin to gain on it. My horse knew this and didn't want to stop, even though I was no longer on his back.

Some of the kangaroos we chased were six feet tall. I have seen them pick up small dogs and run away with them. When dogs corner a kangaroo, he will often make a break, grab the leading dog in his forearms, and bound away to the nearest water hole to drown him. If the dog is not quickly rescued, the kangaroo keeps pushing him under water until he drowns.

Nearly every boy in the Australian back country in my day had a pet young kangaroo or wallaby. They are extremely intelligent animals, gentle and friendly when they are young. But at four or five years of age they become dangerous and often injure their owners. They attack by gripping with their forearms, at the same time balancing on their tails and ripping with their hind claws. In no time, they can strip a man's clothes off and tear his flesh to shreds.

Our living was precarious because we never knew what weather nature held in store for us. Our land was fertile and in seasons of sufficient rainfall it yielded abundantly. Then the countryside was prosperous and happy. The tens of thousands of sheep grazed well, multiplied, and were fat; the horses were sleek; and living on the farms was agreeable. But following a good season there might be a killing drought, which brought tragedy to our lives.

Anyone who has seen the slow starvation of tens of thousands of animals, day after day, can know fully what I mean. It was horrible to watch them getting thinner and weaker little by little, to hear their ceaseless bleating and moaning in the heat of day and through the long nights, to see the dry earth turned to dust by their desperate pawing for roots. Finally, they could stagger no farther and they just stood, mutely dying. All the time, one good rain could have saved them. Yet it was impossible to say whether or not the rain would come in time.

It was the uncertainty about the weather that ruined us in the years of drought. If we could have foreseen the rainless seasons we could have guarded against them by stocking fodder and reducing our herds, and so we should have saved ourselves and our animals. But we could not foretell the weather. It was this ignorance of what was coming that ruined us when the drought set in and made the entire country a scene of disaster and despair.

As a youngster I began to realize that all this agony came from our own ignorance. I became especially interested in the science of weather forecasting, and I determined to read everything I could find on meteorology. At the same time, I was becoming aware of the great strides that were being recorded in science and mechanical invention far from the "out-back" country of South Australia. At the end of the nineteenth century and in the early 1900s, the theories of Darwin, Huxley, Spencer, and Nietzsche were having a pronounced effect on human thought everywhere. Marvel after marvel of discovery and invention was being reported, and man began to feel there was no limit to his power to master and to control nature.

We were fascinated to learn in 1897 that the French Government had supplied funds with which Clément Ader built a machine resembling a bird. He tried to fly in it, but failed. Even so, his experiments hinted at the coming of aviation. Then I read in 1900 that Count von Zeppelin on three different occasions kept his long, cigar-shaped, powered balloon in the air for a sustained period with several men aboard, at times actually attaining the speed of 18 miles per hour.

If men could accomplish things like this, I asked myself, was there anything they couldn't do? Could they not eventually conquer the weather? I do not remember how young I was when I first thought of the possibility of our being able to foretell the weather for a long period ahead, but it must have seemed then only a dream even more fantastic than the age-old dream of flying machines. But with the exploits of Ader and Count von Zeppelin, and later the Wright brothers, my boyhood dreams began to appear somewhat more realistic.

Several times while I was a boy my father was completely ruined by droughts. It seemed that no sooner did we recover from one dry year, pay our debts, and begin to prosper, than another merciless drought seared the land once more, starved the flocks, and ruined our work.

In the great drought of 1902, however, my father did not do so badly. With some premonition of trouble coming, he had conserved dry feed. When the dry spell hit our land, my father was able to save our animals. He could even buy additional stock, keep them alive, and rent some pasture to neighbors. After the drought he found that he could at last retire on a meager income. He was then past sixty-six years old.

My brother Frank took over the land, and my parents took me to Adelaide to live. Although my father and mother had enjoyed their life out back in the bush country on their own station, Adelaide was a much better place for them in their years of retirement. And they knew it would be of greater advantage to their young son in his middle teens. It was time for me to be getting on with the serious business of training for my life's work.

2

Off to Adventure

There were both a university and a school of mines in Adelaide. I found that the South Australian School of Mines and Industries offered a better practical course in electrical engineering, but the University of Adelaide had a better mechanical engineering laboratory. I therefore entered as a part-time student in both, and simultaneously I studied music at the Elder Conservatorium, which was part of the university.

Surprising as it might seem in a boy from out back, I was passionately fond of music and eager to master the means of making it. I had never been allowed to touch a piano. To my strict Methodist parents, the piano was an instrument associated with amusements in the public house and cheap music hall. I was permitted to play an organ, but a piano was supposed to be as immoral as a deck of cards. Although we had lived practically isolated, twenty-five miles from any semblance of a town, my parents would have been horrified at the thought of exposing my morals to the corruption of a pack of cards or piano music.

In Adelaide I continued to live under the same kind of restrictions. At the conservatory I learned to sing and to play the organ, violin, flute, and cello. I played them for many years afterward with the greatest pleasure and, I hope, some skill. But I did not touch the supposedly immoral piano in Adelaide—or later.

Even though we now lived in the city, I had no boy or girl companions because I was simply too busy. In the mornings I worked as apprentice to a mechanical engineer, in the afternoons I was at the university or the school of mines, and in the evenings at the conservatory. My Sundays were occupied with singing at church services. I was paid to sing in the Wesleyan choir, and the pay was important because the Wilkinses had little money.

My pay as an apprentice was seventy-five cents a week for the first year. I was supposed to receive an apprentice's pay for four years, but I caught on so rapidly to practical engineering that at the end of two years I was given the job of general supervisor, earning more money than anyone else in the department.

Most of my professional course was at the school of mines, where I studied in almost every department. My subjects covered manufacturing, electrical motors, internal combustion engines, blacksmith shop and foundry work, fitting and turning, electric motor and dynamo construction, arc lamp manufacturing, gold plating, all kinds of electrical installation, and motor car and bicycle work. At the same time, I was studying theoretical science.

One day in 1905 when I was installing electric wire in a new theater in Adelaide, someone came to me and said that there were some fellows with a traveling motion-picture show in a tent nearby who were having quite a time making their gasoline-powered generator work. Would I have a go at it?

Always keen on tinkering with engines, I walked over to the tent. Sure enough, the show people were in a stew over that balky generator. They were covered with oil and grease, and they had been sweating and straining to make her go, but the generator would just cough and backfire and stop. More people had gathered around to see the struggle with the engine than were going into the tent to see the motion pictures. It appeared the show people were relying on that generator to furnish power for their show when they toured the country districts where there was no central electricity. In Adelaide they had hitched up to the city power lines, but they were preparing for a tour.

After I spotted the trouble and got the motor going for them, I was curious to examine their motion-picture projector. Stepping inside the tent, in no time at all I was asking the operator to explain it to me. Off came the cover almost at once and I was given my first guided tour to the motion pictures. I was fascinated immediately. This chance introduction to the wonderful world of the cinema was to lead me into a series of adventures shaping the future course of my life.

I soon became an avid devotee of photography, and spent as much time as I could spare at that cinema tent, learning not only how to operate and repair the projector but also how to take motion pictures myself. Occasionally, when the master of ceremonies during the vaudeville part of the show called for volunteers, I was daring enough to come to the stage to sing a popular number, like "In the Valley Where the Bluebirds Sing." Sentimental colored illustrations were thrown on the screen to put the audience in the right mood for the particular song.

At age seventeen, the rules of my apprenticeship required me to work either in the central electric light station or to take full charge of some small electric plant for six months. Show business had already opened its doors to me as to a new world; I loved everything about it. So quite naturally I chose to take charge of the electric lighting outfit for a carnival company on tour.

The carnival carried about a hundred people—singers, dancers, acrobats, and roustabouts. I had such a good time traveling with them that I forgot my studies in Adelaide and remained with the show. For eighteen months we toured all the big towns of South Australia and part of Victoria, until the show broke up. So far as Adelaide was concerned, I had finished all the courses that interested me, and I now decided to strike out in the world for myself.

I spent the better part of a year in Sydney, the biggest and most active city in Australia, as a tent-cinema operator. Between times I was out with cameras, learning everything I could about taking action motion pictures. I realized that the old still cameras were all right for scenery or to show people posing. But only the motion-picture camera could catch the drama of a speeding automobile, or a galloping horse with a daring trick rider doing stunts on his back, and bring a thrill to hundreds of people in a theater long afterward. I knew motion pictures were going to develop into a big thing.

In 1908, when I was twenty, just as the Strand Picture Theater opened in Pitt Street, Sydney, I found that my interest in motion pictures had finally paid off with a job offer. The Gaumont picture people in England wrote asking me to come to work for them. I was overjoyed and quickly returned to Adelaide to say good-by to my mother and father and to gather up the rest of my belongings. Oddly enough, considering the strictness of my upbringing, my parents did not object to my plan, and gave me their blessing. Nor did they withdraw it even when I told them I was going to return to Sydney as a stowaway on a coastwise cargo ship, a journey of a couple of days, and write a story about my experiences. A ship was supposed to leave for Sydney early the next morning. As I said farewell to my father, then aged seventy-two, little did I know I would never see him again.

After addressing my baggage to Sydney and leaving it at the express office, I went down to the Adelaide docks and approached the ship I planned to board. I hung around until dusk, trying to appear inconspicuous. Loading was going on, and there was always someone going up or down the gangplank, leaving me no chance to get on board unnoticed. It was not until late evening that the loading was finished. Finally I found the dockside clear. On deck the hatches were closed, and no one was to be seen on the wharf or on the ship's deck except one watchman standing at the head of the gangplank.

Then along came a couple of drunken sailors, beer bottles in each hand. Under his arm one of them carried a newspaper bundle from which crayfish claws and tails protruded. The two men staggered up the gangplank; there was a lot of talk and badinage which I couldn't hear clearly, and then the watchman went off with the two men to some place on the ship. That was my chance; up the gangplank I nipped and into the first open door. The place was floored with an iron grating, and a spiral gangway led down below. The lighting was so dim that I had to step cautiously. Down one deck I moved, then seeing a narrow passageway I slunk along it, trembling and in a nervous sweat. Suddenly a strong hand grasped my arm. I nearly jumped out of my skin.

"Hah! A stowaway, eh? Just wait till the old man catches you. He'll beat the daylights out of you—any of them deck swabs would."

"But," I protested to my captor, whose rugged face I could barely make out in the gloom, "I'll work. I'll do anything. I must get away from here—get somewhere. Anywhere!" I tried to tell a tale of being homeless, out of work, haunted by the call of the sea.

"Ah," the man said, his tone seeming to change slightly, "Come in here and we'll talk about it."

He took me into a cabin and closed the door. I could see he spoke with an air of authority. In a thick Scottish accent he asked, "Well, now, what do you think you could do on board a ship?"

At this point, I was stuck with my original story, and I certainly did not want to tell him about my parents, the university, and my Gaumont job. So I made up a fanciful tale of wanting to work on a ship until it came into port, then go ashore and roam about to see things—and write about them.

"But that don't make sense," he said. "Sailors, especially engineers, are always busy in port. They get no time to run around. What work have you done before?"

"Well," I said, "I have never really worked. I can ride horses; I know a bit about animals and insects; and I have been studying engineering—electrical engineering—as a sort of apprentice with a large engineering firm."

"Ah!" he said. "Electrical engineering! Do you know anything about dynamos?"

"Yes," I said, "I know dynamos—how to wind them and how to work them. I know motors, too." I gabbled on, my words tumbling out as I strove to convince him.

Finally he said, "Well, if I help you to stow away, will you promise to help me wind a dynamo, no matter what the old man tells you to do? I've got one to wind, and I don't know too much about it. But don't tell the old man you have spoken to me."

I promised. He led me into a dark and dusty alcove through the grated floor of which I could see the sweating stokers at work far down below. At each shovelful of coal the dust rose in a cloud and almost choked me. So great was the heat above the boilers that the sweat ran the soot into my eyes until I was almost blinded.

Suddenly some bells nearby sounded—clang, clang, clang! I was in a fever of fright. To me, bells suggested fire. The ship was on fire and there I was stuck in the middle of it, not knowing which way to turn to reach the deck!

I stepped out of the alcove, prepared to run anywhere to find an exit, but I noticed that the firemen below were not alarmed; they kept on shoveling. So I sneaked back into the stifling heat.

Then came the thump, thump of engines turning—slow at first, then faster. More bells clanged, the engines stopped, they started, then they raced. More clanging and jangles, followed by a steady beat of the engines. The vibration of the ship and an almost imperceptible draft of cool air coming to my hideaway from somewhere let me know that the ship was moving. I was exultant. On to Sydney! I had stowed away and no one but the friendly engineer had found me. At least not yet!

But soon after, a figure, appearing as if from nowhere, poked me sharply in the ribs. "Come on; art of it! Up on deck afore the ole man. You'll ketch it proper, you will."

"No, no," I stammered, "you can't take me. The engineer put me here. He's going to give me work to do."

"Oh, 'e is, is 'e? The ole man'll 'ave some'at to say abart that. 'Op to it, an' look lively!"

But I refused to move, and with some coins finally managed to persuade him to let me stay—for a few hours at least, until we got away from shore.

Suddenly bells clanged again. The thundering of the engines slackened, then stopped. I was terrified. Had my presence been reported after all? Were they going to put me ashore? But soon I was relieved to hear the engines wheeze, then take up their steady clank, clank once more, growing more rapid as we picked up steam.

Later I was told that the ship had stopped to let off the harbor pilot. As narrowly as that, I had missed an ignominious return to Adelaide!

But I was not to be left alone very long. Another sailor, rougher than the first and with a flair for drama, shoved me out and booted me up the gangway to the deck. Dawn had broken, raw and rainy; the damp wind struck through my sweat-drenched clothes and chilled me to the marrow. I shivered violently—so violently I could scarcely answer when the first mate, looking down from the bridge above, yelled, "Hey, Clancey, what you got there? A bloomin' stowaway? How the blankety blazes did you get on board?"

I babbled the story of the two drunks, the crayfish and the beer, and the faithless watchman. Then, hearing a throaty snarl beside me, I turned and saw that the man who had flushed me out was the very same watchman.

"I'll kill you for this!" he spat.

Then the captain looked over the bridge. "What's this, mister? A stowaway? Wasn't the ship searched before the pilot went ashore?"

"Err, uh—Yes, sir. I had the ship searched. Don't know how this-un could have been missed. Never happened before, sir." At that moment I could sense how he felt about me.

"Well, it's too late to put you ashore now. Bosun, take him below. Clean him up and then send him to my quarters."

My captor shoved me forward roughly. As he did so, the captain's final words rang in my ears: "You'll have to take what's coming to you when we reach Africa."

Africa! The ship was not going to Sydney at all, but to Africa!

My first sudden visions of my distraught parents, my waiting baggage, my camera, were quickly blotted out by the thoughts that flooded into my addled brain. Africa! Adventure! The other end of the world—gold, slaves, lions, Arabs, Zulus! My feet moved as if I were in a trance.

The bosun muttered threats as he drove me to the fo'c'sle and, as soon as he was out of sight of the bridge, he slugged me down the gangway. That was too much. I turned angrily and slugged back. The next thing I knew, I was coming to with a bunged eye, a split lip, and a roaring headache. I was no match for the experienced bosun.

Later I took on the job of winding the dynamo's armature for the third engineer, and kept out of sight of the bosun for the rest of the voyage. I had plenty of time aboard ship to think, as we made our way through the Indian Ocean, up the narrow sleeve of the Red Sea, steamed slowly past the shifting sands of Suez and into the blue Mediterranean. I had courted adventure and found her. Home now seemed very far away.

3

Algiers, Abduction, and Arabs

After my tangle with the bosun, life on board ship was not unpleasant. Although there was a great deal of hard work to do,
with each task I learned something useful about running a ship
and about the sea. It was exciting to observe the many faces of
the ocean as it stretched away into the distance, and the many
variations of sky, cloud, light, and shadow in this endless new
world. Time passed quickly, especially when I thought anxiously
ahead to what might become of me when we reached port, which
I learned was to be Algiers.

Would it mean jail, as the captain had threatened? I did not
think so, but then I could not be sure. What would I do in this
foreign town, away from my own people and my mother tongue?
I could speak a little French and German, thanks to my language
instruction at the conservatory in Adelaide, but I knew I would
need a practical vocabulary for eating and housing and transportation, instead of the "love" and "my soul" stuff the classical songs
were made of.

When we reached the dockside at Algiers, I was greatly relieved
when the captain looked at me gravely and gave his verdict: "Well,
young man, you have earned your keep. Over the side with you,
now. And don't let me see you again on my ship!"

I lost no time in scrambling ashore. It was not difficult to leave
the docks in that teeming, bustling port of Algiers, and to lose
myself in the crowds of the main part of the city, which was a
modern French metropolis. In those days, with the tensions growing between the two big alliances of European powers, and with
the bitter rivalry between the French and Italians over colonial

25

control of parts of North Africa, Algiers was a hotbed of unrest and intrigue. The French police were everywhere, keeping an eye on foreigners. But the Italians had their secret agents in the city too, trying to track down the source of gun-running to the hostile Arabs in the desert south of Tripoli, whence attacks were launched on their colony in Libya. Even without this tense big-power situation, the city was a melting pot of Europeans, Arabs, Negroes, Jews, and just about every other racial and religious grouping under the sun. It was fascinating, and at the same time a bit frightening, to a young fellow used to the homogeneity of Australia and the orderliness of Adelaide.

While wandering about the city near the waterfront not long after leaving the ship, I soon struck up an acquaintance with a man who spoke passable English. It turned out that he was a member of the Italian Secret Service. He offered me a job watching the waterfront for the discharge of arms, and I promptly accepted. I did not know that the Italian was a marked man, inexperienced Australian youth of twenty that I was; otherwise I would have been more careful. One night, as we were making the rounds of the slum bars, drinking, keeping our eyes and ears open for information about arms, and watching the native girls perform their provocative dances, we were approached by a sleazy-looking, burnoosed Arab. He told the Italian that if we would go with him we could get some interesting information. My employer seemed to think that the Arab was to be trusted. Coins changed hands, and we were off into the night.

We followed our guide for a long while through winding, smelly streets—indeed, this seemed to me like something out of the "Arabian Nights." We were not going into the old native quarter, the Kasbah, with its steep, winding rabbit-warren of alleys and stairs, where we would have been conspicuous. Instead, we went out to a respectable suburban section. Here, entering a house, we were introduced to a group of men who might have been of almost any Mediterranean nationality. The one who acted as spokesman seemed to know our business, and said that for a price he would put us on the track of caravans used for smuggling arms over the border. My Italian friend, after some discussion, agreed to pay for the information and gave the man a note which, he said, should be presented to a certain contact for decoding and the payment of the money.

The job of tracing down the gun-runners would mean a trip of some days, first eastward along the coast to Philippeville, and then south to Biskra, near the Tunisian border, at the foot of the Atlas Mountains, at the edge of the Sahara, where other agents were to meet us.

At this point, I thought of my job with Gaumont in England, but almost at once dismissed it as something that could wait. Here I was at the eve of an adventure in the desert, the kind you read about in lurid novels, and who was I to pass it up? Gaumont and England could wait.

After several days of traveling we reached Biskra, where we were met according to plan and taken again into a house to discuss our next moves. Finally, our hosts proposed that we drink to the success of the enterprise. We drained our glasses and departed, and shortly after I felt my head swimming. A glance at my companion told me that he too was in trouble. Our Arab guide assured us that we must just be feeling the desert heat. This seemed odd, because the night was cool.

A moment later my friend said, "They've drugged us!" Then everything went blank for me.

I remembered nothing more until I felt myself slowly coming to consciousness—and being shaken, swung, and bumped. I awoke to find myself draped over a donkey and tied to its harness. We were in a caravan, crossing a rocky plain. I raised my aching head and recognized one of the men who had met us a few hours before.

About midmorning, we came to a well, where my captors let me drop to the ground. Horses, camels, donkeys, and Arabs milled about, all drinking water. My companion, though as dazed as I, was much more crestfallen. He, a government agent, had been taken in by the oldest trick in the book. We were permitted to talk together, though there was always a native within earshot.

A fine situation for an Australian youngster heading for a job in London! How, we asked ourselves, could we have been so stupid as to fall into such a trap? More important though, where were the Arabs taking us?

In the late afternoon, when our caravan saddled up, we could see that the loads were arms and ammunition. So we had been shanghaied by one of the gun-running units—caught by the very fellows we were supposed to be tracking. There was nothing we could do except mount the ponies the Arabs provided for us and follow the caravan as it wound its way southeastward around the edge of Chott Melrir, the great salt lake of that part of the desert. That evening we camped on the plain beside a water hole, where the sandy soil was covered with a layer of dry loam a few inches deep. In some places it had gathered in mounds about the clumps of thorny brush. Here and there a stunted eucalyptus tree reminded me of my own Australian bush—which I wished I had never left!

In the early morning a wind from the north soon had the air filled with fine, brown dust. The sun shone through it only dimly. At first I thought the storm might offer my companion and me our chance to escape. Then, as the wind rose and the sky was completely hidden, the choking dust knocked out all idea of escape. We had to lie with our faces buried in our arms, for we had no burnoose for protection, as the Arabs did. As we huddled there we wondered if we would be abandoned to die of thirst and hunger or if we would end with our throats slit.

For two days that north wind blew. Nearly blinded by the dust, our nostrils and throats raw, we were at least given water and some parched grain. On the third day, to our relief, the storm abated and the caravan moved on.

My friend learned from one of the men with whom we had originally bargained, and who joined the caravan that morning, that we were to be taken to Tunis. There, one of us would be sold to the Arabs, the other probably held for ransom. Suddenly, I realized how hopeless and helpless I was, far from my home and family, without passport or papers. No one in North Africa knew my identity. There would be no ransom forthcoming on my account.

But with the Italian it was different. He was a captive for whose release a price would doubtless be paid. He promised to do what he could for me, but at best it looked as if I would be sold as a slave. However, I was young enough and optimistic enough to believe I could somehow get out of this mess. I consoled myself, too, with the thought that here was *adventure*.

After two more days of travel we entered a region of sand dunes. When we camped at an oasis, my companion was suddenly whisked away. I never saw him again. Some years later I heard from his family that he had indeed been ransomed, that he had returned to Italy broken in health and died a few months later. He had told his family about me and had worried because he had been unable to help me. But perhaps he had helped, as we shall see.

After being in the camp for some days I was given the freedom of the place—at least enough to see how these people lived. At first, boys threw stones and spat at me, but I pretended not to mind their insults. As any young man might do, I made the acquaintance of a young girl whose dark eyes seemed to twinkle a little as she peered at me above her yashmak, the heavy veil worn by Moslem women. For several days my advances met with nothing but shy retreats.

Meanwhile, I made friends with the younger children, showing them string games I had learned from the natives in my own country, drawing mysterious figures in the sand, speaking to them in the sign language of the Australian aborigines. I also tried to curry favor with the men by behaving soberly and attempting to follow them in their morning and evening devotions. The Moslem worship involves postures, such as kneeling down and placing hands and brow on the ground while reciting prayers, and is almost a gymnastic exercise.

As the days passed, the young girl became less and less timid, and sometimes would join the children when I played with them. Then one day, in answer to my broken French, she surprised me by replying in perfect French. She had been to a French school at Algiers, she told me. As well as I could, and without arousing the men's suspicions, I told her that I was an Australian, and outlined my adventure as a stowaway.

This seemed to arouse her sympathy. Perhaps she realized I was not an Italian, not a part of the war. Or maybe the Italian had spoken for me. At any rate, one day she said she would get me some Arab clothes and maybe smuggle me into a packload bundle that would be strapped to a camel in a caravan heading northwest, back to Biskra.

By then I was darkly sunburned, and had a fluffy beard. It seemed that if I watched my step and kept silent, I might just pass as an Arab—with luck. One night when a caravan was being prepared to leave in the morning, my young friend led me to the outskirts of the camp, where I crawled into a bundle that was to be put on a camel. We whispered hurried farewells, then she left me to spend the night as best I might in nervous anticipation. I must have dozed off eventually. Later, I felt the bundle lifted, heard shouts and bells, then the jolting as the pack camel raised to its knees and stood up; then the steady swing, swong of the camel's awkward gait.

When we came to the noonday rest, the bundles were unloaded and dumped. It was almost unbearably hot; I was cramped and sweltering in my cloth prison, but I dared not move.

Up again and once more the nauseating swing of the camel's movement. Then again rest, at last. There was no way I could tell if it was nightfall. I was afraid to disturb the bundle to peek out until I was sure no one would see me. Finally the sound of activity died down. I waited and waited. Then came the swishing sound of wind and sand, and I felt the cool night breeze.

Finding an opening, I cautiously looked out into the darkness, with the desert stars shining overhead. I slid out, crawled a few feet, bumped into a prone figure that moved and muttered. My heart in my mouth, I slumped beside it and remained silent, awake and fearful throughout the night.

Could I be inconspicuous in the crowd? Would I be found out

now, after my good luck so far? I knew I couldn't stand another day in the stifling bundle. Undecided, my head half buried in the sand, I was puzzled as to what to do. In the gray dawn, later, I could see that men were moving. They had discovered the disturbed pack and the loss of the things the girl had removed to make room for me. There was shouting and gesticulating, but apparently none thought that the merchandise they were missing had turned into an extra traveling companion. Covering my face, I joined the crowd. Fortunately, thieving in the caravans is common. There was nothing to show which way the "robbers" might have gone. The drifting sand had covered any tracks made the previous night.

The journey back to Biskra was a nightmare, because I was constantly afraid of giving myself away. Scraps of food were offered me now and then, and I watered with donkeys at the wells. Then at last a crossing of a dry wadi, through the oleander trees and palms, and we rode into the town. Once there, I got safely away from my escorts and managed to get into contact with British authorities who started me on my way to England. I was properly clothed and washed for the first time in weeks.

By any reasonable standard, the whole experience since leaving the ship might have seemed a useless adventure. But this brief encounter with the Arabs probably helped prepare me for some of the experiences I was to have just a few years later during the Balkan War of 1912. I was again to see Moslems at close hand, to have to use my wits in getting about, living on minimum supplies of drinking water and eating foods to which Anglo-Saxons are not accustomed. It at least had been a lesson in survival.

4

Shooting the Balkan War

Once arrived in England, I soon found myself working in a double capacity for two employers—for Gaumont as a cinematographic cameraman, and for the *Daily Chronicle* as a reporter. I was so busy that any plans I may have had in the back of my head to continue my study in electrical engineering quickly went out the window. My work gave me all the chance I wanted to travel.

For about three years I toured the British Isles, Europe, Canada, and the United States on special assignments, photographing the 1909 revolution in Spain, German military maneuvers, English military maneuvers, a trip through Ireland, a trip across Canada, and so on.

One day, a chance experience at Hendon Aerodrome, near London, added an entirely new dimension to my photographic work. Ever since I had read about Clément Ader and his attempts with a flying machine in France, I had been fascinated by the prospect of flying myself. I often visited aerodromes, to see what was going on and to talk with the flyers and mechanics. Aviation had come a long way since the time, only five or six years before, when I had helped build a model plane back in Adelaide and seen it sail into some telephone wires and stay there.

This particular day at Hendon, I fell into conversation with a stranger. He and I were talking about airplanes, and I spoke of the celebrated pioneer English flyer, Claude Grahame-White, a contemporary of the Wright brothers, and more recently winner of the Gordon-Bennett International Aviation Cup. With my Australian frankness and the cocksureness of youth, I told him exactly what I thought. For one thing, I said I had heard that

Grahame-White was what the English call a conceited ass. But I added that whatever he was, I admired him because he was working at a science that some day would bring great benefit to the entire world. Then something made me ask, "You don't know Grahame-White, do you?"

"Well," he said, "yes. I happen to be Grahame-White."

Naturally I was embarrassed, but Claude Grahame-White put me at my ease at once, and we enjoyed a laugh over my stupid blunder. Later that day, this great pioneer of aviation took me up for my first real flight. I can still remember the thrill of feeling I had the power of the eagle, soaring over the rooftops and the trees, while the people down below resembled so many ants, growing smaller as we winged away from them. The air rushing past our ears, the roar of the motor, the vibration of the ship—it all gave me a new sensation of speed and power, spiced with a sense of risk, that is almost completely lacking in the enclosed cabin of the modern airliner.

Later Grahame-White made arrangements for me to take flying lessons at Hendon. Although I took the pilot's course I did not attempt to qualify for a license, lack of money being the main obstacle at the time. But with flying churning within me, it was not long before I had made contact with Lieutenant Porte of the Royal Navy, who was experimenting with a new Déperdussin monoplane, in which he was installing a 100-horsepower Anzani engine. This was a daring "first"—putting an engine of that power in a plane—and some thought it might shake the craft to pieces. Porte wanted me to go up with him, in a plane built to lift one man, and shoot some advertising film *from the plane in flight!*

I was just daredevil enough to say yes. We fixed my camera to the starboard side of the fuselage, about two feet to the rear of the whirling propeller, and I was to perch astraddle the thin body of the plane and crank away at my apparatus, while the pilot operated the controls from the cockpit a couple of feet behind me. Since I was just about at the center of gravity of the plane, it was agreed that if we nosed down I was to try to push back a foot or so, and if the tail dragged I was to do my best to pull myself forward

—of course taking care not to put my head or hands into the path of the prop.

The single-seater plane was a frail, parasol-type thing, so-called because its members were stabilized by guy wires leading outward from two short masts jutting upward from the body. As the 100-horsepower motor was revved up, the whole contraption shook like a leaf in a storm. Whatever I felt, I could see that Porte was rather nervous about it all, as a good test pilot should be—not quite sure the machine would prove as stable as most other planes were at that time.

My camera was strapped to the bracing wires and I was astride the fuselage, picturing myself at the moment as the Australian bush boy about to ride the fastest, noisiest, and most dangerous horse he had ever mounted. My nose was just a few inches from the trailing edge of the propeller, and the engine was idling when Porte shouted to ask if I were ready. I opened my mouth to reply, when he shoved the throttle forward, the engine suddenly roared, and my cheeks and lungs were blown full of wind from the propeller. I was almost choking as the machine bounded over the ground, and before I could even get my breath we were in the air. The machine, unbalanced and unstable in every imaginable way, was twisting and turning like a bucking horse. I hung on with grim desperation. It dipped and reared, fell off on one side, then the other. From the ground it must have looked less like a horse than like a barnyard fowl fluttering about in a gale. We managed to circle the aerodrome, and as soon as possible we came down to a bumpy landing. We had been in the air only a few minutes, but that was time enough for me to turn almost completely numb with fear and cold.

My pictures that time were not worth much. But within a few months I had taken aerial motion pictures several times. I particularly remember one assignment in France when I took pictures of a hare hunt. I was perched in the front of a Farman plane, on a bicycle seat with my camera strapped between my legs. I well recall the thrill of skimming along within a few feet of the ground, filming a hare as it ran before us. These were, I believe, the first motion pictures ever shot from an airplane.

In the fall of 1912, war having broken out in the Balkans between the Turks and Bulgarians, I was ordered off to Constantinople. My mission was to film the war from the Turkish side. Up to that time, there had been no moving pictures of a war, and Gaumont was eager to score a "first" in this respect. The exact causes of this little war in the far-off Balkans were not clear to the average man-in-the-street, although he knew that for centuries the Moslem Turk had been trying to keep his foothold on the continent of Christian Europe, which long ago had trembled before his power. But with the recent increase in European tensions, not only among the big powers such as Britain, France, Russia, Germany, Italy, and Austria, but also among their smaller allies like Turkey and Bulgaria, everyone was intensely curious to see how a twentieth-century war would be fought. The military buffs had not observed a really first-class fight in Europe since the Franco-Prussian War in 1870–1871; the technology of arms had improved greatly in the forty years since. So everyone—government leaders, military men, and the man-in-the-street—was curious about the vestpocket war in the southeastern corner of the continent, as if it were a kind of rehearsal for something bigger.

When I reached Constantinople, now Istanbul, that sprawling city was in a state of pandemonium. To impress the Bulgarians with the size of their forces, the ill-prepared Turks were seizing men everywhere, putting them in any kind of uniform, and parading them through the streets. The government was also seizing every horse. Soldiers and police stopped cabs and took the horses on the spot, leaving the cabby to drag away his cab as best he could.

I was one of twenty-seven correspondents and cameramen who had come from various parts of the world. We found the Turkish authorities as confused about how to handle the foreign press as they were about fighting the war. We press people wanted to get out of the chaos of the capital and to the fighting front, where we could see the war and report it.

The Turkish commanding general sent for all of us one day and said, "If you correspondents want to join the army, we'll take you out, but we can't furnish either transportation or food. Every man must have a servant, and an interpreter who can speak Turkish and Bulgar. Every man must have a horse for himself and one for each of his servants. Also, you will have to carry two months' provisions, and show us you have money enough to pay your way."

Twenty-seven of us. That meant twenty-seven servants and twenty-seven interpreters, each to be provided with a horse! Yet just about everything on four legs had already been seized by the government. It looked hopeless.

Bernard Grant of the London *Daily Mirror*, a chap named John Banister, and I agreed to join forces, and get along sharing three servants. We could work together without rivalry, for Grant was a still photographer, Banister was a writer, and I was taking movies. Grant and Banister were Londoners who had never been on a horse or ever camped. So we decided that I, with my experience with life in the outdoors, would look after the horses and the camp, Banister would get the provisions, and Grant would cover us on the news.

By then the only decent horses left in Constantinople were in the hands of the police. Whenever a policeman saw a better horse than the one he was riding, he simply took it and handed over his own. From the police force I managed to buy three fairly decent mounts, paying the equivalent of about three hundred dollars. Then I got hold of a pack horse, and another animal that would do for the interpreter. But I couldn't find a sixth one anywhere.

One day my interpreter came to me and said, "There's an old fellow, a Greek, who wants to speak to you."

"What does he want?"

"He will tell nobody but you."

The old Greek came into my hotel room, and the interpreter told me that he was a cabby, and that the government had taken his horse.

"He has seen you riding, and he wants to work for you because you know horses."

I said, "But I haven't enough horses. Can he tell me where to get one?"

The old Greek said he could, but would not tell the interpreter. He would take me to buy the horse, but the interpreter must not come. Also, I must take enough gold to buy the horse. The interpreter warned me not to go alone with this old Greek, with gold in my pockets. But the old fellow looked honest, and I was grasping at a last straw.

Next morning the Greek arrived at the hotel with a cab drawn by a nag so pitifully feeble the police would not want it. We drove for what seemed two full hours through the back streets of Constantinople. I had no idea where we were. Finally, I lost patience and tried to tell the old Greek I could not waste all day. But the only English he knew was, "All right." The madder I got and the more I protested, the more he said, "All right, all right," and kept on whipping his weary horse.

Finally we stopped in a mean part of town, before a row of dirty, tumbled-down houses. The old fellow got down and led me through one into a courtyard. Ominous looking men and women poured out of the house and engaged the Greek in a vigorous discussion, utterly unintelligible to me. They kept looking me over and arguing. I saw that the old Greek wanted them to do something or other about me, and they seemed afraid to do it. Finally they gave in and beckoned me up the outside stairway of the house.

In a bedroom on the second floor stood the most beautiful Arab stallion I ever saw. He was a bay, with a black stripe on his back. One of the old Turks who could speak a few words of English got the idea across to me that they loved that horse so much they had hidden him, to prevent his being stolen by someone in the government or the police who would be cruel to him. They had seen me handle a couple of the other horses and could tell that I knew how to care for a good mount.

The old man said they did not ask any price for the horse because they would not sell him. But he said I might make them a little present and they would give me this horse if I would promise to bring him back when I was through with him.

I gave them a hundred pounds. They said, "Let us hold him for you. When you are ready to leave on the military train, come out here the last thing, after dark, and get him."

We were scheduled to leave Constantinople at four o'clock in the morning. I went out late at night, got my horse, and rode him straight onto the train. By this time the old Greek had attached himself to our party, and we were glad to have him. He had some unpronounceable name, so we decided to call him Marcus Aurelius.

The second morning out of Constantinople the train stopped not far from Adrianople in Thrace. The horses had to jump from the cars to the ground. When my beautiful Arab took a flying leap, out among the miserable animals the others had picked up—well, there was a sensation. I was young and this was my first war, but that horse gave me some unexpected prestige with older correspondents.

We were all dumped out onto the plain—horses, goods, provisions, and equipment—and we were told to reach the press camp as best we could. There were all nationalities among the correspondents, as well as servants and interpreters from every race in the polyglot Levant. You never heard such a babble of tongues. We three had Marcus Aurelius as hostler, a Maltese named Godfrey as interpreter, and a wandering Englishman named Henry for general servant. He was old and physically broken down with drink, but fairly dependable.

For days the Turks kept us cooling our heels in camp. The Turkish officer in charge of us was supposed to show us the war, but what he did was virtually to keep us prisoners. We had to show him our pictures and such news stories as we could get. He sent them to Constantinople, and in three or four days the story just might appear in London. But it wouldn't be the story you had sent. The Turks cut everything but the few parts they wanted printed.

Occasionally we were taken fifteen miles or so across country, to the top of some hill from which we could see nothing, and there the Turkish officer would tell us what the army was doing. Then we were brought back to camp again. We were furious, and made so much of a row that at last, on the thirtieth of October, the Turks announced, "Tomorrow we will take you out and show you a real battle."

We started toward the front under Turkish guard, the officers riding with us and telling us how the army was cleaning up the Bulgarians. They really did expect this battle to be a tremendous success. But long before we drew near the front we could see it was anything but. While their liaison officers kept telling us about the glorious victory, we could plainly see that the countryside was in a panic. Turkish peasants were running for their lives, with their families, hens, sheep, household goods, donkeys, and bullocks. Our Turkish officers explained that the army was making a strategic move, but finally they said, "We can't take you any farther today." So we had to turn around and start back toward camp. That was all right for the correspondents; they had seen enough to know what was happening. But we photographers wanted to see the actual fighting and get pictures of it.

I was riding with Francis McCullagh, veteran correspondent from the Russo-Japanese war, and sharing a pack horse with Saul, a Pathé cameraman. I said to them, "I see only one thing to do. We've got to get away from this party if we want to see the battle. I'll cut the pack saddle's girth and let the load fall. Then when I stop to fix it, you come back to look for me."

I did this and the girth gave way, and all our stuff went on the ground. I dismounted to repack, but the Turkish colonel set two orderlies to watch me. Before I could get away from the orderlies, the colonel himself came back to reclaim me.

However, I managed to cut the girth again. By this time, the frantic peasants and the fringe of the retreating army were overtaking us. We were riding just ahead of a traffic jam of bullock carts, sheep, soldiers, artillery, children, donkeys, and veiled women. This time two more orderlies were told to keep an eye on me, while the other correspondents hurried on, out of sight. I gave the orderlies some gold coins. Although my Turkish was *nihil*, I didn't need to explain. When they pocketed the money, off they went. So I adjusted the pack and headed back toward the battle.

In a little while, Saul and McCullagh and Bernard Grant overtook me. In the confusion they had come back, against the colonel's orders. Saul had lost part of his camera; had to go back to look for it, so we lost him. Grant, McCullagh, and I went on to the top of a hill, where we had a view of the rout of the Turkish army.

Streams of fleeing peasants were going out of sight to the south. Behind them the whole country was dotted with disorganized groups of soldiers. Along the river bank below us, thousands of panic-stricken Turks were jammed like sheep, with swarms of soldiers on foot and on horseback struggling across the bridge and through the water, in the face of their own Turkish cavalry, with drawn swords, trying to halt them and drive them back.

When a troop of Turkish cavalry came past the base of our hill, we left Godfrey with our pack horse and heavy gear, and rode down to see the cavalry charge. We got there just in time. When the cavalry broke into a gallop, we were swept along with them. I couldn't have held my spirited Arab if I'd tried, and I didn't try.

Nothing in the world quite compares with the wild madness of a cavalry charge—riders with sabers drawn, rushing headlong on the enemy. Down the slope we went, but not toward the enemy. The cavalry, we found to our amazement, were charging their own rabble of Turkish foot soldiers and peasants!

On we went, storming across the bridge. Dead and dying men were under the hoofs, rolling and screaming and falling into the water. It seemed that the main body of the Turkish army was still ahead of us. We got out of the shambles on the bridge. Ahead was a long line of infantry spread out, with cavalry behind it, and we thought it was the main Turkish army coming back in good order.

Suddenly shells began striking all around us. A bit of shrapnel stung me in the face. A shell struck right between McCullagh and me; it was a dud. Then we realized that we were facing the advancing Bulgarian troops—in fact, we were in the hot center of a battle.

The Bulgarians evidently took the three of us for Turkish officers, with our fezzes on our heads, and our riding breeches and boots. A group of Bulgarian cavalry swung out from behind the infantry and galloped to cut off our escape. We cut around a little hill, trying to get away; the cavalry came right behind us. They didn't shoot, they wanted to take us alive. Around the small hill we went, and they were so close we didn't dare to make a bolt across country. Around the hill we went again, then we made a dash, full speed into the river. The Bulgarians opened up on us with rifles, but we swam our horses across the river and luckily got away.

Next day we got back to our camp near Chorlu. Although Grant and Banister and I had three tents in the correspondents' camp, we shared them. That is, we used one for sleeping, one for eating and photographic work, and the third for our servants. I now had some action film—probably the first ever made of a battle.

On Sunday, November 12, we heard the guns again. The Turks promised to take us to the front, but few of us believed they would. Ward Price of the *Daily Mail*, Grant, and I decided to stick together, taking along only our man Godfrey, a wonderful linguist, at home in seven languages. A Maltese, he had been first dragoman of the British Embassy. His manners were perfection, and he was well known socially in Constantinople, a member of the best clubs.

I said to Godfrey, "This time Mr. Grant, Mr. Price, and I are going into the front lines. We can take only one interpreter. We can use you if you will come along, but I warn you, it's going to be dangerous."

He not only told us what a brave hero he was, he even swore

he'd rescue us if we were captured by the Bulgars. Yes, oh, yes! There was nothing he would not do.

This day I got more unusual film showing men, guns, and geysers of earth where the Bulgarian shells were striking. While I was grinding away, a Bulgarian shell struck right in the middle of a Turkish battery and blew the whole thing up.

When we moved on, Godfrey stood behind and shook. I couldn't get him to move or speak. He just stood there, his knees knocking together. Angrily I told him, "Get up on that horse and come along."

He began crying and pleading, "We'll be killed! By Allah, we'll all be killed!"

He grabbed hold of my horse's reins and wouldn't let go. I was riding my Arab, leading the pack horse and his horse, and with the heavy camera under my arm I couldn't break loose from him. He begged me not to leave him there alone. When I pushed him off, he groveled on the ground, then hung on to my legs. I lost my temper, and took out my pistol.

Ward Price quickly wheeled his horse and knocked the gun from my hand with his riding crop. He said we'd better go ahead without an interpreter. I was too angry to care what happened, but I knew Price was right, and we were wasting time.

When we went on toward the fighting, Godfrey got safely back to Constantinople much later, dressed up, went to the Pera Palace Hotel, and told his friends all about his exploits and how he saved my life. Saul, who happened to be there at the time, and had already heard the true story from us, took Godfrey by the neck and the seat of the pants and threw him bodily out of the room.

When the Turkish officer in charge found that Price, Grant, and I had not returned to camp, where all the other correspondents had been rounded up and hustled back to Constantinople, he ordered our arrest on sight. In fact, we were classed as outlaws. But the Turks were too disorganized to pursue us systematically, and old Marcus Aurelius and Henry stayed faithfully with us. We never could have done what we did without that loyal and crafty old Greek. He was the most accomplished thief imaginable.

When our supplies gave out, we lived entirely on what Marcus Aurelius could scrounge. Any time he saw a stray pig or turkey, we dined in style.

I wore the costume of the country—deep-seated Turkish trousers, the short sleeveless jacket, and the kind of kerchief-cravat worn by the Turks, a bit of rag under the fez, its ends wound around the neck and the lower part of the face. My films were concealed in the mass of tattered clothing I wore. While the sentries at city gates seldom searched a man, they always poked through the packs on the horses. My skin was tanned brown, and by the time I had walked ten or fifteen miles I was dusty and grimy enough to pass anywhere for a low-class Balkan Turk. Waiting until there was a crowd pushing through a gate, I assumed a stupid air, and pretended not to understand what the sentries wanted. Finding nothing suspicious on the horse, they'd impatiently hustle me along. In this way I went back and forth through the lines whenever we had to send off our news stories and photographs.

In November the Turks were forced back on the Chatalja Line, the last row of defenses in the narrow peninsula before Constantinople. The war was a miserable affair. The Turks had few really trained soldiers. Many of their men had no idea how to handle a gun, didn't even know enough to close the breech. When they pulled the trigger they sometimes blew off a hand, or lost an eye.

There were a few hospitals, but without sufficient medical supplies. Doctors operated day and night without anesthetics, and with very few antiseptics. The wounded died by cartloads. The soldiers preferred to lie in the field to being taken to the hospitals. The average Turk or Bulgar would struggle along with great courage until he lay down and died. Usually when I tried to give a wounded man a drink from my flask, he would turn away his head. Good Moslems will not drink liquor. Not one complained of anything.

We saw such a massacre of men in that forerunner of World War I that human life seemed valueless. I saw thousands dead in the village streets, and other thousands dying of cholera. By

mistake one dark night we camped in a graveyard. Next morning
while eating breakfast, up came a procession of carts, and cholera-
blackened corpses were dumped into the ditches beside us.

Some time after this, Ward Price left us and went in to Constantinople. Grant and I moved farther to the rear, where we set
up in the house of an old Armenian priest, in a village not yet
abandoned. Here on my Blickensdorfer typewriter we wrote dispatches, and got our pictures ready.

One day a car came driving up to the priest's house, and out of
it stepped a well-dressed Englishman who introduced himself as
Ellis Ashmead-Bartlett. He was an experienced reporter with a
fine reputation, and on the strength of this he enjoyed special
privileges from the Turks. He was reporting the war for the *Daily
Telegraph,* while his brother Seabury was taking pictures. Thanks
to their good connections, they had been allowed to drive up from
Constantinople.

When he came in, he said, "May I join you? This seems to be
the only decent place in town."

Of course we told him to move in and make himself at home. He
offered us cigars, and said he'd provide dinner—caviar, soup, real
bread, and meat and vegetables, even champagne—supplies he
had brought from Constantinople. We had been living on rice,
raisins, and dried corn, and rolling our own cigarettes from local
tobacco that we found hanging in stables, so we were delighted at
the prospect.

Later that evening Ashmead-Bartlett said, "Oh, by the way,
I must go out and look up my chauffeur, and ask him to get a horse
for me tomorrow. I want to ride out and look over the situation."

He was gone more than half an hour, and our hunch was that he
was writing a news dispatch. We were sure of it when he came
back and told us he had found that by some mistake there was no
bottled water among his supplies, so he would send the car back
the forty miles to Constantinople to get bottled water for all of
us. While Grant kept Bartlett talking, I slipped out and bribed his
chauffeur to take our photographs and stories along.

During the evening the veteran reporter told us tales of his experiences and entertained us royally. He was a charming fellow: an Oxford man and a correspondent of world-wide experience. Although always the gentleman, he was a bit inclined to think there was nobody in the world but Ashmead-Bartlett. Anyway, his caviar and champagne were excellent.

Later, when the chauffeur came back with the bottled water, Ashmead-Bartlett got to feeling quite merry, and at last he said, "It's too bad, really. You're young fellows without experience. But the joke's too good to keep. You thought I was sending the car back just to get that bottled water. The fact is, the water was here all the time. What I did was send off a dispatch. It will be a wonderful news break. So far, nobody else has gotten a word out of here. You told me just what I wanted to know. Really, you young fellows shouldn't be taken in so easily."

We laughed right back at him, and I said, "Don't worry. You helped us too. We also sent out our stuff. Your chauffeur was most accommodating. Cheerio, Old Man!"

I don't think he ever really forgave us. For what we had sent off was actual first-hand stuff. What made it all the harder for him was that we were not in his class. He was the famous ace of Fleet Street, and we were only a couple of young scalawags who carried cameras. Back to Constantinople he went next morning.

That same day word reached our village that the Bulgars were coming. All the villagers cleared out, including the Armenian priest. We were alone in the village and were packing up when old Marcus entered in triumph with half a dozen turkeys. They were too good to leave. I cooked the turkeys in a couple of kerosene tins over a fire in the yard. Just as they were done, some Turkish deserters came along, and we shared the meal with them. In no time at all Grant and I were in agony—hit by cholera.

About four o'clock Bulgar artillery began to shell the town. Henry and Marcus tried to get us up, because the place was being blown to pieces all around us. But we were only semiconscious and in such pain that we didn't care what happened. They put our two saddle horses to a cart and loaded all our equipment into it. Then they slung us face downwards, unconscious, over the backs of the horses and tied our hands and feet together under their bellies. The jolting may have saved our lives, because it made us horribly sick to our stomachs. Old Marcus drove over the hills until he got us four or five miles behind the Turkish lines, where he untied us and laid us out on the grass. The weather was warm and sunny, and there we stayed. Little by little we recovered.

As soon as we could travel again, Grant and I made our way toward the Chatalja Line. All along the roads men, horses, and oxen lay dying; carts and artillery were broken down; soldiers in filthy rags were trudging along barefoot. These were starving, utterly beaten men.

Grant and I didn't dare risk sending the true story and pictures of this retreat from Constantinople, because there wasn't a chance we could get them out. We thought of Rumania; there was a wireless station in Constanza, more than 150 miles up the Black Sea coast to the north. The only way to reach Rumania was by sea, because the invading Bulgarians held the land.

We took our interpreter and went down to a little village on the coast. The only boat in the harbor was a tug, freshly loaded with coal and ready to leave early next morning for Constantinople—exactly the wrong way for us. We tried to persuade the skipper to take us north to Constanza, but it was useless. That evening while he was ashore, we rowed out to the tug and tried to bribe the engineer to get up steam and take us to Constanza. When he refused, Grant poked the muzzle of a revolver against his stomach. At first, the engineer raised a row about piracy, but when he saw we meant business, he got up steam, and off we went. While Grant stood over him with the revolver, I took the wheel.

At that time, I knew almost nothing about navigation. Nor had I ever been along that coast, which sweeps west and then north from Turkey, past Bulgaria to Rumania. But I knew you had only to follow it north and you would come eventually to Constanza. Fortunately the weather was fair, and we did not encounter any of the storms for which the Black Sea is notorious.

When we came into Constanza after more than a day's steady puffing along the coast, we offered the engineer money if he would stay by while we went ashore and filed our dispatches. This time he decided he might as well take it. There was no censorship to worry about here, and we sent off news that day that the Turks would not permit anyone to dispatch from Constantinople.

The weather was still fine, and the engineer was friendly on the return trip, so Grant and I fell asleep. When we were awakened, we were approaching our starting point. We armed the engineer with a good story for his captain, plus some more money, and shoved off from the tug in a rowboat. Then as we drew closer there seemed to be a strange excitement on shore, and loud voices. Suddenly our Greek interpreter whispered, "They're talking Bulgar!"

Bulgarians they were. They had captured the village while we were away, and here we were rowing right into their hands. We backed water, swung round, and got back to the tug as fast as we could.

About twenty miles farther on we rowed ashore again. Everything seemed quiet, so we left the rowboat and the tug and started to walk to Constantinople. It was a long, hard trip of a couple of dozen miles on bad roads. We made no effort at disguise, but simply showed our correspondents' permits to the sentries and walked boldly in.

Just at dinnertime that evening we reached the Pera Palace Hotel, where we had kept our suite of rooms. We walked in, dirty, bedraggled, foot-sore, covered with dust. It had been a week since we had had a bath or a shave. The moment we appeared, there was an uproar. All the correspondents came piling out, shook our hands, thumped our backs, and congratulated us on our escape. We couldn't understand it. They dragged us into the dining room, grimy as we were, and insisted that we tell them all about our escape from the Bulgarians.

We now learned that while we were steaming to Constanza on the tug, word had gotten to Constantinople that the Bulgars had captured the village where we had been seen the night before. When nothing more was heard of us, our fellow correspondents concluded we had fallen into the hands of the other side. They had even organized an expedition and hired a boat to go to our rescue. That is, they intended to go out under a white flag to parley for our release.

When they appeared, in a Turkish boat flying a white flag, the Bulgarians opened fire. The gallant correspondents kept right on, put a boat ashore under fire, and offered to ransom us. When the Bulgars swore we were not there, they kept on raising the ransom, until they offered so much for us that they were sure no one would have refused it, if we were alive. The only plausible explanation was that we had been killed and that the Bulgars were trying to conceal this. So they had returned to Constantinople, and telegraphed their papers the dramatic story of our demise.

That was why we had received such a rousing welcome. But when we explained where we had been and what we had done, their expressions changed in an instant. While we had been off getting the better of them with the war news, they were risking their lives to rescue us from a danger we hadn't been in at all!

The next time Grant and I went out to the front we did not expect any trouble of any kind, for we had taken the precaution to get letters from Prince Aziz, of the Sublime Porte royal family, requesting that we be shown every courtesy and given all facilities.

First, at Chatalja we were shown the Turkish trenches—some of the first trenches used in modern warfare. The Germans were instructing the Turks. They had German artillery and German officers. The French, supporting the Bulgars, had equipped them with French guns. The Turks had a few airplanes, as well as searchlights and signal lamps, with British and German experts teaching them how to use all the new equipment. But when the instructors went home, within a few days all the planes were smashed, the searchlights and signal lamps burned out, and nobody knew how to fix them. The Turks simply did not bother with them any more.

When Grant and I went up to the front lines again, I got some good pictures, and was busily turning the hand crank of the camera when I heard horses galloping up behind me. It was some cavalry officers who had warned us not to take pictures. We showed the leader our permits, but would not hand over our letters from Prince Aziz, for fear we would not get them back. The captain brusquely put us under arrest, and his officers took us back to his camp and put us in a tent, guarded front and rear. When I protested, they explained they could not let us move because the whole area was infested with cholera. They asserted that Prince Aziz would hold them responsible for our health.

When we demanded to be taken to the headquarters of Nazim Pasha, the Turkish minister of war, the answer was, "Tomorrow." This went on for a week. For several days we had no food and no water, but one little stroke of luck saved us—it began to rain. The tent was old and leaky, and the rainwater poured through it. We drank all we needed.

On the fourth night one of our guards backed up to the flap of the tent and stealthily put his hand inside. He held out a handful of raisins to us and went away quickly. He had not said a word, and would pay no attention to us afterward. This handful of raisins was all we had to eat during the seven days. We were becoming exhausted from want of food, from the dripping water and the damp chill in the filthy tent.

Sometime before midnight on the seventh night we heard men and horses outside the tent. The sentries came in and ordered us out into the rain, and told us to get on our horses. Weak from hunger, we had no idea what was about to be done with us. We rode through the camp, and were joined by the captain, Haji Ali, and his aides. In the dark and the rain, we started across country. The rain was pouring down in sheets, and we rode through it all night. We swam two rivers. In the middle of one of them my Arab slipped, floundered, and threw me off. I couldn't swim, and almost drowned before I got hold of his mane.

We were overjoyed when we found that our destination was Nazim Pasha's headquarters. Grant and I were skin and bones, wet, and filthy. Our riding clothes had not been changed for ten days and nights, and our faces were covered with ten-day beards.

In that state, we were hauled unceremoniously before Nazim Pasha, and I handed him my letters from Prince Aziz, requesting that we be offered every courtesy. The Minister of War was an imposing, big-bellied man wearing huge medals on the breast of his tunic. His gray mustaches, turned up slightly at each end, made him appear the complete aristocrat and boss. When he looked at us his face was a study. He sent at once for an interpreter, and began to explain and to apologize to us. He ordered hot baths, fresh clothes, and food for us—immediately. We were quick to take advantage of his generosity, and soon we felt like decent human beings once more.

Nazim Pasha insisted that the least Haji Ali could do in reparation was to be our personal escort and servant. The captain accordingly begged us to allow him to travel with us to Constantinople. Enjoying the swift reversal of roles, we let him come along.

We started early next day on horseback, and in the village where we stopped for the night the first thing Haji Ali did was to take charge of our comfort. He had ridden ahead, and when we arrived we found the best house in the place prepared for us, with hot baths waiting. When we saw Haji Ali laying about him with his whip, we understood how he had produced this miracle in a sleepy Turkish village.

That night we were served a wonderful banquet, complete from *apéritifs* through many courses to liqueurs. Constantinople could not have done better. At table, Haji Ali entertained us with amusing stories, told in French and German, and he joined us in the drinks.

Next day he said that he would send our dispatches to Constantinople by a trusty messenger. We must not go into the city, looking as we did. He prevailed on us to come home with him and rest for a few days, promising that if we would come he would show us the real Turkish life that foreigners did not see.

It was an intriguing offer, and we accepted readily. The outside of his home was of forbidding appearance, with high, dull walls, but inside it was a veritable palace. Servants escorted us through courtyards and magnificent rooms. As soon as we arrived, we were offered hot baths and provided with silk robes. A tailor from Constantinople was announced; he had come to measure us for new clothes. Until they were ready, we were to live in these silken Oriental robes.

The end of it was that we spent two weeks in the most amazing Eastern luxury. Haji Ali, who was not a Turk by birth, but a Persian, proved to be a charming fellow to us whom he treated as equals. But to those whom he considered inferior, he was brutal, slashing them unmercifully with his horsehair whip which he always carried. When he wanted a servant, he had only to clap his hands and one came running.

He had collections of marvelous antique weapons made of Damascene steel and silver, carved and inlaid chests and tables, and any number of wonderful rugs with intricate floral and geometric designs. Our table service was from Paris; our sheets and pillowcases were hand-woven silk. Always before a meal the servants poured perfumed water over our hands.

Dancing girls from this Oriental captain's harem entertained us. Haji Ali had twenty-seven dancing girls, who were really a theatrical troupe. They put on dances, pantomimes and tableaux, and sang and recited poetry. There were two English, six French, and some Armenian and Russian girls among them. They were not at all the type you might expect, but cultured girls, artists kept to provide entertainment for Haji Ali and his friends. He had three Turkish wives in the harem, and I believe some concubines, but they were kept out of our sight.

Although Haji Ali was a man of wealth and influence, he was not of high rank. He was merely a bey, captain of a cavalry troop. I suppose there must have been a few thousand households like this in Turkey then.

With an understandable reluctance, we finally had to be taken to Constantinople and formally returned through the Turkish War Office. There we learned that an armistice had just been concluded and was likely to continue. The war was over. In no time at all, I received orders from Gaumont to report to London. The day before I left Constantinople, old Marcus Aurelius and I returned the

Arab stallion to his owners, safe and sound. They wept over him with joy, and he rubbed his head against them like a dog happy to be home.

I said good-by to my colleagues of the little war in the Balkans, packed up my camera and suitcase, and boarded the Orient Express for London. My three months in Southeastern Europe had been more of an adventure than I had anticipated.

5

Balloons and Cocoa

I arrived in London a few days before Christmas, only to find that when news is breaking there is no such thing as a rest for the motion-picture cameraman. On the morning of December 23, Gaumont sent me down to the Brixton gas works in the Battersea section of southwest London with instructions to film a balloon ascension.

The flight was to be a publicity stunt for Sandow's Chocolate, named after Sandow, the German strongman, who publicized his product as a health food: "A Perfect Sweetmeat and a Perfect Food." A daring flyer named Captain Penfold was to parachute from a balloon wearing a flowing white beard and dressed in a red Santa Claus suit. Upon landing he would distribute Sandow's Chocolate from a sack to the children in Hyde Park.

It was a risky stunt, because Hyde Park lay two miles to the north of the gas works where the balloon was being filled. If the wind held true from the south, the flyer could drop into the big park safely. But if the wind should shift, the leaping Santa might find himself almost anywhere over the jagged roofs and chimney pots of London.

The balloon was owned by the Spencer brothers, a pair of Australians who performed in demonstrations all over England. Their entire capital was tied up in the craft.

When I arrived at the gas works, the weather had taken a turn for the worse, with a gusty wind shifting from south to southwest. Low clouds were scudding over the city. But the balloon boys were game to go. Frank Spencer was troubled because there was not enough weight in the basket—a wickerwork affair just about big enough for three, with ballast bags hanging over the edges.

On an impulse, I said, "Why don't you take me along? I can add the weight, and take pictures from the air."

Without even thinking it over, Frank said, "Come on, Bert. Hop in!"

I climbed into the basket clutching my precious motion-picture outfit and a still camera, and squeezed in between the parachutist-Santa and Frank Spencer, while his brother directed the crew in preparations to cast off. But now the difficulty was reversed, because with the added weight, plus the wind and the chill air, the Spencers feared we might not rise quickly enough to clear the massive iron framework of the gas tank just downwind of our starting point.

The large envelope swelled and swelled; every foot of gas possible was forced into it. Someone shouted, "Boys, unless you give the basket a mighty heave she'll never clear."

The boys heaved with a hearty, "Up she goes!" And up we went, angling steeply toward the menacing iron girders. We didn't clear them. The basket caught, almost capsized, and it was a miracle we were not thrown to the ground. My cameras were strapped in, but I was photographing with one when the jolt came. I was flung halfway out of the basket, but Frank, hanging on for dear life with one hand, grabbed my collar and prevented me from falling. It was a narrow escape. The great balloon swung and bobbed, straining at her ropes. We pushed and heaved, and after a few minutes of desperate struggle managed to free the basket from the iron framework, and lurched clear, sailing up at an angle. The houses sped by below us.

We caught a glimpse of the Thames beneath us and then we were lost in the clouds—clouds so thick they blotted out every sign of the great city down below. I suddenly realized what kind of pickle my impulsive offer to join the party had got me into—but there was no point regretting it now. We were cold and miserable up there, and felt quite alone in our strange and somewhat ridiculous situation, yet each of us wanted to carry out his job: Penfold somehow had to deliver those "palatable, digestible, economical" chocolates for the Sandow Chocolate and Cocoa Company; Frank Spencer had to do his best (despite the wind and clouds) to deliver him; and I had pictures to shoot and then deliver to Gaumont. Naturally enough, all three of us wanted to get out of all this alive and in one piece.

We drifted for a long while, during which it became obvious that wherever Penfold jumped, it would not be in Hyde Park, which must have been left behind in the first five minutes of our wild ride. He had intended to swing out from the basket on a trapeze to give the viewers down below a thrill before dropping earthward on his Yuletide errand of good will. But that part of the show was definitely out now.

We were discussing the dilemma when suddenly beneath us there was a patch of clear sky and open country. Whereupon the parachutist, without a moment's hesitation, stepped to the basket rim and jumped with his load of chocolates, and I leaned overside desperately trying to snap him as he fell.

What with the relief from his weight and the mighty shove he gave as he leaped into the air, the basket tipped and swung violently. Frank and I almost went over the side with him—and we had no parachutes. But we managed to hold on as the balloon shot skyward. The plan was for Frank to release gas at the time Penfold left, so that the balloon, relieved of so much weight, would not rise too quickly. By the time we had recovered our balance, however, we were up to fifteen thousand feet, with the gas release cord whipping violently as we swung, and so entangled in the shrouds above us that the gas valve could not be operated. The more we pulled, the tighter the tangle. Now we *were* in a fix, because there was no possibility that we could climb into the shrouds and release the valve by hand. We would have to wait until the gas cooled and for much of it to escape through the fabric before we could hope to descend. Frank estimated we might be aloft twenty-four hours, perhaps thirty.

It was bitterly cold at that altitude, we had no suitable clothing, and we were still rising. Soon we were up to twenty-two thousand feet. The wicker-work basket gave no protection from the wind. But we were at least thankful that a balloon drifts with the air currents, so its occupants are not blown too hard. Otherwise, at the temperature we were in we would soon have been stiff and frostbitten. We shivered for hours and rubbed and slapped ourselves for warmth, except when we were in clear sunshine now and then as we swung from cloud top to cloud top.

But it was not long before we were aware of a new hazard, for the wind was fast carrying us toward the cold seas to the northeast of England. By the time the gas should cool we would doubtless be over the North Sea. We struggled with the ropes and finally risked climbing the shrouds but, with our frost-stiffened fingers, we could not budge the valve. By nightfall, hungry, frozen, and miserable, we were resigned to our fate in that runaway balloon.

How we spent the night we could hardly remember afterward, but when dawn broke we were thrilled to find that we could still see the coast. The wind had changed; we were drifting over the Channel, and the balloon was descending. As we swung down within three thousand feet of the sea, it looked as if we were on our way to a watery grave. Then, a bit lower, we saw we were drifting toward a tugboat. We watched anxiously and talked of this fortuitous succor to buoy our hopes—but luck was against us. The wind carried us past the vessel while we were still two thousand feet above it. The men on board signaled to us, but of course could do nothing to help. As the sun rose we again ascended and drifted farther out to sea on another stream of air.

That day passed as though it were half a lifetime. Again in the late afternoon we saw we were once more approaching the coast, but what part of the coast we couldn't tell, for we had lost all track of our movement.

As evening came the balloon sank rather sickeningly. The gas was cold now, and much of it had escaped. We felt sure we would soon be in the water. But if we could keep aloft until we drifted over land, we would be all set to throw overboard my cameras, the sand bags, and our boots if necessary.

Slowly we inched toward the coast, dipping and bobbing in the turbulent air. Twice we almost swept the water. My cameras went overboard. Up we went. Next our precious ballast. With this gone, we knew we would not be able to control the balloon when over land, and would strike heavily. Having hit the ground, it would be almost impossible for us both to jump at the same instant, and with the loss of the weight of one, the other, if still aboard, would go up again.

Down we came and were swept into some treetops. The basket lurched crazily, and the branches ripped our fingers as we clung to its edges. Eager though we were to save our lives, Frank also wanted to save the balloon, for it represented all his and his brother's worldly possessions.

We hung in a tree for a moment; the balloon dipped, struck the ground, then bounced and jerked. The basket was yanked from the treetop and smashed into the ground with such force that Frank was temporarily paralyzed by a blow in the small of the back. Here was a further predicament. How was I to get the balloon under control and get Frank out of the basket? Fortunately, we were in open farm land. It was late evening but several farmers were still out trying to finish their winter plowing. They shouted to us as we bobbed past. The balloon, pushed by the strong wind, took giant steps, each time banging our basket into the ground and on occasion dragging us through a thick hedge. Then, with the balloon still jerking us along, we headed straight for a team of horses, which bolted in fright at this strange apparition. Off they went, dragging the plow across the field while the farmer desperately hung onto the reins. I didn't see clearly what happened next. I was busy in the basket trying to protect Frank from further injury, when we snapped to a full stop. Then more heavy bumping. The basket had hitched itself to the plow as it passed!

The balloon bobbed and bumped as the frantic horses dragged us over the field. There was nothing I could do except seize the rip cord and tear a strip from the balloon. At least we were on the ground, and I cared not at all that the balloon would be useless for days until the rip could be repaired. The balloon collapsed, and the horses were quieted. The farmer brought a dray and drove the empty envelope, Frank, and myself to a nearby village. There Frank got medical care, and I caught a train to London. A fine Christmas Eve!

When I reached the office, I found the place in an uproar. Everybody supposed we had been lost. Steamers and tugs were searching for us in the Channel. The whole countryside was roused and looking for us. My boss looked at me, speechless. When he got his voice back, he barked, "Wilkins, haven't you any better sense than to take chances like that when you know we've got no insurance on you?"

Not a word about my safety. The office had carried insurance on me at a heavy rate all the time I was off covering the Balkan War, but the policy had not been renewed. They thought it was imprudent of me to risk my life when it wasn't insured, especially since I didn't have any worthwhile pictures to show for all my effort.

I found from the newspapers that our aerial Santa Claus had landed on the back of his head in a field near Chelmsford, about thirty-five miles northeast of Hyde Park, and had needed about ten minute's rest before his senses cleared. By the time he could see people instead of stars, he was surrounded by farmers and children who had come running to his assistance, so he was at least able to distribute his chocolates and get some publicity for Sandow. One little boy, taking him for the real Santa Claus, assured him gravely, "Don't forget, I want a pop-gun tomorrow."

About this time Philip Gibbs, Bernard Grant, and I finished writing a book about the Balkan War. Philip Gibbs, who was later knighted during World War I, had been with the Bulgars. Bernard Grant and I, when we returned from Turkey, met him in London, and he said, "Let's hurry and get out a book. It will be the first one from the Balkan War, and Methuen will publish it."

Gibbs was a very skillful, fast writer, with good publishing connections. His idea was that the three of us should write the book, covering the story of the war from both points of view, Turk and Bulgar. Grant and I thought that three names on one book would be overdoing it, so we decided to write our story together and then toss to see whose name went on the cover. Grant won the toss, so my name went inside the book. It appeared as *Adventures of War with Cross and Crescent,* by Philip Gibbs and Bernard Grant.

By the time the book came out I was far away in the West Indies, filming and writing up the cocoa industry for Cadbury, Ltd., a chocolate manufacturer with somewhat more restrained publicity methods than Sandow's.

Life on the Caribbean island of Trinidad was quite a contrast to war and cholera in the Balkans. I had a charming house and garden, a staff of servants, and every day I went by train to the nearby cocoa plantations. An old West Indian met me with his cab and an aged white horse. The old horse was so pokey I usually strolled ahead of him. In the evening we would return in leisurely fashion with the films I had taken. During the night, working in my house, I would develop them.

I found the cocoa industry fascinating. The trees grow as high as twenty feet and have leaves so glossy they appear artificial. Their odd-looking purple fruit protrudes directly from the trunk. These trees must grow in the shade, and are planted beneath a taller tree called "Mother of Cocoa."

Workmen gather the purple fruit, cutting it open and scooping out the gluey pink pulp, full of seeds. The pulp is left to ferment for ten or twelve days, until the seeds separate from the sticky mass. Then they are washed, dried, coated with clay, and roasted like coffee.

The whole scene was picturesque, as if made to order for the camera—the glossy black laborers naked from the waist up, working with the purple fruit and pink pulp in the tropical light and shadow. Leon Gaumont hand-colored the film I shot and produced it under the title, "Food for the Gods." This was the beginning of color cinematography.

Indentured labor was used on the plantations, as in the British colonies of North America in the seventeenth century. The native laborers had strict caste rules and moral laws. White men were kept at a distance. The women's compound was separate, and only the husbands of the married women were permitted to see the women's dances. Perhaps for this very reason I decided to try to film them.

It required some persistence, but eventually I got the overseer's sister to agree to help me take the pictures. She arranged a feast in the women's quarters on a day when the overseer sent all the men to work on a distant part of the plantation. Then I was dressed as a woman, and the overseer's sister introduced me to the dancers. They knew who I was, but we argued that as I was a photographer and dressed like a woman, I should be considered merely a part of the camera. After all, said I, their moral code didn't forbid a camera seeing their dances. After much persuasion, the women agreed to let me stay and crank away. Dressed in colorful, voluminous skirts but otherwise naked, their coal-black hair falling about their shoulders, they made a fascinating sight. The music grew louder, and the dance grew wilder.

When the excitement was at its height, the women made so much noise with their drumming and singing that the men heard it, and one of them stole back to see what was going on. He dared not come into the compound, but stayed outside peering through a crack in the wall until he was sent away. I was told that he had recognized his wife, and me. That evening after dinner, I was sitting on the veranda of the overseer's house with some other people, when suddenly we heard screams in the women's quarters. We rushed down to investigate, and saw this fellow chasing his wife with a machete. Just as we appeared, he caught her and slashed off one of her ears.

At first the woman was in disgrace, for it was their law that when a woman transgresses the moral code, her husband shall cut off one or both of her ears, to brand her for life. In this instance, though, the others decided within a few days that she had done nothing wrong, on the ground that only a camera had seen her dance. They all then turned against the husband, and she became the heroine of the compound, proud to tell the story and display her battle scar.

When my work at the cocoa plantations was finished I planned
to join a French expedition bound for the Orinoco, and take pictures of the white Indians said to live there—if we found them.
The expedition was not quite ready to start, so I filled in the
time with a trip around the Lesser Antilles, filming the beautiful
scenery. I was in Barbados visiting friends when word came that
I must return to London and join the Orinoco expedition at once.
A boat was just about to leave. We piled my luggage into a car
and raced to catch it, but before we reached the wharf the boat
had sailed. I hired a fast motor launch and set out in pursuit.
Some little distance out to sea we overhauled it and came alongside, and the captain and my friends held the launch while I
clambered up to the boat's deck with my photographic gear. As
I came over the side, the steward handed me a cablegram. I
ripped it open, saw it was from my London office, and read:

WOULD YOU GO IMPORTANT ANTARCTIC EXPEDITION? MEANS
TWO OR THREE YEARS ABSENCE. GOOD TERMS. EXCELLENT
OPPORTUNITY.

I was overjoyed. To me the query meant only one thing—that
the one leader above all others with whom I had for years dreamed
of making a trip to the Antarctic, Sir Ernest Shackleton, had succeeded in getting another expedition together. I had met this famous explorer a couple of years earlier in England, and had boldly
said that I was at his service for a trip to the South Polar regions
if he should ever want me. In the months that had passed, my hope
that he even remembered me had faded. Now this cablegram meant
I would be able to tackle the great, grim continent that lay at
the bottom of the world!

Shouting to my friends in the launch to hold on, I scribbled
an affirmative reply and tossed it to them. They promised to cable
my message the moment they should reach shore. When they
were gone, I went down to my cabin to settle my luggage. After a
little time I looked at the cablegram again. The news was so
good I wanted to assure myself that it was true. This time I read:

WOULD YOU GO IMPORTANT ARCTIC EXPEDITION?

In my hurry I had mistaken the key word. I knew that Shackleton was not going to the Arctic, and I wanted to go with Shackleton. It was my ambition to do some extensive and valuable work in the Polar regions, and I knew that I must have a great deal of training before I could undertake to handle an expedition myself. Shackleton, I believed, would be the man to give me the training I needed. Another leader might not give me much opportunity to learn what I needed to know.

In 1913 we had no telegraph on shipboard. We would not reach Trinidad for some days, and during that time I was cut off from any communication with London. I realized that in the meantime my office would be acting on the basis of the cablegram my Barbados friends had sent for me. I could not see anything to do but abide by my mistaken assent.

Arriving in London, I hurried to the Gaumont office. As soon as I came in I asked, "Who's making this Arctic expedition? I agreed to go with it by mistake. I thought I was going with Shackleton, and I know he isn't going to the North."

"No," the manager told me. "It's Stefansson."

"Who's Stefansson?"

"He's a Canadian. He's been to the Arctic several times, and this promises to be quite an important expedition."

The boss explained that Stefansson wanted a photographer along, and I was recommended as the logical man. Maybe they thought I lived a sort of charmed life, with my penchant for getting into scrapes and out of them. I wondered whether Stefansson was perhaps a kind of daredevil himself, so I asked, "What sort of fellow is he?"

"Oh, he's an interesting chap. I have met him and talked with him. He tells me he is going to the Arctic to travel with dogs, and he will expect you to work like a dog, work with the dogs, and eat the dogs if necessary."

Well, I had agreed to go and could hardly back out now, so off I went to Canada.

6

North with Stefansson

I met Vilhjalmur Stefansson for the first time in Victoria, British Columbia, where the Department of Naval Service was assembling the equipment, supplies, crew, and scientific staff for his expedition. I found him a slim, small-boned man just under six feet tall, with an impressively large head and brow, a wide, expressive smile, and soft manner of speech that put the other fellow at his ease at once. He was informal, and asked others to call him Stef. He had studied religion and anthropology at Harvard University, and although now only thirty-three was already known far and wide for his explorations in northern Alaska and western arctic Canada. This remarkable man, I had learned since betraying my ignorance in London, had actually lived for five years among the Eskimos and come back to civilization announcing his discovery of the so-called "blond Eskimos" of that part of the world. Stef was rugged, adaptable, and immensely learned in the ways of the North.

I realized quickly how fortunate I was that he had turned to the Gaumont Company for an expedition photographer, and how lucky I had been in misreading that cable weeks before in the Caribbean. Coming into contact with Stefansson in this chance way was another turning point in my life.

The purpose of the expedition was soon explained to me. Stefansson planned to explore the Beaufort Sea and Coronation Gulf area —two bodies of water washing the northwestern coast of mainland Canada. The land there included Victoria and Banks Land, now called Banks Island, two big islands which were known in only the most hazy outline. The expedition was to last five years, and would carry out research of many kinds. The scientific staff would be large, in comparison with what was then usual on polar expeditions. Not counting the captains and mates, some of whom were scientists in their own right, the staff numbered sixteen, including Stefansson and his second in command, Dr. Rudolph Martin Anderson, head of the expedition's southern or Coronation Gulf section, Stefansson heading the northern. When I joined we had only one ship, the *Karluk,* but we gradually picked up others, first the *Alaska,* then the *Mary Sachs, North Star,* and *Polar Bear.*

For me the prospect was fascinating, not only to explore and to take pioneering motion pictures of the Far North, but also to learn about weather observation in the Arctic. This harked back to my boyhood dreams, where the possibility of some day knowing the weather weeks ahead had seemed to me the answer to many of man's problems. The hope of studying the meteorology of the Antarctic had originally attracted me to Shackleton, but now here I was about to see the picture at the other end of the world, so to speak.

The first day I went to the Esquimolt Navy Yard I came upon a fellow sauntering along a footpath. He looked to me as if he had been having a bad weekend. When I asked if he could tell me where to find the *Karluk,* he snapped, "What do you want with the *Karluk?*"

"I'm going on the expedition."

He looked me up and down and said, "What? In those clothes?"

I was wearing spats and striped trousers, and a topper. He had on ordinary gray trousers and jacket. I must have appeared an English dandy to him.

"No," I said. "But that has nothing to do with it. Can you tell me where I can find the ship?"

He said, "Have you any money?"

"Yes. But I never ask for money—neither borrow nor lend."

"All right," he said. "Come along and let's have a drink. Then I'll take you to the *Karluk.*"

As we started out, he said, "I'm Mackay. Surgeon with the expedition."

Then I realized that I had fallen in with the famous Dr. Alister Forbes Mackay, one of the heroes of Shackleton's first trip to the Antarctic. Presently he took me down to the *Karluk,* assuring me she would prove to be a much more comfortable ship than she looked.

She was a cramped old whaler of 250 tons, a barkentine rigged with square sails. She stank of whale oil. The quarters were like nothing I had ever seen—unpainted, crowded, smelly, and swarming with cockroaches. I saw no place for any decent food or comfort.

That afternoon I met the ship's commander, the already legendary Bob Bartlett, who had skippered Robert E. Peary's ship, the *Roosevelt,* in his conquest of the North Pole. I began to wonder what kind of cruise I was in for. Although appearances certainly seemed to be against the ship, yet these were famous and capable men, among them Diamond Jenness, anthropologist and Rhodes Scholar from New Zealand, Professor Henri Beuchat of Paris, known for his work in American ethnology, the oceanographer, James Murray of Glasgow, who had also been with Shackleton in the Antarctic.

Assuming I would have time to put to use during the journey north, I decided to study navigation, and, in order to get experience, asked to be assigned to a watch. Bartlett agreed to take me in hand.

We sailed from Victoria in June, 1913, in the *Karluk,* and had a pleasant trip up through the Inside Passage, which provided a magnificent spectacle of rugged mountains and ice capped islands, glaciers and crags, with our route of chill, blue water weaving amongst them. Stefansson followed us on a passenger steamer and joined us in Nome. No sooner had he arrived than there was almost a mutiny in the expedition. A number of the other men would not agree to his plan for living on, or off, the Arctic; they demanded additional provisions and water tanks.

Stefansson told them they would get water from the ice. This they did not believe, though they were scientists. The fact is, and Stefansson knew it from experience, that the ice in the ocean is bitterly salt only at the start, getting fresher month by month till in a year it is fresh enough for strong coffee, while in two it will make excellent tea, and in three years it is fresher than almost any mountain brook. There are great ponds of fresh water on top of the Arctic ice in summer. One only needs to dip it up in buckets.

After the doubters were satisfied, we moved on to Teller, a few miles up the coast from Nome, to take aboard sledge dogs and a supply of fish for their food. Then, when we were about to start, the engineer of the *Mary Sachs* came aboard raving drunk and refused to start the engines. The skipper could run them, but the engineer, James R. Crawford, wouldn't let anyone else touch them while he was in charge. He was so drunk that all he wanted was to flop in his bunk and sleep. But he protested in his drunken way that he couldn't sleep with the engines running. Our other two boats were lying idle in the stream, and delay could be dangerous. So I went to Stefansson and volunteered to run the engines. This was the first time he had heard I knew anything about engines. He said, "Well, if you can persuade Crawford, go ahead. It will be a real service to the expedition."

I went over to the *Mary Sachs,* and the skipper and I tried to persuade Crawford to let me run the engines until he felt like doing so. He was in a fighting temper, and getting him to agree to anything was out of the question. Without consulting Stefansson further, the skipper and I locked Crawford in his cabin, I started the engines, and we set off. At the end of two days we judged it would be safe to let the engineer out, but we were mistaken. He was a bad actor, especially when drinking. It was no longer safe for me to be on the same boat with him, so I transferred back to the *Karluk.* Crawford never forgave me.

The *Karluk* leading, we passed north through Bering Strait into the Arctic Ocean, then worked our way northeastward through the ice toward the Beaufort Sea.

Some distance past Point Barrow, the northernmost tip of Alaska, Bartlett believed he could use the principle of ice navigation followed for many years on the Greenland coast, namely, to go out into the ice instead of remaining in the strip of open water near the shore. He failed to allow for the fact that the Greenland ice drifts away from the shore, while in the Arctic Ocean there is no regularity to the movements of the ice. It seldom opens twice in the same place.

Bartlett, not understanding this, took the *Karluk* out into a lead away from shore, expecting it to open again next day. It never did. That night, under the stress of wind and current, the floes pressed in, one against the other, and we were solidly frozen in the ice. The *Alaska* and the *Mary Sachs* passed between us and the shore and went eastward out of sight.

We were frozen in about fifteen miles off shore. As the cold continued and the ice became thicker Stefansson thought we might be stuck there for the winter. This was most inconvenient, because some of our party's equipment was on the other ships, and some of the men from Anderson's group were aboard the *Karluk*. We had meant to make a redistribution, separating Anderson's party from Stefansson's in the Arctic at Herschel Island, off the Canadian coast, about 400 miles east of Point Barrow.

This was not going to be a routine photography job—I could see that right off. I was being introduced to the Arctic with a bang. The emotional effect of that immense solitude was overpowering, awe inspiring. There was something terrifying in the way the ice had gripped the *Karluk,* and now held it. Our party seemed abandoned in an empty world.

After some days Stefansson's secretary, Burt McConnell, told me that Stefansson was planning to go ashore and get some Eskimos to stay with us through the winter. At first Stefansson intended to take no one with him but McConnell, but when I said this would be an opportunity to get pictures of the ice and the Eskimos, Stefansson said I might go along. He then added Jenness to the group.

None of us except Stefansson had had any experience either on the ice or in low temperatures. We were all wearing summer clothing; the fur garments were aboard the other vessels. In order to demonstrate his theory that men can learn to live with minimal supplies on the resources of nature in the Arctic, Stefansson took little food, either for us or for the dogs. I took with me only one small camera.

Early on September 20, the four of us set out with a dog team. Everything was new and strange to me. I was surprised to find how difficult it was to travel over the rough ice, and how complicated the management of a sled and dogs. We had to look ahead constantly to choose the smoothest route, help the animals at the roughest places, and be alert to separate them when they snapped at each other. We traveled only a few miles that day, and that night the *Karluk* could still be seen in the distance. I then had my first lesson in making camp on Arctic ice in a temperature far below zero. This meant pitching our tent by a windbreak, staking out the dogs separately, cooking with minimal fuel and no waste of rations, and finally managing a sleeping place with rock-hard ice less than an inch beneath our weary bodies.

Some time in the night we were awakened by the howling of a terrific storm. It continued without a break for two days and nights, and practically all that time we stayed in our sleeping bags, huddled in the tent. Never had I been so cold and stiff in my life. Outside, we could see nothing for the whirl of snow, nor hear anything but the screaming wind and the crunch of broken ice.

I shall never forget the jar and then the wavering motion when we were set afloat. The storm was breaking up the ice, and we found ourselves floating on a cake barely large enough to hold our small tent and the dogs. The grating jolts when we struck against other floating ice cakes shocked me into a numb fear.

On the third day, when the storm cleared, we could see no trace of the *Karluk*. In every direction, to the far horizon, we could see nothing but ice adrift in open water. Nor did we ever see that ship again.

Stefansson had instructed Bartlett, in case of a breakup, to set beacons on the ice and if possible to send a party ashore with a message and a flag, so we might know the *Karluk*'s new position for our return. But we saw no beacons, and we could not reach the shore. Although we made several attempts, we always came to open leads too wide to cross. The ice was drifting slowly westward, but Stefansson was not alarmed either for us or for the *Karluk*. We were well inside Harrison Bay, and the probability was that the ice would hang on Cape Halkett, a point to the west, and remain there for the winter.

Our food was soon gone, so we began living on the Arctic, as Vilhjalmur Stefansson had trained himself to do. He showed us a good many of the survival tricks he had learned from the Eskimos. We shot seals and foxes, but saw no polar bears. These are the three forms of game that venture out on the ice. Other animals never leave the shore, because, no matter how deeply land and sea are buried under solid ice, they always know when land is beneath them and they stay on it.

We were afloat for a week or more before the open leads froze and we were able to reach land. By that time, thanks to Stefansson, the rest of us were getting used to ways of living in the Arctic, and I found it not so difficult. He was one man in the world to teach this art, since he had added the special knowledge of the Eskimo to his own scientific training.

As soon as we reached the shore we set out with all speed, going westward along the coast to overtake the *Karluk*. Evidently she had drifted with the ice, and we were hoping she might have gotten locked in so we could get back to her. But we saw neither ship nor beacons—nothing but the rough, hummocky ice, and the snow. We were hoping to find Eskimos, but there were no Eskimos on that barren coast. The only game was an occasional raven.

Stefansson did not dare risk going inland to hunt, for fear of missing the *Karluk,* so we pushed on day and night, with only occasional pauses for rest. After some days even the scrawny ravens deserted us, so we were reduced to small rations of seal oil and a few tufts of reindeer hair. Naturally there is no nourish-

ment in reindeer hair, but we felt that we wanted something under our belts. The most satisfying thing we could do was swallow
a few tufts. This gave the sensation of something in the stomach
to ease the gnawing pain.

One day we came to a place where foxes had been digging in the
snow. We dug down and found what was left of the carcass of a
whale. There was no blubber left, just a little lean meat on the
bones. We decided the best thing to do was to eat it raw and
frozen. It was almost tasteless, and because it was frozen we got
no smell. After eating sparingly of it, we carried the rest along
with us, living on it until we finally came to an Eskimo camp.
These Eskimos had seen nothing of the *Karluk,* but they welcomed us into their houses warmed with blubber lamps, and
gave us frozen fish. The Eskimos dug them up from a cache outside the igloo, and showed us how to trim and skin them, and they
were very good.

After resting for a day with the Eskimos, we continued along
the coast. I was more or less crippled because I was not used to
walking in shoes without heels. My shoes had worn out, and I
was now traveling in Eskimo mukluks, a soft, wrap-around foot-
gear without support, which strained the tendons and caused the
painful condition called "Achilles' heel."

We eventually reached Cape Halkett, but still found no trace
of the *Karluk.* There was no sign of beacons on the ice or messages
on shore. We had all along been confident of finding the ship
somewhere in the bay or at Cape Halkett. Beyond that point, because of the contours of the shoreline, it was impossible to guess
what might have happened to her.

We traveled on, and next day met an Eskimo family who gave
us our first news of the missing ship. They had seen her drifting westward along the coast, locked in the ice, well within
sight of land. They had made an attempt to reach her on foot,
but were stopped by open water. They wondered why nobody
attempted to come ashore from the *Karluk* with a boat. The
ship remained in that neighborhood, they said, for almost two days,
and then slowly drifted farther westward and out of sight.

That was the last anybody on shore ever saw of the *Karluk*.

Stefansson was amazed, because anyone familiar with the Arctic must have known that once the ship passed Cape Halkett there would be little hope of leaving it and reaching shore. The currents around Point Barrow, summer and winter, break up the ice so badly it is impossible to move without a boat, and difficult and dangerous even with one. It seemed mysterious that Bob Bartlett had not sent someone ashore while he could do so, especially as there were several men aboard whose equipment was on the other ships. It seemed incredible that he had not at least sent a party ashore to leave a message for us.

The only thing for us to do now was to strike out on foot for Point Barrow, which lay 120 miles up the coast, a little north of west. There, at the trading post, we could buy winter equipment and wait out the worst of the season's cold weather. When we pulled in after several days' hard traveling across the many frozen bays which indent the shoreline, we found that here, too, there was no word of our lost ship. In any event, the four of us were quite safe, and I had come to the end of my first Arctic trek much wiser in the ways of the Far North than when we had set out from the *Karluk* on September 20.

The journey had been a severe one. Wearing summer clothes and finding little game, we had suffered from cold and lack of food. My feet were in bad shape. Still, I realized that if a man agrees to go to the Arctic he should be hardy and put up with any suffering that comes along. I thought it was an explorer's duty to suffer and be a martyr. I had yet to learn that, properly prepared, we could be as comfortable in Arctic conditions as if we were down in civilization.

At Point Barrow we described our journey to Charley Brower, the trader who had lived there so many years that he practically *was* Point Barrow to those who visited this most northerly settlement in the Western Hemisphere. A husky, smiling, cheerful optimist, Charley Brower loved his northern life and wouldn't have returned to so-called "civilization" in the temperate zone for any amount of money. Stefansson, in his book *The Friendly Arctic*, called Charley "the most northerly citizen of Uncle Sam for forty years."

When we told him about finding the whale on the beach, Charley said, "Yes, I know that whale. I killed it four years ago."

It took us about a week to recover from our trip and be outfitted with proper suits of Eskimo clothes. Meanwhile we lived at the trading post. Mrs. Brower was an Eskimo, and there were a number of Brower children. The Browers' cook, Fred Hopson, had also married an Eskimo girl.

Going into the kitchen one morning, I was appalled to hear the language Hopson was using to his wife. He swore at her for at least ten minutes before he caught sight of me. Then he broke off with a laugh and said, "Don't worry about her. She doesn't understand a word I say. We've been married twenty-eight years and have sixteen children, but she doesn't know a word of English. I just swear at her to let off steam. It doesn't mean a thing." And true enough, Mrs. Hopson had amiably and placidly continued to help cook breakfast the whole time.

We ate with the Browers, and slept in unoccupied corners of the store, using our own equipment and sleeping bags. The store was a frame building, about 30 by 40 feet, with shelves around the sides, and a number of tables on which goods were displayed to the Eskimos. There was a big coal-burning stove in the center, with chairs around it. Often when we woke in the morning the chairs were occupied by an Eskimo family who sat watching us with interest. The Eskimos would sit in these chairs and spend an hour or more quietly looking around the store, before they began their bargaining.

They brought with them sometimes three or four plump bags, whose contents remained a mystery until at last one would produce a fox skin and begin negotiations with Brower. When the price for that skin was settled, he would begin to look at goods and take his time about selecting what he wanted, up to the full amount. Then he would make an unsuccessful application for credit, and that failing, he would reluctantly produce another skin double the value of the first. In this way, little by little, all the contents of the bags would come to light. The finest skin was invariably held until the last. The Eskimos were keen traders and since the school had been opened at Point Barrow, they had learned the use of money. They often demanded to be paid in dollars and cents, only to spend the money in the store immediately. They liked to feel they were spending money like the white man.

We had been at Point Barrow about five days when Stefansson asked me to take a dog team and travel along the coast to a fishing lake, to get fish for ourselves and the dogs. He gave me minute instructions, telling me precisely where I was to go and what I was to do, which included waiting for him at the lake. I started out with Jenness and two Eskimos hired at Barrow.

We traveled for two days in the direction Stefansson had indicated, and then came to a wide bay. The Eskimos halted at the shoreline and said we must not cross because a storm was coming. They insisted we go around the bay. I consulted my map and found that to go around meant an additional forty miles. Deciding the Eskimos wanted to make the trip longer because they were being paid by the day, I said that we would cross the ice, and made them start. They lagged behind for some time, then hurried to catch up with us and tearfully begged me to come back. In my ignorance, and my determination to follow Stefansson's instructions to the letter, I would not listen.

We had not traveled more than a mile when a storm hit us head on. The dogs became unmanageable at once. It is their nature to den up during a storm, and though they will travel through a storm in harness, it is their instinct to keep their backs to it. I found it almost impossible to make any headway, but I kept doing my best to drive them on. For some time I struggled forward against the wind, and I began to suffer badly from the cold. After a while, not feeling the pain so much, I concluded I was getting used to it.

The violence of the storm finally made it impossible to go farther, so we built a snow house for ourselves and the dogs and, crawling into it, dragged a tarpaulin over us. In a few minutes we felt the ice heaving up and down beneath us and knew we were afloat. All night the Eskimos sat up and prayed and sang hymns they had learned from missionaries. Jenness and I got as much sleep as we could. One thing that bothered me was a queer, numb stiffness of my hands and face. My face especially puzzled me; it felt like a mask.

In the morning the storm was not quite so bad. I could make a course without driving straight into the wind, so we started out again. We found the ice broken, but by avoiding the wider leads we managed to make fair progress.

When full daylight came, the others saw that my face was covered with blisters. Jenness did not realize the seriousness of this condition, and the Eskimos said nothing. They were sullen. Later, I learned that I had made them risk their lives the day before, and had camped for the night in a most dangerous place, where other parties had been lost. I went ahead of the team, fighting against the storm until we reached the other side of the bay. Meantime the blisters covered my whole face.

We traveled all day, and came at last to an igloo. Thank God, we found Eskimos inside! We went into the warm igloo and, in spite of the heavy stench of blubber, furs, and human bodies, it was a tremendous relief to be sheltered from the storm.

Before I could even sit down, an Eskimo woman seized hold of me and hastily thrust me outdoors again. I thought I had been guilty of some breach of etiquette, for which they were putting me out of their house. I stood there for a moment in the storm, not quite knowing what to do. Then my two Eskimos came out rather sulkily, still resenting my treatment of them. They took me into the igloo by stages to ease the damage to my frozen face —first just inside the outer house, then little by little along the passage. As I came slowly into the warmer air, I began to feel the pain of thawing out. I carried the scars of that freezing for more than a year, and for some weeks my nose, chin, and mouth were one big scab.

We stayed two or three days in the igloo, treated kindly by the Eskimos. Then we went out to the fishing lake and piled up our store of fish, while waiting for Stefansson to come along. When he arrived he was well stocked with winter equipment. McConnell was with him as well as several Eskimos Stefansson had hired at Point Barrow. This time we made far better speed going back on our tracks eastward to the rendezvous point he had arranged with the other two ships back in August. This was Collinson Point, 300 miles away. Stefansson had now given up hope of finding the *Karluk* this season, and we could only wonder at the fate of Captain Bob Bartlett and the others we had left aboard her.

At Collinson Point we found that the *Alaska* and the *Mary Sachs* section of the expedition had taken up quarters in an old hut built of earth and logs. Tired and hungry after our long march, we arrived just in time for Christmas dinner.

To add my share to the party, I broke out the motion-picture projection machine after dinner and put on a show. The machine and generator had been on the *Mary Sachs,* and it was all I had of my equipment. The rest was on the *Karluk.* Our Eskimos had never seen a moving picture, and we wondered what the effect would be on them. They watched several short dramas and comedies with interest but without pronounced reaction. But when I put on a wild animal picture, showing lions and tigers and elephants in action, the Eskimos bolted under benches and through doors.

Early in the new year, 1914, Stefansson announced that he was going on with his plan to explore the Beaufort Sea. Though he had lost his ship and his equipment and the men on whom he had relied for help, he intended to carry out his plan on foot and short-handed. He asked for volunteers, and I was one who decided to go with him.

Immediately there was a controversy about equipment. Stefansson, as leader of the expedition, naturally had a right to what he needed. But the members of the Anderson party meant to keep all the equipment they had. They said it was not their fault that Stefansson had been left without equipment, and that to divide with him would upset their own plans.

This quarrel over equipment delayed our start for weeks, and we set out at last on March 16, not very well armed to meet the challenge of the Arctic. We were aiming for Banks Land, 800 miles away across the frozen sea, and knew, with our late start, we were racing against the spring break-up of the winter ice. We had been traveling only a few hours when a blizzard struck us, and were able to keep going only two days with our poor equipment when we had to halt. Several sleds had broken down, most of our kerosene had been lost, and a number of the dogs could go no farther.

We made camp and discussed the situation. There were six of us with Stefansson, besides the Eskimos. The chances of completing our journey, depending entirely on the resources of the Arctic, did not look very encouraging. It seemed absolutely necessary to get another supply of kerosene, fresh dogs, and new sleds from the Anderson party.

I volunteered to go back and fetch the needed supplies, and this was decided upon. The party would wait in camp until I returned. Stefansson sent Natkusiak with me, an Eskimo he had known for years. He was the most capable Eskimo I have ever met—a roly-poly little fellow, always jovial and good-natured, with a keen sense of humor, interested, and wideawake. Taking the strongest sled, as nearly empty as possible, and the best dog team, we set out to cover the two days' journey to the shore and back in forced marches.

Early the second day we encountered another blizzard. A 70-mile gale blew out from shore, full of stinging snow, and we had to face directly into it. The dogs turned vicious when we pushed them. In any other circumstances we would have camped, but we had no choice. We struggled on in the blinding snow, fighting the ferocious dogs every yard of the way and constantly having to straighten them out in harness and right the upset sled. Finally the dogs became completely unmanageable. Suddenly they broke away from us and disappeared in the blizzard, still harnessed and taking the sled with them.

Although Natkusiak and I managed to get safely through to the outfitting camp, the storm became so furious that it was hopeless to venture out. In that smother of snow we could not hope to find Stefansson's camp. As soon as the storm showed signs of decreasing in fury, we set out, with new dogs and sledge. Some miles from shore we came into clear weather, and with the wind behind we made good time, traveling day and night without stop until we reached a place a few miles from the spot where our camp had been. There we came on wide stretches of open water.

Every trace of Stefansson's party had vanished. There was nothing to be seen but the open water and cakes of floating ice.

It seemed evident that Stefansson and his men were marooned on a floe somewhere out at sea, short of food and supplies. There was a chance that we could find them by getting across the open leads and traveling in the direction of the ice-pack's drift. We spent five days trying to find a way across the open water to the off-shore ice, and always came to open leads too wide to cross. Then we retraced our trail and tried again. I kept setting out flags and messages, but I was forced at last to admit that the attempt to find Stefansson's party was useless.

Stefansson had vanished as the *Karluk* had vanished, on heaven knows what currents, and all we could do now was return to Anderson's camp with all the supplies I had brought—appearing there as if I had deserted my leader on the ice.

7

Exploring the Arctic Isles

I remained at Collinson Point for weeks, as spring warmed into Arctic summer, hoping that a message from Stefansson would somehow get through—if he and his men were still alive.

Anderson's group had an excellent library, and from the scientific collection I had a chance to read for long hours and fill in the gaps in my knowledge of Arctic science. In its own way the delay was a blessing: I had no equipment with which to carry on my photographic work, so I could study to my heart's content.

In all the books, I failed to find a definite statement that a scientific study of polar meteorology would provide a basis for worldwide weather forecasting; but I was excited to find references to the International Polar Year conducted by twelve governments back in the 1880s, during which the exact kind of weather stations I had conceived as a youth in Australia had been maintained in a big circle around the globe. In fact, one station, under Lieutenant Ray of the United States Army Signal Corps, had been located at Point Barrow, where Charley Brower now had his trading post. Another American group was the Lady Franklin Bay party, under Lieutenant A.W. Greely, where the tragedy of starvation of the abandoned men had overshadowed their success in bringing back every one of their scientific records. The trouble was that the International Polar Year reports were only a beginning, from which continuous study could have been extended. Yet no one had carried on the work so well begun thirty years earlier.

In the late spring a trading schooner came in to Collinson Point. Aboard was a photographer with a spare camera. I was able to buy it from him, and at last I could go on with my work while waiting for word from Stefansson. I decided to go to Point Barrow and get pictures of floe whaling, Barrow being one of the few in the world where this technique was practiced. The Eskimos would go out on the ice and wait for the whale to rise, then attack him with spears or harpoon guns and drag him ashore.

Anderson and his men required most of the dogs and all the good sleds for their own work, and I was, after all, just a displaced man from Stefansson's party. The best I could get from Anderson to make the 250-mile trip west along the coast to Point Barrow was a broken-down sled and five of the weakest dogs. The dogs didn't even have the strength to pull our light load, so Natkusiak and I took turns in the traces along with the animals.

I had heard the other men talk of snow-blindness, but I had never experienced the misery of this ailment until Natkusiak and I were well out on the trail. Traveling in the glare of spring sunshine on the snow, I soon had the feeling that my eyeballs were coated with a dense and painful film, through which it became steadily more difficult to see. My eyelids grated on the cornea, as if they were covered with dust. I remember calling out to Natkusiak by the nickname we used in camp: "Hi, Billy! What's the matter with me? My eyes are full of dust, but there isn't any dust here."

"No dust," said the Eskimo, shaking his head. "Maybe you get snow-blind now."

Soon it seemed as if the dust were red hot, and I hardly dared move my eyelids. But even with my eyelids closed, the red hot dust continued to pelt my eyeballs. Then I developed a splitting headache, my limbs began to stiffen, and my joints were sore. I could no longer walk ahead of the dog team.

"It's no good trying," I said to Billy. "I can't lead the way. You go ahead and I will walk beside the sled."

I was afraid if I stopped to rest we would reach Point Barrow too late to get the pictures I wanted. So, blind as I was, I kept on, dragging the sled and stumbling over the rough going, in the hope that I might recover on the way. Natkusiak had to do all the work of guiding the sled, making camp at night, beating the frost out of my clothes and foot-gear, and feeding me. That spring traveling was a new experience to me, too, because one cheek would be burned by the sun and wind, while the other side of the face was actually freezing. I gradually recovered, and resolved to take precautions in the future against exposing my eyes to snow glare.

Just before we reached Point Barrow we struck the trail of the whale hunters. We followed it quickly out to the edge of the floe, glad to know we had arrived in time. That very morning they had killed a whale, and were cutting it up when we reached them. Still hoping to get some pictures, I stayed there week after week, until six weeks had gone by and the thaws brought an end to the sledding season. Unfortunately, we never caught sight of another whale.

Natkusiak helped me as an interpreter, but after a few days I caught on to enough words to express basic thoughts and to understand simple messages. While I stayed with the Eskimos we lived on fish. Believing in nature-spirits and in the power of mind over matter, they invoked both in order to get their supply of fish.

I watched them as they gathered in a circle about the shaman, their leader in these occult matters. The old medicine man started to sway in time to a rhythm which he hummed, back and forth, then in a circular motion. He kept his body moving, gradually increasing in speed. Then he began to swing his head from side to side in time with his body movements, and the swinging and sweeping of the head became faster and faster. The whole crowd, including myself, were hypnotized into following his movements. Our bodies swayed and our heads swung, and I soon realized that the old fellow was not only hypnotizing himself, but he was rapidly inducing a harmony of thought in the minds of everyone.

Then he began to talk of fish, how they had been scarce before and how he had often succeeded in making them appear in the river. Everybody united in muttering words of agreement: Yes, he could make fish. Of course he would make them again. There will be plenty of fish in the river, and we will have a big meal. We'll get a lot of fish! We'll get a lot of fish!

The words were repeated as in an anthem. Then suddenly the old man started to babble in an uncanny high-pitched voice. Some-one told me that now he was in the control of his great spirit; he was talking magic words which could not be understood. I could see and sense the awe of his audience. But I was a determined skeptic, and realized the old man's object was to detain the people in his tent, so that they would not go out and frighten the few fish that were coming up the river.

I cannot now venture how long all this went on, but when at last, because of their cramped positions, the people began to get restless, the old man's tempo began to slow down. When his gyrations came to an end, this was, apparently, the recognized signal for him to be brought out of his magic trance. An old woman took up her heavy copper *ulu,* a curved flat knife, and cracked the old man heavily on the forehead. He came to with a start and looked around in such realistic surprise that it was difficult to believe the whole business had been extremely clever acting. Then he began to talk in a language his audience could understand.

"My magic has made many fish," he said. "I can hear them in the water. You," he said, pointing to one man, "you will spear many. You," pointing to a woman, "you will find many fast between the rocks, but you must be quick to catch them. You," he said to another man, "you are not to get any at all. It's not worth your while even going to the river. This boy, he will catch one or two, three or four perhaps. You will catch one. You will not get any no matter how hard you try."

On he went, pointing to nearly everyone in the tent. I was waiting for him to predict my lot, but when he turned in my direction I was given no prophecy. However, I thought I caught a gleam in the old man's eye which said even plainer than words, "Now you will see how clever I am. These people really will catch some fish."

By that time I had his scheme pretty well figured out. Naturally, if there were any fish at all in the river, they would by now have swum up to the weir because no one had been near the river to frighten them for hours.

Suddenly the old man exclaimed, "Now we go out and see."
There was a wild scramble to get out of the tent; the people
grabbed their spears. This urgency was especially noticeable on
the part of the ones who had been told they would get plenty of
fish. But those who had been assured it was not worth their
while even going to the river were not in such a hurry. However,
I noticed that some of them did, rather shame-facedly, pick up
their spears and move toward the water, but they were not in
time to profit by it.

Of course there were now quite a few fish in the water; spears
were jabbing here and there; and the women were in almost up
to their waists and leaning over, feeling in the rock crevasses for
the fish that were hiding, and occasionally they found one. Soon
there was quite a pile of fish on the strings held in the fishermen's
hands and on the river banks where the old man and I stood idly
by. We had no need to join in the effort to take the fish, for we
knew that he, as his reward for magic performed, would get his
full share, and I, as a guest, would be welcome at every pot in
which the fish would soon be cooking.

I winked at the old man and said, "That was very clever. You
made plenty of fish. You are a wonderful magician."

"It is not difficult when you know how to do it," he replied, "but
I must tell that old woman not to hit me so hard next time. Now
my head aches."

In my hope of getting a picture of floe whaling, I stayed with
the Eskimos so late in the spring that all the solid ice was covered
with rivers and pools of water. I shall never forget the trip back
to Collinson Point. Much of the way we were knee-deep in water,
and in places we had to swim the dogs and carry the sled over our
heads. It was slow, tiring work, especially as I still had not learned
to swim—which is unusual for an Australian. Later, I saw to it
that I learned, for my own safety in such situations. We got back
to Collinson Point, pretty well exhausted, on the last day of June,
1914.

I was overjoyed to find two messages from Stefansson waiting for me. The first had been found under a flag, fifty miles down the shore. It was dated a day or two after we had lost contact in March and in it he said it would be impossible for me to find him because his party had been carried fifty miles on the broken ice that first night. His party was intact, and if they could find game, he would push on northeast across the breadth of the Beaufort Sea to Banks Land, his island objective, which lay 800 miles away. If they could not find game, they would turn back.

It turned out that Stefansson decided to go on. First, however, he sent three men back to Collinson Point with the second message, asking me to take charge of the *North Star*, a 40-foot fishing schooner he had bought some time before. I was to make every effort to join him on Banks Land, sailing the schooner as far north as possible along the coast of the island, so that he could use it for work farther north.

Stefansson's schooner was lying on the beach about a hundred miles up the coast, east of Collinson Point. I did that bit on foot. Natkusiak and a one-eyed Swiss cook from Anderson's party went with me. When we reached the schooner, a snug two-master, I had to overhaul the engines and put her into the water. The three of us managed to move her down the beach, inch by difficult inch, by means of block and tackle, log rollers, and back-breaking labor.

We then sailed to the Northwest Mounted Police Station on Herschel Island, which lay just off the Canadian coast east of the demarcation line with Alaska. It was one of the few year-round settlements in this stretch of hundreds of miles of lonely shoreline. Here I was to pick up navigation instruments, sextants, watches, and Stefansson's mail. Once a year in the summer, as early as ice conditions permitted, a whaler would bring in a full year's mail from the outside world, and on its return journey carry out our year's writings. Having to wait for a few days for its arrival, I had time to write a long letter to my parents in Adelaide, who now seemed a million miles away. I reassured them that I was getting along well, that my health was fine, and told them about the ferocity of the northern mosquitoes, which buzzed constantly around me as I wrote. I put this letter in the mail sack with others written months before.

The same day that the mail ship arrived, the *Mary Sachs* and the *Alaska* came in to get the mail for Anderson's party. Anderson himself was aboard one of the boats. After we had sorted the mail and I was ready to go, I learned that the crew of the *Mary Sachs* refused to try to reach Banks Land with me. Stefansson had asked Anderson to send the boat, and I knew he was relying on her to bring the bulk of the supplies he needed. But months had passed since Stefansson sent that message, and during those months nothing further had been heard from him. The crew of the *Mary Sachs* did not believe Stefansson could have reached Banks Land. In fact, they were convinced that if he had survived at all he must have been carried far west on the ice floes, and was by now somewhere on the coast of Siberia. Because I had traveled over the ice with Stefansson, I had more confidence than the rest of them in his ability to survive and go where he wished to go.

Anderson and I discussed the situation. I was still determined to carry out Stefansson's instructions, and Anderson said, "Well, if you're determined to go, I won't stop you. Stefansson is probably dead by this time. But if you are set on going anyway, why don't you take a real boat?"

I thought the *North Star* was too small to carry enough provisions to enable Stefansson to go on with his work for twelve months, and told Anderson so.

He replied, "If you succeed in getting to Banks Land, I don't believe you will find Stefansson. But you can carry on with the work if you take the *Mary Sachs*, which is bigger than the *North Star*. So let me take the *North Star* for my work along Coronation Gulf."

This plan seemed the best way out of a bad situation. Stefansson wanted both boats, but nobody else would try to take one to Banks Land, and I could not handle the mutinous crews of two boats alone. So I agreed to switch vessels with Anderson.

There were only two crewmen on whom I knew I could rely:

Natkusiak and the one-eyed Swiss cook. Together, we worked a variation of the old shanghai trick that had been used in every port in the world for centuries, and which the Italian agent and I had fallen for back in the land of the Arabs. I procured a case of the expedition's liquor supply, with which Natkusiak and the cook got the engineer and the crew of the *Mary Sachs* dead drunk. Then the three of us sailed her away from Herschel Island.

Seventy miles out in the Beaufort Sea we tied her up to an ice-pack because I didn't think it safe to take her farther without the help of the crew, and they were still lying in their bunks below, dead to the world. When they began to recover and stagger up on deck, I was the target of bitter words from the engineer, Jim Crawford, the same man I had locked in his cabin at Nome. He had not forgiven me for that, and now he fancied he had reason to hate me all the more.

However, I managed to keep the situation fairly well in hand, and the crew agreed to go eastward along the Mackenzie coast district as far as Baillie Island, there to discuss the matter further. Baillie Island was both on my route to Banks Land and on that of Anderson's party, which could join us there. Crawford agreed to this plan with the rest, but I soon noticed him drinking—a bad sign.

On the way to Baillie Island, we had to pass the mouth of the Mackenzie River where there are shallow seas. Here a storm struck us and for fifty-six hours we hardly knew from minute to minute whether we would be able to save the schooner. Half our gasoline was washed overboard, and we barely managed to save the dogs. Every man aboard was at the point of exhaustion.

When at last there was a lull, I decided to tie up for the night in the lee of a grounded iceberg. I put a man on watch and went below to get a little sleep. The next thing I knew, Crawford burst in shouting that the engine was awash. In the rough sea, the iceberg had broken up, the boat had drifted on the beach, and staved in her bow. The sailor on anchor watch had slept through it all.

The seas were pouring in all night, and all that delayed our sinking was the fact that we were now stern to on the beach. At first it seemed impossible to gain on the water, but the crew worked for their lives. We managed to hold the water level down while we made temporary repairs, and then pump the boat almost dry. Keeping the pumps going, we started the engines and moved off-shore, only to discover that both our rudders had been shaken loose.

Thus crippled, we continued eastward toward Baillie Island through pack ice. It was dangerous going at best, and all the more difficult because we could not depend on the rudders and had to keep the pumps going in order to stay afloat.

During all this I got no chance to rest or even to change my wet clothes until we had worked through the worst of the ice and reached a fairly clear strip of water off Baillie Island. Now that there was only one strip of ice between us and the beach, I left the crew to work the *Mary Sachs* through it while I went below to clean up.

I had been below a few minutes when I heard a yell and felt a jarring crash. The whole boat shook, and one of the engines be-gan to race. Rushing on deck, I saw that we were on the beach. The crew had worked the boat in to shore, where the ice had closed in on her and smashed one propeller.

Crawford, raving drunk, jumped overboard and started to swim straight out to sea. I put a small boat overside and rescued him, but we had to tie him into his bunk. With him out of the picture I had to handle the engines as well as the navigation. When we tried to unbeach the boat, we found that the propeller's driveshaft had been broken off at the hub. It was impossible to repair the propeller without unloading the boat; yet I dared not do that, knowing that once the cargo was unloaded, nothing would induce the crew to leave Baillie Island.

With one engine and one propeller, we managed to edge the boat along the island coast until we got to the most northern point, where we could strike out straight north toward Banks Land, about a hundred miles off. But since this was also the place where we could depend upon being picked up by Anderson's party, the crew flatly refused to leave the point. Furthermore, they saw no sense obeying orders from Stefansson when the orders were months old and they believed Stefansson lost or dead. That they might be choosing to leave Stefansson's party to starve on Banks Land did not seem to them even a remote possibility.

The only thing I could think of was to offer them higher and higher wages. Finally they agreed to go on, if I would leave a conspicuously marked record for Anderson's party, stating that if we were lost, these payments would be given to their families. I went ashore and left the message, marked with a flag, and then with the crew in this mood of desperation we headed north into the strait.

As soon as we were in the current we were out of control, because we had only the one propeller. The floating ice constantly threatened us, and the rudders were not dependable. I didn't dare leave either the engine or the deck for any length of time. However, no man ever had a more anxiously willing crew. They worked without rest or food, with only the one thought of keeping afloat till we could reach Banks Land. For the first time on the whole trip, we were all of one mind.

It was really luck that got us through. At last we saw ahead of us the hard ice on Banks Land. Searching the shore, we could find no sign that Stefansson had been there—no cairn, no flag. He had expected the *Mary Sachs* to come to this southern end of the island, and it seemed certain that if he had reached Banks Land he would have left a beacon for us. The island was only 180 miles long, and if he were on it and able to travel, he could surely have come down to that point. My disappointment was profound.

We needed a beach on which to repair the boat, so I worked her slowly northward along the west coast until we came to Cape Kellett. With pumps going day and night, one useless engine, and a crew growing more restive as our search continued fruitless, I decided to go no farther north until repairs had been made. We put in at Cape Kellett, where the hard ice gave us the beach we needed. That night the autumn freeze-up came, and I determined to make this place our headquarters for the winter.

The men were furious with me for having brought them there. We had been at sea a hundred and twenty days, only to reach this desolate and uninhabited coast, and now have to stay there till spring. I had them unload the schooner and get everything in readiness to overhaul her, and laid out the plan of the snow-huts, which they could build as soon as the snow came. Then I built a sled and set out to find Stefansson.

I was determined to go all the way round the island—some 400 miles—and make sure that he and his party were not starving somewhere on it. There was no danger of our starving because we had the supplies brought for Stefansson. I wanted to travel as fast as possible, so I took very little food with me, intending to depend on game I hoped to find. The feeling against me in camp was so strong that I thought it advisable to leave Natkusiak and the cook there. Taking two Eskimos, with a dog team and a sled, we struck a little inland and then north. Seeing no game except a few white foxes, after traveling three days and making about ten miles a day over difficult going, I found our food supply was almost gone, and I decided to camp and hunt.

In order to cover as much ground as possible, I sent the two Eskimos in one direction while I went in another. I hunted all day, not seeing anything worth shooting or finding any trace of human beings. At night when I returned to camp I found the Eskimos had encountered only wolves.

Next morning we set out again. A few miles along I climbed to the top of a hill. Scanning the open country with my field glasses I made out a little beacon built of stones. With a thrill I told myself it must be a message for us from Stefansson, for no other party but his could be on Banks Land!

When I reached the beacon, sure enough it contained a tiny piece of paper in Stefansson's hand. It was not addressed to us and made no reference to our being on the island. It read:

MAKE CAMP $\frac{1}{4}$ MI. S.E. OF HERE

Evidently his party had separated for hunting, and this was a message he had left for the others. So I knew Stefansson and at least one of his companions were alive. I hurried to the southeast, expecting to come upon them weak and hungry, dragging themselves along, ready to collapse at any moment.

When I came to the place where they had camped, I could tell from their trail that there were at least three men and some dogs in the party. Nor had they been gone from that site very long. Recognizing I could not really help them if they were in distress, I returned to my temporary camp, only to find that my Eskimos were out on the hunt. Leaving them a brief message, I set out to walk the thirty miles back to the main camp to report my discovery and return with a relief party. On the way, I thought it wise to shoot all the game I came across, with the result that by the time I reached our beached boat I had left in my wake seven dead caribou, a couple of polar bears, some hares, and several wolves.

I told my story of finding Stefansson's message and trail. All hands were at first amazed, then some were skeptical. It was agreed we should first bring into camp all the edible meat I had killed, as winter was fast closing down on us, and then go after Stefansson and his companions. Natkusiak and several of the crew hurried out with me to skin the animals and carry the meat to camp on the sledges. After a sustained trip of some thirty miles, traveling day and night, we returned from this task about four in the morning, worn out and ready to sleep around the clock. To my amazement, as I entered my tent, whom should I find but Stefansson himself, sound asleep, stretched out in my sleeping bag as peacefully as though he owned it! He looked as comfortable as if nothing had happened to him in the past nine months since he had floated out to sea.

I looked at him with anxiety, but he didn't appear either weak or emaciated. His two companions, sleeping on the boat, looked to me fatter than when I had seen them last, in March, at Collinson Point. Also, all six of their dogs were tied and sleeping by our dogs, and they were fatter than our dogs.

We sat around till breakfast time, not daring to wake Stefansson and his two companions. But I still couldn't believe that they were not suffering from exhaustion after the better part of a year alone in the Arctic, without supplies. When they finally awoke, we had a cheerful reunion. The three men had been living on caribou meat for months, they said, and felt wonderful. I believe that some of our party who had doubted Stefansson's ability to live on the country were convinced that morning.

Once the greetings were over, I could tell from Stefansson's manner that something was wrong. Crawford and the other men who had stayed in camp while we went out to bring in the meat, had had time to talk with him. I learned later they had told him a tale of their own heroism—how they had striven and suffered to come to his rescue, and how my stupidities and arrogance had hindered and delayed them. Small wonder that Stefansson now thought if anyone in the world was useless and exasperating, I was that man. Of course, Crawford and his pals were as silent as the grave about the part that liquor and bonuses played in their heroism.

One fact I could not deny was that I had failed to follow instructions, and had not brought the *North Star*, which Stefansson considered the better ice boat. He felt I had exceeded my authority in delivering his schooner to Anderson's party at Herschel Island, for he had instructed me to bring it to him. I tried to explain my reasoning—that I thought he could best use the larger boat if only one could be sailed to Banks Land—but the earnest declarations of fidelity of the four crewmen seemed to outweigh my argument. At any rate, Stefansson did not think I had done the right thing and was seriously annoyed.

We settled down there at Kellett Point for the winter, and were comfortable enough in our sod house. We went out frequently on hunting trips, spending the night in snow igloos when darkness found us far from our base, and by the end of the winter I had learned the art of cutting the hard snow blocks with my knife to the right shape and placing them in position almost as well as an Eskimo. I agreed with Stefansson that there was nothing too difficult about building a snow house—that the ability to put one up was not a mysterious racial quality belonging exclusively to the Eskimo, as some old-time British and American explorers had maintained.

I shall never forget the great good luck we had in discovering a whale carcass on the beach, buried in the snow. It was a first-class game lure. Over a period of many weeks in the winter it attracted foxes, wolves, and bears, which we trapped or shot pretty much as we pleased, and it also gave us an unlimited supply of dog food. I spent much of the winter, when it was too dark for photography, preparing the skins and bones of these Arctic creatures for later mounting. To make certain that the dimensions would be right, I labeled each with the measurements of the carcass before dissecting it. These specimens later went to a number of museums.

Both on the trail and in the evenings in camp, Stefansson and I conversed for hours on many topics. I suggested to him that I thought an airplane could profitably be used in Arctic travel, because the level, snow-coated ice floes at the right season offered ideal landing places. He was inclined to doubt this, but was not dogmatic about his views. In his turn, he offered me food for thought in his observation that perhaps the submarine offered a more practical method of navigating the Arctic Ocean in comfort. He pointed out that the seas of the far north, though nominally covered with ice, are dotted every few miles with lakes of open water because of the constant shifting of ocean currents below the ice pack and of the winds above. Furthermore, Stefansson told me that whales were known to search out thin spots in the ice above them and crash up through it for air when they failed to find a natural opening. All this was interesting speculation back in that winter on Banks Land in 1914-15.

Determined to have the *North Star* at Banks Land, Stefansson sent me south in early April, 1915, to find Anderson's party and bring the boat as far north as possible, with provisions for the following year's work. He sent Crawford and Natkusiak with me.

Stefansson, of course, knew little or nothing of the trouble I had had with Crawford, and there was no point in his knowing, because in any case I would need an engineer on the *North Star* while I navigated.

It was 500 miles to Coronation Gulf and Anderson's party. Setting out with a small sled and five dogs, we came down Banks Land from Cape Kellett, mapping the country on the way, then crossed the ice eastward to Victoria Island and followed down that coast to Dolphin and Union Straits. It was so late in the spring that the ice was covered with water, varying in depth from 6 inches to 3 feet. A cold spell at one point covered the water with ice as thin as window glass, and we had to break it for the dogs so they wouldn't cut their feet. We took turns, one going ahead and breaking the ice, while the other two came behind to manage the sled and dogs. Where the water was too deep for the dogs to wade, we unhitched them and swam them across; then we came back and carried the sled over the deep water, holding it above our heads.

We did this for 400 miles, day after day. At night we lay down in our wet clothes, and next morning got up and started again, wet to the skin the whole time, yet none of us caught cold. We were living on nothing but seal and caribou meat. It took us twenty-two days to cover the 500 miles, averaging a little more than 20 miles a day. Toward the last we were getting rather tired and weak, because we were working and traveling all the time, and we ran out of food.

The spring was so far advanced that we knew we would soon not be able to get any more seals, and if we failed to find Anderson's party at Coronation Gulf we would be stranded without food. Therefore we decided to make camp, hunt seal, and put up some caches of meat. When I got my snow house built I was so tired I lay down in it and went to sleep. Pretty soon, something woke me and I sat up, expecting to see Natkusiak. Instead, it was a white man I had never seen before.

"You one of Stefansson's outfit?" he asked.

"Yes," I said, still groggy from sleep.

"I just came from the house," he said.

"What house?"

"At Bernard Harbor. I'm with Anderson."

I was still so sleepy I didn't say anything. He asked me, "Have you heard the news?"

"No, not very much."

"Wilkins and all his party went off last year and have never been heard from. Must have been lost to the last man, looking for Stefansson. Stefansson is all right, so it doesn't matter a lot. Wilkins didn't amount to much."

Then he went on and told me there had been a war in Europe. The last news, he said, told of the British advancing through Germany toward Berlin at a rate of 20 miles a day, so, the show was doubtless over by this time.

I said, "I happen to be Wilkins, so how much can I believe of the rest of this news?"

"Oh!" he said. "I thought you were Cox! Where have you been?"

"Banks Land."

"Well," he said, as if chastising me for thoughtlessness, "we thought you would come down and let us know if you were safe."

Next day Crawford and I went on to the Bernard Harbor camp, and there I heard again about the war in Europe. This was late in May, 1915.

I found that the *North Star* had been crushed by the ice and had gone down in the harbor. Fortunately, she was at a shallow berth, so that at low tide we could walk about her deck. But we would not know how much damage the water had done her engine until we raised her and dried her out. Stefansson had given me written authority, making me second in command of the entire expedition, with the right, therefore, to take the boat from Anderson. I had her dragged out of the water, and Crawford and I chipped the ice off the engine and cleaned and repaired it. When we got the engine working, I set to work to repair the hull.

Meanwhile, the authorities in Ottawa believed that Stefansson was dead and consequently had ordered Anderson to take charge of the expedition and all its equipment, including the *North Star*.

Word of this decision was brought to camp by an inspector of the Royal Canadian Mounted Police, who had come to that sector to make an arrest.

At this juncture all I could do was put the conflict up to the men. Practically without exception, they agreed that I should be allowed to take the *North Star*. They were not against Anderson, but simply felt that Ottawa had acted without knowledge of the facts, and that as Stefansson was alive he was therefore still in command of his own expedition.

I said that if the ice opened first to the eastward, I would be glad to take Anderson's party in that direction before starting north. If it opened first to the west, I would have to hurry on to Herschel Island for supplies and then sail north as soon as possible. The ice opened eastward first, so I took Anderson's party across Coronation Gulf to the eastern shore. They had barely disembarked when a terrific gale struck us. I knew this would open up the ice to the west, and there I was, the full width of Coronation Gulf from the place where I should have been in order to take immediate advantage of the ice-break. And there were only the three of us to handle the craft.

Wanting to make all possible speed and at the same time save fuel, we put up sail and ran before the storm. It simply flung us across the gulf. This was in the dusk of an early summer midnight, so early in the season that the daylight was dim at that hour. We could not see land at all and could barely see the white crests of waves dashed up by the storm.

Suddenly we struck Dolphin and Union Strait, a treacherous uncharted channel dotted with jagged, black rocks around which the seething water was churned into white foam. There was nothing for it but to sail on, taking advantage of the wind astern, and trust to luck in the murky light. We raced through at eight or nine knots, and how we ever got through alive I don't know. Luck's a strange thing.

At Baillie Island I got a message from Stefansson saying not to go to Herschel Island for supplies, but to return to Banks Land at once, sailing as far north as possible. This surprised and puzzled me, for the object of my getting the *North Star* had been to bring supplies. However, I headed at once to Banks Land, picked up a few supplies at Cape Kellett, and after leaving a record of my visit in a cairn, took aboard Castel and the Swiss cook, then went on up the west coast. Stefansson, I knew, was exploring the unknown island above Banks Land and would want to fall back on us for a base.

We worked our way through the ice, going steadily northward until we reached Cape Prince Albert, the extreme tip of the west coast. Here we were farther north than any ship had ever gone before.

Once more we faced the problem of beaching the schooner. Short-handed as we were, and without machinery, it was quite a difficult job, but we had to get the boat ashore to save her from being crushed by the ice. We shifted the cargo, putting her down by the stern, and then under full steam we drove her up on the beach. We unloaded her to bring the stern up, then dragged her all the way ashore by the windlass and rollers method. It was a struggle, but we did it. We then set about making camp. No further word had come from Stefansson, and we had no idea where he was, so we established ourselves in comfortable snow houses and settled down for the winter.

It was not until late December that a couple of men bringing a message from Stefansson pulled into our camp by dog team. It turned out that he was not north of us at all, but southwest at Cape Kellett, our camping place of the previous winter. In response to his written request, I returned to Kellett with the dog team and met Stefansson there at Christmas time. There he told me of his comings and goings since we had last seen one another in early April—how he had first gone north to explore, then had returned south to Herschel Island for supplies during the summer, had bought still another boat, the *Polar Bear,* had sailed her up the east side of Banks Land only to be caught in the autumn freeze-up. Leaving the boat there for the winter he had then crossed Banks Land on foot to the base at Cape Kellett and was, I believe, the first white man ever to cross that island. He had found the record

I had left in late summer, and therefore sent the dog team north to summon me to a conference.

All this had happened in 1915, and the whole distance crossed and recrossed so painfully, so many times, was only 500 miles. An airplane would do it today in three hours. Radios today would keep us in communication with each other and with the whole world, as simply as if we were in the same room. It seems strange that such a short time ago we were crawling over the land, groping about in the dark, losing touch with each other as we did. Yet it seemed perfectly natural at the time.

Stefansson told me the war in Europe was not ended. Word on this had recently come from Anderson's party, who had received more news from outside via the mounted police. Instead of England capturing Berlin, the German forces were said to be in France. Also orders had come from Ottawa recalling the expedition, and Anderson was going back. Stefansson, however, had decided to go on with the work.

We talked about plans for the following year, and renewed an old discussion between us about the use of airplanes in polar exploration. Stefansson knew almost nothing about planes, and was still strong on his idea of using a submarine. At this moment, neither of us even dreamed that this idea had been advanced three hundred years before by my ancestor Bishop Wilkins, but had never been acted upon. I maintained that airplanes, which are so much less costly, should first be used for general reconnaissance, whereas one could resort to the submarine to travel under the ice for oceanographic study.

Stefansson gave me the opportunity of waiting until I got my mail at the *Polar Bear* before deciding whether to stay with him in the Arctic or go out with Anderson's party. I made the trip alone, and when I reached the *Polar Bear* camp I was surprised to find John Hadley there. Hadley, an Englishman, a veteran Arctic hunter and traveler, had been aboard the *Karluk* when she had drifted away in the ice pack in 1913. He told me the tragic story of her fate, and that of more than half the men aboard

—an episode doubly tragic because it all could have been prevented.

The ship had drifted far to the west, past Point Barrow and Bering Strait, to a point near Wrangel Island off the Siberian coast, where she was crushed in the ice and sank. Captain Bob Bartlett had led everyone safely ashore on a tiny islet, but one man after another took it into his head to disobey the advice of the few experienced Arctic men among them, like Hadley and the Eskimos. They fell into small quarrelsome groups and sought their own safety, some setting off over the ice too heavily laden or in the wrong clothing, others taking the wrong direction. Bob Bartlett and a few others finally made their way out. Had each of them had the benefit of traveling with Stefansson and learning how to live on the resources of the Arctic as he had done for years, I feel sure that not a man would have been lost.

The letters I read at the *Polar Bear* camp early in 1916, written many months before, brought word from my brothers that my father had died. They urged me to return home to Australia to help settle his estate. I realized, too, that my mother must be provided for.

My mail also included a number of old letters and cablegrams from London, sent by the *Daily Chronicle* and the Gaumont people, ordering me to return at once and help cover the great war in Europe.

8

Cameraman on the Western Front

When I came out of the Arctic that spring of 1916, it seemed incredible to me that almost the whole world was engaged in a war that had raged for nearly two years while we were cut off from news. I traveled to Ottawa by way of Nome and Vancouver, in order to report to the Canadian Ministry of Marine on the expedition work thus far. The Ministry insisted that before I should be released to go home and join the Australian Flying Corps, which was my wish, I would have to reduce my enormous mass of Arctic notes into some kind of orderly report. I finally got permission to sail for Australia and write the report on the long journey home.

It was a roundabout trip, for instead of sailing down across the Pacific to Australia from San Francisco, I had to go the other way round the world—that was where the shipping lanes were in wartime. We plowed in convoy through seas infested with German U-boats bent on torpedoing allied shipping, and when we reached Plymouth our steamer waited in the harbor a month for the chance to make a run for it. During this period seven captured U-boats were brought into port. When we did get under way, one poor chap aboard was so jittery over the possibility of being torpedoed that he stopped shaving. He said he was in such a state of nerves he didn't dare shave for fear of cutting his throat.

In all, it took us more than two months to reach Australia by way of the west African coast, Cape Town, and the Indian Ocean. The greater part of my work on the Arctic report was wound up before we landed. I went at once to Adelaide to greet my widowed mother and to see the other members of my family once again.

Unfortunately, the time was short for catching up on all that had happened to each of us since I had stowed away in Sydney Harbor eight years before. The war was on and I had to get into the fight.

At first, I applied for a commission in the Navy, since all that time at sea, coming on top of my experience sailing in Arctic waters, had put a touch of salt in my veins. I wanted to get into the motorboat patrol, where my engineering training and my love of the water seemed to point. But I was disheartened when the Navy officers in charge said they wanted me to organize a motor-boat patrol to train recruits. I just could not see myself, at age twenty-eight and as physically fit as any man in Australia, running a training school. I pointed out that the war was already two years old, and I wanted action, the sooner the better.

I was in Melbourne when General Hubert John Foster, a family friend, advised me that the only men who would get to France quickly were the flyers. I eagerly told him about my experience with planes, although I confessed that the last time I had been up was with a half-trained, devil-may-care Turkish pilot one day during the Balkan War in the fall of 1912. Nonetheless, aircraft pilots were rare birds in 1916, and the general thought maybe I would do. He proposed, "Let's drive out to the training squadron and see what you can do."

When I went up and handled the plane with the dual control, the officer who was training recruits found I knew almost as much about flying as he did. I told the general I must go to Sydney, but would come back to Melbourne to see if he could get me a commission. For this he said he would have to have special permission from the Army Department and also from the Prime Minister. Yet the very next morning when I reached Sydney a telegram was waiting for me:

RETURN TO MELBOURNE AT ONCE. COMMISSION GRANTED.

Two days later I was back. The general helped me get a tailor to make my flying uniform double quick, told me to collect my equipment and be at camp next morning ready to sail. There was no delay this time, and off we went to the war in France.

I had walked 600 miles from Banks Land to reach a boat, then had journeyed from the Alaskan Arctic to the United States west coast, thence to Ottawa, to England, around the Cape of Good Hope, to Australia. Although I had my commission in only three days, it had taken the better part of a year, and a journey of some 33,000 miles before I got to my second war. I arrived nearly three years after it had broken out.

Our detachment of reinforcements for the Royal Australian Air Force arrived in England in July, 1917. When we went up for medical examination, the doctor did not approve the way my feet and ankles looked, or my gait. I told him about the injury from my first long trek over the ice.

"Your feet are in a hopeless condition," he said gravely. "You did not have medical attention in time, and now it is too late. Nothing can be done. You will never be able to walk properly again."

When I told him that since the original injury I had averaged fifteen miles a day on foot in the Arctic, he said that from a strictly medical viewpoint, such a performance was impossible. Since I already had my RAAF commission, I decided not to argue the point.

Next I took the eye test and was told I couldn't hold a commission as a pilot because I was color-blind. This astounded me. I had always had a keen appreciation of color, had even painted a bit in water color and oils, and had read the skies as a navigating officer, so I found this hard to take. The examining officer tried to convince me that there were other jobs quite as interesting as flying, but finally he consented to my being tested again by a specialist outside the military. The verdict, after an exhaustive examination, was that my eyesight was normal but that my knowledge of color names was poor. I could distinguish every color tone, but did not always know exactly what it was called. I wonder how many good men were thus lost to their country's service because the test, rather than the tested, was faulty.

Next morning when I went back to the examining officer at headquarters he told me to report direct to General Griffiths, the commander-in-chief, whom I had never seen before. He received me cheerfully and joked, "Well, I hear you're color-blind and can't be a pilot!"

I showed him my certificate of normal eyesight and my pilot's commission.

"There are other important jobs," the General said. Then he told me that Captain Frank Hurley had been appointed official photographer for the RAAF, and that Captain Charles E.W. Bean, the official Australian war historian, had selected me to be Hurley's assistant and official photographer of historical events in the war. He said I could keep my rank in the flying corps, that I could fly whenever it was desirable to get pictures from the air, and that I would be expected to be with every section of the army in turn and photograph it in action.

A few days later, Hurley and I went to Boulogne-sur-Mer and met Captain Bean. "Anzac Charley" Bean was an honorary captain who had the confidence and respect of both officers and men. Everybody liked him, and he acted as a sort of unofficial go-between within the ranks, smoothing out difficulties. He had absolute integrity, plus courage and ability of the highest order.

In Boulogne he explained to us the nature of our duties. Hurley was to photograph only such scenes as were suitable for public release, that is, for propaganda. I, on the other hand, was to make a record of actual conditions—the grim and sordid along with the heroics. This meant I would often work in the smoke and dust of battle. My films might turn out to be bad photographically, yet from a historical point of view they would be most valuable.

This was hard-slugging trench warfare, with the Germans dug in directly opposite our lines, all the way across northern and eastern France from the English Channel to the Swiss frontier. The British, under whose command the Australians, New Zealanders, and Canadians were placed, held most of the left flank of the Western Front, with the Belgians squeezed between us and the Channel. The French, and later the Americans, made up the center and right of the Allied lines. Although there was hard, bitter fighting in all sectors during this four-year war, the muckiest, filthiest, most miserable part of it seemed to be in our fairly level sector of northern France, which was too damp, it seemed, ever to dry out, and not cold enough to freeze firmly. In this, men were supposed to keep their rifles clean, to fight, to eat and sleep, and I was to take pictures of them trying to do it. No cinematography this time—we wanted still picture records, not a show.

Approaching headquarters near the front, we saw for the first time the awe-inspiring display of shellfire and signals against the sky. Hurley and I were mightily impressed. We went into our tents with our equipment, but before we had time to unbuckle even one strap, a German air squadron came roaring over and began dropping bombs. All the experienced men dived into dugouts, but Hurley and I, not knowing where to go, ran out in the midst of the exploding shells looking for some kind of shelter. After that, on first arriving in a new place we would quickly learn where safety holes were located. Quite an exciting first night that was. After the air raid we sat up till morning, watching the titanic struggle along the battlefront—countless flashes from the big guns, exploding shells, and signal rockets.

The next night we got our first taste of battle. Charley Bean took us up to the front line of the Ypres salient, by way of Hell Fire Corner and Bloody Angle—all to become familiar historical names. Through a deluge of rain we went on to a crater on Hill 60 where we were to spend the night. Just north of Zillebeke Lake the Germans were taking our front line trenches. Our troops were fighting desperately. Except for the flashes that blazed along the battle line the night was pitch black. There was a morass of slimy mud on either side of the narrow duckboards which the troops had laid down in sections to make it possible for men to walk in the rain-soaked trenches. We struggled along the duckboards with the replacements. They were trying to get up to the battle in double-quick time, in the rain and the dark, whereas a stream of stretcher-bearers and wounded was struggling in the same narrow walkway to get back to first-aid stations. Finally we got through the crush into the dugout occupied by front-line headquarters, tunneled out of the clay about forty feet underground. There we sat and listened to the pounding of shells up above. Every shell that struck near the top of the dugout drenched us with water and mud shaken down from the saturated earth overhead. Our clothing and even our mess kits caught their share of it.

It was this first time up front that I first heard a joke that later spread through all the Allied armies. A wounded, mud-covered Tommy was supposed to have told his comrades, "I wish I could go back to Blighty and work in a munitions factory. Just think of those blokes getting five bob a day for making those shells— and us getting only one bob for stopping the gorblimey things!" After a few hours in the trenches, I knew precisely how he felt.

This was far bigger and more deadly frightening than the Balkan War which I had covered with my motion-picture camera on my beautiful Arab mount. When the Germans attacked, shortly after we had come forward, it seemed like a trip into Hell—that black night lighted by flames of guns and by signal flares, the air shaking with noise, and the earth shaking underfoot. Human beings seemed insignificant in the midst of all this. It didn't seem possible that men could go through it and live.

The next day, Hurley and I shot pictures of troops marching up through Ypres, and for the next several weeks during the hot fighting we were every day at the front. During these days, I made battle scenes of front-line infantry at grips with the Germans, machine guns in action, heavy artillery fire from the valley, and twice a week made a low-level flight over the entire front-line area.

Once a week we took our photographs to censorship head-quarters at Montroix. From there the pictures passed for press and propaganda were sent on to England, and the others were stored in the library to be used in the history of the war that Captain Bean was compiling. Hurley and I each had a car and a staff of assistants. We reached the battlefront every morning at dawn as soon as daylight photography was possible. At dusk we returned to our cars, drove to headquarters, and developed our plates. Then we dined, having had nothing to eat since five in the

morning. After dinner we examined prints of photographs taken
the day before, and read the comments on them made by the
censors and headquarters staff. We could rarely get to bed before
midnight or later, and before dawn next morning we were once
more on our way to the front. The work was so strenuous that Captain Bean made us take one day's leave each month in London.
But for this day of rest, I doubt if we could have kept up the pace.

When the Australians were not in action, Hurley and I were
with other troops. We tried always to be in the thick of things,
with the English, the Irish, the Scots, the South Africans, the
Canadians, the French, and when the Americans came we were
often with them. We soon came to know the systematic German
methods, especially as we had access to military intelligence reports. We learned that the safest time to visit an area was immediately after it had been severely strafed by German artillery.
There was usually a let-up for a few minutes when we could dash
in, get photographs, and be out again before the attack was resumed.

The Germans on this front avoided shelling hospitals. They
would shell towns all around a hospital, and never put a shell into
one. For example, the small seaside resort of Lapanne, not far
from Dunkirk, was never touched. All the towns around it were
destroyed, but the Germans never touched Lapanne, because there
was a hospital there and the Queen of the Belgians used to visit it.

Hurley and I covered the whole of the Allied front from Dunkirk
on the coast to Nancy in the Moselle. We were with every branch
of the service—intelligence, artillery, engineers, tunnelers, infantry, machine guns, and the flying corps. This last, of course,
was my special interest. As often as possible I would fly over the
lines with an aerial escort. German planes often attacked us, but
we rarely stopped to fight; instead we would turn tail and head
for home. Our machines were sometimes riddled with enemy bullets, but we were never wounded or forced down.

My pictures included battle scenes showing Germans attacking,
Germans surrendering, Germans running from their dugouts,
bodies hurtling through the air after shell explosions, men strug-

gling from debris thrown up by shells, and the wrecking of almost every type of equipment.

The destruction of tanks was especially grim. Many of these ponderous primitive vehicles of war would burst into flames when hit directly by artillery fire, and the men were rarely able to escape. For a long time after I imagined I still could hear them screaming for help in their pain, as they roasted alive. The wounding of artillery horses was another blood-curdling experience, and many a shrill cry from a suffering beast was silenced by a merciful pistol shot. But worst of all to me was the sight of airplanes falling in flames. Many times I was nearby when a plane fell, and I had to photograph the charred body of the aviator. One night I saw three Zeppelins brought down of the seven the Germans lost that night. I was flying at the time and, observing the fight from the air, I saw those Zeppelins go down in flames. Hydrogen, a highly inflammable gas, was used in Zeppelins then. The craft would have been far safer with helium gas which does not burst into flames like hydrogen, but the Germans did not have a supply of helium.

Even amid all this destruction, my thoughts often went back to my wanderings in the Arctic, and I was more than ever convinced that the airplane was the answer to exploring unmapped regions with speed and safety. Some day, when the world would return to normal, I hoped I could sail through polar skies in pursuit, not of an enemy man, but of the secrets of nature that would help conquer the natural enemies of all mankind.

I suppose the most striking aerial event I witnessed was the death of the Black Knight—the German ace of aces, Baron Manfred von Richthofen. I was on the way up toward the front in a car when we stopped to watch an aerial dog-fight. There were some thirty or forty planes in that whirling battle, split roughly into three groups, and they were fighting at such an altitude it was difficult to distinguish the allied planes from the Germans, except by the character of the attacks.

One plane seemed to be lagging, then went into a nose dive and came down. As it approached we saw that it was an allied plane. A German swooped in pursuit, and as it came down on our plane's

tail we saw that it was all red, the distinctive coloring of Richthofen's plane, of which we had all heard. Our man plainly was
in difficulty, diving straight for the ground. The machine in the
lead came out of its dive just as it neared the ground, zoomed
steeply, banked, and went out of sight behind a hill. Richthofen
followed the maneuver exactly in pursuit. There was the sound
of just one machine gun firing. Over the very top of the bank we
could see Richthofen's red plane apparently go out of control,
sideslip, and then it also disappeared. I didn't see the actual crash,
but it was evident that the red plane had been hit when we lost
sight of it.

From a colonel's headquarters nearby, I called up flying corps
headquarters and was told that von Richthofen had just been
killed. I drove to the scene as soon as I could and by that time
the body of the German ace had been carried to British RAF headquarters. I did not go to view the body, but photographed his
wrecked red plane and then went back to develop my pictures.

Later, I learned there was a dispute as to who had killed von
Richthofen. The report had come in that Roy Brown, a Canadian
flyer, had attacked the famous German during the fight and the
English maintained that one of his bullets had been fatal. But the
Australian troops on the ground had seen, as I did, that von Richthofen's machine came down in the nosedive under perfect control.
An Australian machine gun outfit claimed that one of their men
had brought it down, firing at it from the ground as it banked.
That was my impression also. The machine gunner was stationed
on the hill, and apparently in a lucky burst he had got the red
plane as it banked steeply on the upward climb. The question as
to who killed Baron von Richthofen became such a sore point
between the Canadians and Australians that we decided not to make
a controversy of it then, but simply put the evidence in the official
history.

Richthofen was buried with full military honors by the combined Allied Flying Corps in France, while German pilots were
permitted to fly unmolested over the grave and drop wreaths of

flowers. The propeller of his plane was set up in the form of a cross at the head of his grave. Although this was a long, cruel, bloody war, there was enough of the old-time gallantry left in Europe to permit this kind of salute to a popular knight of the air. World War II saw nothing like it.

From the time we reached France in July, 1917, until the Armistice, my work took me into every battle fought by the Australians. The big German attack of March, 1918, came a day earlier than we expected. I had gone for my day's leave in London, fully expecting to be back in time for it, but I was caught at the Channel in such bad weather, that it was impossible to travel by boat or plane. When I managed to get back, I found the Germans had broken through our lines twenty-four hours earlier. The whole area over which they were advancing was in the utmost confusion. All communications had broken down, and on the surface the Allied retreat appeared to be a complete rout. Disorganized troops were scattered all over the country. Artillery, infantry, labor corps, tanks, wounded, cavalry, and medical units were all jumbled together and pouring toward the rear without any apparent organization or control.

That retreat would have been disaster, but for our well seasoned troops, who fought delaying actions. Each infantry commander set up his unit and slowed the Germans whenever he could. Artillery roaming the country independently with their guns would halt and swing them into position, take a few pot shots at the advancing enemy and stop them. Meantime a small party nearby would bivouac off the road, undisturbed by the firing or by the shells coming from German long-range guns. Everybody seemed to realize that a victory for a day was not all-important.

Our troops were pillaging the country as they retreated, carrying off all kinds of food from the French farms. Some had wheelbarrows loaded with fowl, clothing, army rations, and perhaps a sheep. There they were, happily trundling their loot along the road in the midst of ammunition wagons, armored cars, and automobiles filled with staff officers who had lost their units.

In my car, I went forward through this crazy, mixed-up army until I was stopped by German machine-gun fire. About this time, I noticed some French armored cars coming along the road. When they too encountered the German fire, they turned about and drove hastily through the troops, then changed their direction and went on out of sight.

After exposing all my negatives, I hurried back to the town I had marked for use as a base. It had been fairly undisturbed when I passed through it that morning, but when I returned I found all civilian inhabitants evacuated, and the principal hotel occupied by headquarters staff. Foch and the British generals were there in conference. A friend in the Intelligence Service told me they were considering abandoning the town and retreating still farther. He said the Germans had broken through with armored cars and were advancing on the town.

I inquired where these German cars had been seen, because they had not been reported to me and it was my business to find them and photograph them. My friend described place and time, and I realized that what they were talking about was in fact the French armored cars that had passed me that day. This seemed to have an important bearing on Allied plans, and I was asked to report my information at once. Messengers were hurriedly dispatched to verify my report, and as a result it was decided that our lines could be held after all. I received special mention for the service I chanced to render that day, although it was quite by accident that my information had such value.

Hurley and I went through all the battles of that spring when our troops regained the area taken by the Germans. I shall never forget the battle of Villiers Brettoneux. The way for the British attack on that little town was prepared by two Australian units, in perhaps the most daring maneuver in our experience on that front. These two units were to advance, one from either side, and meet behind the town, cutting it off. This advance would, of course, expose them to each other's fire if they used their guns. The Australian troops advanced practically in silence, just going in with their bayonets and cleaning up the German lines. They met behind the town, and then the British attacked it in front. The Germans trying to get out of the trap found themselves surrounded and outnumbered, and most of them tried to surrender. But the British troops attacking them were young boys of eighteen to twenty-one, new troops brought out as replacements. They were taking no prisoners. The ferocious blood-lust of those boys forced the Germans to stand their ground and fight till they were killed almost to a man.

When I came back through the little village and the surrounding orchards, the perfume of apple and cherry blossoms mingled strangely with the powder smoke, and the delicate pink and white tints of the flowering trees rose like a bizarre funeral spray over the blood-soaked corpses sprawled beneath their soft branches.

When the Americans joined the Australians in 1918, I was taking pictures of their march through a town in which our troops were billeted. Imagine my shock when I heard an Australian sing out tauntingly, "Well, Yanks, so you've come over to win the war?"

An American soldier marching by turned to him seriously and said, "Aussie, if we do as well as you fellows have done, anyway we'll have done our share." The Australian turned away, shame-faced.

That was the type of incident that soon led to excellent feeling between Americans and Australians. They got along splendidly together. Our men learned from the Americans straight from the shoulder that they did not overrate themselves in comparison with veteran troops. On the other hand, many of the English thought the Americans were braggarts. But that was not the spirit shown by a single American I met. There was a natural affinity between the Yanks and our men from down under.

July 4, 1918, was to be celebrated by one of the most perfectly organized battles of the whole war, fought by Americans and Australians side by side. The plan was to give experience to the newly arrived Americans, and the idea aroused a keen interest in our men. Carefully planned, it was so small that everyone could get a comprehensive idea of the action. The men were able to understand it perfectly, and they were all looking forward to it.

For the first time in history, tanks and planes were to cooperate directly with infantry. The tanks were to go over carrying small groups of men and quantities of supplies and munitions, clean up the German machine-gun positions, and deposit men and munitions at the advanced line. Overhead, planes would also transport munitions, food, and water, and carry out observation for the headquarters staff. Australians and Americans were to alternate in the lines, in small units.

However, to everybody's consternation, just as everything was poised for the well planned attack, orders came to withdraw the Americans. The American High Command had decided that American troops would fight only as a separate army. It was too late now to replace those who were to be pulled out. The Australian staff did everything possible to keep them, but most of the American units were ordered out of the lines. This meant that the Australians had to cover the section with only 50 per cent of the necessary forces. Many of the American units refused to leave until they received confirming orders, and even then some successfully evaded receiving the orders. In fact, scores of American soldiers exchanged uniforms with Australians who marched back to American rear positions while these AWOL Americans remained to fight.

The zero hour was at dawn. I was with the front-line troops, my camera ready to catch these Yanks in action. When the order came to advance, all but one man rushed forward to the attack. This chap hesitated, seemingly paralyzed by the shock of the barrage. I watched while he stood white and gasping, only for a moment. Then he pulled himself together and rushed out, running to overtake the others.

I went out into the attack and found that these new American troops were not at all behind the veterans in going into the German trenches, doing their full share of cleaning them up, and establishing the new line after ground had been taken. Though it was a successful battle, it was strenuous for everyone because we were short of men.

Late that afternoon, when I was coming back with my negatives, I noticed the same young soldier again. Though he was not a Red Cross man, he was carrying one end of a stretcher. When he put it down at a dressing station, he recognized me and came over and told me how he had felt that morning. He said this was his first battle and that all night he had been quaking with fear. When the barrage started, he just could not make himself go out and face the Germans. He said he knew he would be killed. Finally, it was only a greater fear of being called a coward that made him leave the trench. What happened to him after that I don't know, because I never saw him again. This was the only time I ever saw a man force himself out of such a state into action.

This battle led to the big advance of August, 1918. There was keen concentration on the part of the observers, and many observation balloons were sent aloft near the front. Naturally the German planes attacked them.

An observation balloon moored to the ground is a helpless thing with no protection against an enemy plane. Our observers formed the habit of taking to their parachutes whenever they saw enemy planes coming, meanwhile having the balloons hauled down to escape destruction. Because some men got jittery and abandoned their posts before their balloons were attacked, our headquarters ordered that no observer should leave his balloon until it was actually in flames.

One morning, I was occupying a balloon basket with an observer, third from the end in a line of seven balloons, when a lone German plane came over and started to machine-gun the line. When we heard the rattle of his fire and saw our first balloon fall, we gave the signal to be hauled down. The German got the balloon next to ours; it burst into flames and its observer jumped. My companion told me to climb over the edge of our basket and hang on by my hands, ready to let go as soon as I saw our gas bag explode.

The plane swooped down, letting its machine-gun rip. We could hear the bullets striking the gas bag overhead, but we could see no fire. When the German saw that our balloon had not caught fire, he returned and flew once more above us, raking us. By this time, the balloon was swaying, swinging me by the hands as it was rapidly hauled down, but we were still perhaps 3,000 feet up. By some miracle, which I shall never understand, the balloon again did not catch fire. The pilot circled and let us have it again. A third time we heard the bullets ripping through the envelope and through the wicker basket, but neither of us was wounded. Even after this third attack the balloon was not in flames, and our nerves were near the breaking point from the suspense of waiting to drop.

The pilot continued down the line and set fire to the other balloons. When we realized that ours was not going to burn, my partner leaned over the edge of the basket and told me to climb in again. It was all I could do to keep from letting go and dropping, without bothering to pull the parachute rip-cord. The hardest thing I did during the entire war was to climb back into that basket, even with the observation officer's help. After the suspense of hanging there, waiting to drop, the nervous reaction was terrific. To be hung on a string in empty air, dangling, waiting, with bullets whistling about my ears was not exactly my idea of how to spend my youth.

One fact that was never publicly told was that part of the Hindenberg Line was captured by one Australian captain on his own initiative. I had been out across No Man's Land with a patrol at that point, getting sneak pictures of the Germans. It was hilly country, or we should never have succeeded. When I came back through our lines, this particular captain told me that he had orders to attack next morning. I told him that from my observation the line was very weak in that area. He said it was a stupid waste of lives and ammunition to wait for the morning barrage and attack an alerted enemy. It would be perfectly easy to watch the German kitchens working and know when the men were eating supper and off guard. He said he could go out himself at suppertime and just quietly capture them all.

That night at eight o'clock, when the Germans were all sitting down to their supper, he went out with 40 men and rounded up

300 prisoners. Then he quietly moved his men forward and occupied the German trenches. It was just a little idea of his own, and such a breach of discipline that it couldn't be made public. But take part of the Hindenberg Line was what he did. The neighboring outfits on his right and left flanks did not take their parts until the next day, and made a big fuss about doing it. But this infantry captain from the Queensland bush country did not have to fire a shot or wound a man.

I went into the attack on the Hindenberg Line with the 27th and 29th American Divisions on September 27, 1918. These divisions were supported by the Australians. The weather was so foggy it was impossible to see clearly, and the advancing Americans were badly cut up by the German fire. In the gloom and smoke they had not been able to clean up thoroughly, so there was a hopeless mix-up in the fog. The men were fighting with splendid courage, but they were quite lost in a country new to them. The whole thing was wild confusion.

Knowing the area by heart, I took it upon myself to help as much as possible. I saw some Americans fighting in a trench, and Germans running up with bombs. The Germans met another group of Americans and tried to surrender, but the Americans were new to war and they weren't taking any prisoners. A German officer popped out of the fog, organized his men, and captured the Americans. I rushed back and got another group and we came back and captured both the Germans and the Americans. Then an Australian liaison officer came along and got things reorganized when the Germans attacked once more.

Three of us had just climbed up on the rim of a crater and I was pointing out the location of a German machine-gun nest when a hail of bullets hit us. We all dropped. As soon as I recovered my senses I realized I had been struck. The men beside me were dead.

The troops in the crater were Australians. Without an instant's hesitation they poured over the rim and took the machine-gun nest. Seven bullets had grazed the fleshy part of my chest. I had another wound in my scalp and one in my heel. My uniform was soaking with blood and I looked ghastly, but I really wasn't badly hurt.

The next afternoon I was back at work, a rather depressing spectacle swathed in bloody bandages. I was hit three times the second day, and so covered with blood that I got the sympathy of everybody, though my injuries were superficial. Wherever I went I met men who opened their eyes wide and hauled off their canteens to brace me up with a swig of rum.

A bar was added to my Military Cross because my work that day had been observed by two colonels. I was carrying my camera and that made me conspicuous. The Military Cross had been given me earlier for bringing in some wounded men. Naturally we didn't stick to photography when something more pressing came up that we could do, though we always did our job of getting pictures.

My war work kept me busy for months after the Armistice, finishing the photographic record of Australia's part in the greatest armed struggle man had known up to that time. Some years later, when the volumes of the official war history came off the press, one after another, I derived a deep measure of satisfaction from the use to which Charley Bean had put my pictures by the hundreds.

I went with the air force into Germany, and in January, 1919, with Captain Bean and five other officers, I went out to Gallipoli and Mesopotamia to photograph those battlefields. One day in Constantinople, I was walking down the Rue de Pera when an old Greek driver jumped off his cab and threw his arms around me, weeping. It was Marcus Aurelius, the old boy who had been with us through the Balkan War. He rushed back to the cab and thrust out his Turkish passenger, explaining to me with signs that he was going to drive me all day for nothing. The only English words he still knew were, "All right!"

The first night we were in Constantinople, four of us walked into the Tokatlion cabaret and took a box. A waiter appeared at once with three bottles of champagne and a large dish of Turkish sweetmeats. I said, "We didn't order that."

"It is with the manager's compliments to Captain Wilkins."

I was surprised that the manager knew me, and asked who the manager was.

"He will be here in a moment, sir."

In walked Godfrey in full evening dress—that brave lion from the Balkan War, seven years earlier. "Oh, my dear Captain Wilkins, how happy I am to see you again!"

I didn't know whether to throw him over the balcony or drink his wine. But I decided to drink it and pump him for information. Neither of us mentioned the day I had nearly murdered him, nor the time Saul threw him out of the Pera Palace Hotel. All during the war, it turned out, he had been acting as a spy for both the British and the Turks.

9

The England-to-Australia Air Race

As I was finishing my work on the Australian history of the war, I kept several irons in the fire, with a keen eye open to see which of them would glow first. I was anxious now, as I had been before the war, to carry out a plan for a series of meteorological stations girdling both the Arctic and the Antarctic that would enable us to make the kind of permanent, systematic study of polar weather that had been carried out once, back in the 1882–1883 International Polar Year. My war work both in photography and in flying had impressed on me firmly the tremendous value of accurate weather prediction.

But the principal obstacle to such a plan in 1919 was the fact that the polar regions were still not sufficiently explored. The people who would be responsible for putting up the money to establish scientific stations had to be satisfied that it was even possible geographically to place them where they would do the most good. An area of nearly one million square miles of the Arctic—north of the islands explored by Stefansson in the previous decade, and west of Peary's route to the Pole—was unknown. At the other end of the world, the Antarctic continent was accepted as a fact, but vast reaches of its coastline and interior had never even been seen by man.

Early in 1919, I suggested my plan for polar weather stations to a committee of the Royal Meteorological Society, but they turned it down as impractical. Some day, maybe, but not now, I was told. Next, I got the idea of trying to get possession of one of the captured German Zeppelins which the Royal Navy was trying to get rid of, thinking them a useless expense. I asked if I might borrow one for a flight over the North Pole. Nonsense!—the brass hats snorted. Impossible! Foolhardy! Ridiculous! I was considered all kinds of an idiot for even suggesting such a thing.

Then, I tried to get the Zeppelin people in Germany to build me an airship, to be paid for by some wealthy English friends who had a measure of faith in my idea for a polar flight. The Germans were interested in a paying customer, but their interest turned to hostility when they heard where I wanted to fly the Zeppelin. They wanted nothing to do with a mad Australian who was bound to bring them bad publicity by way of "Zep Disaster!" headlines in the press. When I tried to tell them that I had already spent three years in the Arctic and knew how perfect flying conditions could be in the far north at the right time of year, they would not listen. They were certain of only one thing about the Arctic—that it was the locus of giant storms, with winds of devastating power likely at any moment to rip their delicate airship to shreds. It was not the right part of the world for flying at all.

Then, I became acquainted with an engaging and interesting Englishman, John Lachlan Cope. A Cambridge man, fascinated by the idea of polar exploration, he was organizing an Antarctic expedition. He took me on as second in command, with the program to include the use of a series of planes to explore the continent, much as Peary had used dog teams in the north. All my difficulties seemed over. But Cope's expedition would not set out for some months, leaving me time for other work, and it was during this interval that I became involved in the historic England-to-Australia air race.

As early as March, 1919, the government of Australia had announced it was offering a prize of 10,000 pounds for the first flight from England across Europe and southern Asia to Australia, as a step to bind the Commonwealth closer to the mother country by the swift, new means of transportation that had come of age during the air battles of the World War. Nor was Australia the only one in this, because with hundreds of trained men eager to fly, and hundreds of new planes on the flying fields, the golden age of long-distance air racing was dawning. In June of that first summer of peacetime, Captain John W. Alcock of the R.A.F. and Arthur Whiffen Brown of San Francisco made history with their spectacular flight across the North Atlantic from Newfoundland to Ireland, winning the big prize offered by the London *Daily Mail*. Both were knighted and Sir Arthur became a British citizen. Records were being broken every week. In 1919, the world was witnessing one triumph after another of heavier-than-air craft, driven by engines far more powerful than we had dreamed of back in 1910 when I first went up with Grahame-White at Hendon.

According to the rules of our race, no plane was to start before September 8. The winner would be required to complete the flight half round the world within thirty days. Each plane and all its parts were to be of British Empire manufacture, and every man aboard had to be an Australian citizen. We had eager fellows enough on hand, demobilized from the Australian Flying Corps, and it was not long before various aircraft manufacturing interests, petroleum companies, engine makers, and others with a stake in the growing industry had given their backing to several teams willing to attempt the 11,000-mile flight. The route, for those days, was a rugged one, over vast stretches without landing fields, over jungle and mountains and, of course, wide stretches of water. The improvised landing places included the steeplechase courses at Rangoon and at Singapore in the Straits Settlements, from which the hurdles had to be cleared away against our arrival. But despite all this makeshift arrangement, we were game to prove ourselves and the sky-birds to which we committed our lives.

Public comment was mixed on the wisdom of holding the race. The Melbourne *Argus* thought the flight would prove so simple that there was no necessity to throw away thousands of good Australian pounds on the project. But another Melbourne paper, *The Age,* described it as "a circus flight—a poorly disguised attempt at self-advertisement at the expense of the Australian public." *The Age* expressed the hope that Parliament would reassemble soon and force the government to retract its offer. Across the Atlantic, the *New York Times* gloomily asserted that "Christopher Columbus did not take one-tenth the risks that these bold air pioneers will have to face.... They will be throwing dice with Death!"

My crew, of which I was commander and navigator, was termed the Interstate Quartette, because each of the four members came from a different state in Australia. The pilot was Lieutenant Valdemar ("Val") Rendle, a twenty-three-year-old doctor's son from Brisbane, Queensland, with a brilliant record as a combat flyer. He had worked as a mechanic in an aircraft factory, had been a test pilot, and had flown the official air mail from London to Paris. His assistant, Lieutenant Reg Williams, was born in Victoria and was also only twenty-three. He had logged many hours in the air as an instructor and in the "ferry service," flying new machines from England to France during the war. Lieutenant Garnsey ("Gar") Potts, from New South Wales, had been a pilot and gunnery officer, but in recent months had been working with Reg Williams at the Grahame-White Aviation Company at Hendon. A better group could not have been put together. Of the four, I ranked as the "old man" at age thirty-one, my birthday passing almost unnoticed as we prepared our plane for the start of the race.

Our craft was big for its day, with a 75-foot wingspan and weighing 4 tons when loaded. It was a Blackburn *Kangaroo,* a twin-engine biplane originally designed as a fighting bomber carrying a ton of explosives and a crew of three. Built by the Blackburn Aeroplane and Motor Company of Leeds and Hull in north England, the " 'Roo" had a long fuselage jutting out a good 15 feet in front of the wings, with four open cockpit seats in line, two forward of the wings and two aft. The engines were twin Rolls-Royce Falcons of 12 cylinders, each developing 275 horsepower, and capable of a maximum speed of 107 m.p.h. They were beautiful engines, and I was pleased as I could be with them. In fact, we were in perfect order and all set to go on November 10 when, at the last minute, the Rolls-Royce people decided to change the gasoline strainer. I would not let them because I was satisfied with the strainer already installed.

The evening before we were to start I put police on guard at the machine, with strict orders not to let anyone come near it, and the boys and I went up to London to say good-by to our friends. At midnight we came back to Hounslow Aerodrome, ready to take off at 4 A.M., and found that the Rolls-Royce mechanics had gotten around the watchmen and taken the engine down. They had it completely dismantled when I got there.

I stayed right on the job after that, but it was five days before the Rolls-Royce men had the engine in shape again. Then bad weather held us for another three days. By that time, my crew was beginning to lose heart since another team, led by Captain Ross Smith of Adelaide, in a Vickers Vimy, had got well out in front of us.

Actually, ours was the fifth crew in the race to get off. A Frenchman named Etienne Poulet had joined the race unofficially, starting from Paris, but he was ineligible for the Australian prize. Nevertheless, he was keen on beating us, and we wanted to beat him. By this time, he had reached India, where he was stuck for some days trying to fix a leaking oil tank. He had already used up thirty-eight days.

The Matthews team was also out of it, having wandered far off course into southern Germany, there exhausting the permitted thirty days while snowbound at an airfield in Alsace-Lorraine. Sadly for all of us, the two chaps who had taken off from Hounslow on November 13, Lieutenant Roger Douglas and Lieutenant Leslie Ross, had crashed at Surbiton. They were both dead just a few minutes after take-off, while we were still at work on our engines a few miles away. But Ross Smith and his three companions, nine days ahead of us, were already somewhere above the Arabian desert, sailing along in grand style. It would take great flying and good luck to catch him.

We had to wait for the fog to clear on the morning of Friday,

November 21, but we finally got airborne a little past 10:30. We were happily surprised when Prince Albert, the Right Honorable Winston Churchill, and a couple of generals came out to the field to wave us off. But their "Good luck" cheers didn't avail against the elements: we found the weather at Paris too bad for a landing, so we had to fly on to the field at Romilly, about 60 miles east. Here we spent a precious three days repairing the balky gas strainer and waiting for the weather to improve, after which a 200-mile hop to Lyon was followed by another enforced wait of several days. We finally took off for Monte Carlo on the twenty-eighth, only to run into a frightful thunderstorm. We were blinded by the rain, in the midst of the jagged Maritime Alps, when the controls froze solid. When we tried to jam them loose, one of the throttles broke so that we couldn't control the engine—we could merely switch it on and off. There was nothing to do but take a chance on landing, and we quickly decided on the field at Fréjus, an ancient town with Roman ruins about two miles inland from the Mediterranean coast. The danger was that if we were to miss our target we might ram into one of the many parts of the old Roman acqueduct which jut upward from the meadows surrounding the town.

Down we came through the storm, feeling our way. We could see neither ground nor hangar. Suddenly the whole plain appeared beneath us, covered with rocks, the narrow runway stretching out between them. Fortunately we struck the runway, but too fast. The speed of the plane carried us the length of the field and on into the hangar before we could stop. Another few yards and we would have smashed.

We worked all night on the engine and controls, with the help of a group of British mechanics who had been left at Fréjus with some Handley-Page planes that had burned out on the way to India. They were friendly, and offered to take care of the machine while we went to the hotel to clean up and sleep a couple of hours. Thinking we could trust them, we left the plane in their charge.

Usually we started the engine off the switch, but that morning the British and French flying corps people wanted to get moving pictures of the take-off. One of the British mechanics swung the propeller and started the engines. We took off easily but while we were climbing one of the engines cut out. We switched on the other. Then the first engine picked up, and we went on. But the first engine kept failing, so I decided to follow the coast to an emergency landing field only 30 miles away.

We came down in still another forced landing, examined the engine, and found one of the ignition wires had been disconnected and bound with soft wire to the frame of the engine. Someone had deliberately tampered with the machine, hoping to wreck us. We spent two hours going over the engine and the machine, and could find nothing else wrong. Still, that discovery left us feeling uneasy. This was our ninth day and we were just reaching Italy, while according to news reports Ross Smith already was in India.

Across the Gulf of Lyon and all the way to Italy we flew in pouring rain. Landing at Pisa, we sank in mud and it took hours of hard work to get out of that. Next day, we managed to get into the air again and reached Rome, only to find that because it was a saint's day, no business was being done—not even with an air-race crew. All the gasoline was locked up, the man in charge was away on a picnic and couldn't be found. That delayed us another day, during which we heard that Ross Smith now was in Siam, ready to hop off for Singapore.

With rain still pouring down, we got to Taranto in the south of Italy, whence we flew across the Adriatic, over the Greek coast, and on to Suda Bay in Crete, without calling at Athens. The field at Suda Bay was a marsh, flooded with water, and our wheels stuck deep in the mud as soon as we touched down.

During that night the Royal Air Force dug a 2-foot ditch to drain the field for us, using Turkish prisoner labor. At dawn we were still at work, putting down pieces of wood and old sheet iron —in fact, everything solid we could lay hands on—and filling the gutters with big slabs of timber, in the hope of getting off that day. After a lot of taxiing and straining of the engines, we finally managed to take off. Then we had to fly around the island since our

As Gaumont cinematographer, 1912: setting off with camera and assistant to film army maneuvers at Cambridge.

*A stunt that led to better things: To make his first
aerial films Wilkins rode astride the fuselage.*

*The Balkan War: luncheon stop on the way to the front.
Wilkins standing at left.*

In camp, Chorlu, Turkey: Wilkins (center) talking with Bernard Grant.

Captain Penfold as Santa, Wilkins (black hat) as Gaumont photographer, about to rise from the Brixton gas works.

Aboard the Karluk, *1913,
headed for the Arctic.*

*Christmas Day, 1913:
showing movies at Collinson Point.*

Stefansson's expedition in Nome. Back row: Wilkins, Malloch,
Beauchat, O'Neill, Jenness, Cox, McKinley.
At left: Mamen, McConnell, Chipman. Front: Mackay, Bartlett,
Stefansson, Anderson, Murray, Johansen.

Western Front, 1917: Captain Wilkins, official photo-historian for the Royal Australian Air Force.

End of the attempted flight to Australia—thirty feet outside a lunatic asylum on Crete.

With fellow expedition member C. R. ("Roddy") Carr as the Quest *sailed from London, 1921.*

The Boss, Sir Ernest Shackleton, as the Quest *made ready.*

Australia, 1924. The snake ventured into Wilkins' camp and was collected for the British Museum.

Fairbanks, 1926. The Alaskan's *brief first flight ended badly.*

heavy load of fuel made it unwise for us to try to climb above the mountain ranges.

The mountains of Crete are impressive. From the air one gets a striking view of them as they rise almost sheer from the Mediterranean to heights of 8,000 feet. Isolated villagers and goat-herders on their steep uplands stared in wonder at us as we flew past them, thousands of feet above the sea. Many of them had never seen an airplane before.

We flew around the mountains and set out southeast across the Mediterranean, with our course fixed for Cairo. Eighty miles from Crete, with everything going well, I was about to open a box of sandwiches when Potts, the mechanic in the rear, passed forward a note to me saying that oil was leaking from the port engine. Before I could answer this, Potts tapped me on the shoulder and handed me a second note. The oil crankcase had broken off, and the oil was streaming out under 40-pounds' pressure.

"What are we going to do?" Rendle shouted.

"Climb!" I yelled back, gesturing upward with my hand. "Climb while you've still got oil!"

We had been flying low, so we could get up to only 2,000 feet altitude before the oil gave out. The nearest land was Crete, 80 miles behind us, and according to the makers of the plane, we could expect to fly no more than 30 miles on one engine from 2,000 feet, gradually losing altitude as we proceeded.

It was interesting to sense my own feeling and observe the other men, when it seemed doubtful that we had more than a few hours to live. We knew that when the plane struck the water it would surely sink. We had life-saving suits, but there was no hope of swimming 50 miles, and little chance of our being picked up. There was not a boat of any kind in sight—nothing but blue water. My thought was, "Well, here goes. Only one more adventure, the big one."

But curiously enough, the plane kept going and maintained altitude, with only one engine. I said a little prayer of thanks to the marvelous workmanship of those Rolls-Royce mechanics. We came nearer and nearer to Crete. As we kept edging along, past

30 miles, 40 miles, 50, then 55, we all showed increasing signs of fear. With a chance of survival, we all began to be afraid of dying. The wind was against us, and that helped keep us up. We thought if the wind just held, we might possibly make it. I shouted to Rendle, "If we can get there, crash on the nearest beach."

As we came within sight of the island, it looked like a pale, fawn-colored and rosy cloud low against the blue horizon. The nearer we got, the more solid it looked. Soon we could again see the rugged mountains and green forests and villages. The plane was still holding up at 2,000 feet.

When we reached the coast, there was nothing below us but broken bits of rocky beach, steep slopes, and towns. We decided to try to fly around the island to the field at Suda Bay. We made it around to the northern side of the mountains, and there the wind was against us, blowing strongly on the same side as the good engine. We could not turn the machine against it, and the wind and the engine were taking us on, past the island, out to sea again. Rendle shouted, "We've got to take a chance on the dry engine to kick us around!" I nodded my agreement.

He switched on the engine that had no oil supply and almost at once the water-jackets cracked and blew in pieces. The fragments tore through the fuselage like a bursting shrapnel shell, and the plane went into a flat spin. Luckily, none of us was hit by the fragments. We were just above the town of Canea, falling straight toward a group of houses from 800 feet. Rendle did the only possible thing. He nosed the machine straight down in a steep dive toward the houses, then at the last second he pulled it up and we just grazed the roof of the farthest one.

We reached the field beyond, but there was no time to turn and we had to land with the wind. The plane raced out of control across the field, dropped hard into a 4-foot ditch, burst all four tires, bounded out of the ditch, and ran straight at a solid stone wall. Luckily there was a bank of earth just in front of the wall, and our *Kangaroo* dashed up the bank, stopped with a jolt, and nosed over forward, its long tail sticking awkwardly up in the air.

None of us was hurt. Somebody snickered, and in a moment we were all half paralyzed with hysterical laughter. This broke the tension, and we could then climb out of our cockpits and take stock of our situation. There was a 6-foot ditch between the bank of earth and the stone wall. The machine had nosed down into it. Although the plane looked for all the world like a wreck in its absurd position, there was really very little damage done to the undercarriage. A rope around the tail pulled the plane out readily enough. We at once wired London ordering a new engine, but we learned shortly that it could not possibly reach us until the next boat, two months later. Then came the news, on our second day of waiting in Crete, that Ross Smith and his party had safely reached Australia to win the prize, on their twenty-ninth day out from England. Disappointed as we were in our own bad luck, we were happy to learn that a countryman, a veteran flyer, had proved that such a flight could be made. That evening we raised our glasses to—Sir Ross!

I wanted to finish the flight just the same. I found by wire that I could get two new Eagle-8 engines in Athens, with 80 horsepower more than our engines. They would cost $30,000, but I was willing to try to raise the money to buy these engines myself. However, both the Rolls-Royce engineers and the Blackburn Company wired me that such powerful engines would wreck the plane. They said if I put them in, they would assume no responsibility. Recognizing that the makers of the plane probably knew what they were talking about, I decided not to take the risk.

We therefore concluded, to our great regret, to abandon the flight and claim our accident insurance. The insurance company cabled that we were covered against everything but a mechanical breakdown, and they classified the breaking of an oil pipe as a mechanical breakdown. Therefore, they said we could collect nothing. We claimed that the breakage of anything was an accident, and we were insured against accident. The difference was an interesting one from a legal viewpoint, because there were bound to be more such cases in the air age ahead, so the Shell Oil Company agreed to fight the case for us. The trial was prolonged more than a year and a half. We eventually won it, but the real point at issue was never clearly settled. The insurance did not cover the price I had paid for the plane, and I lost about $10,000 on the abandoned trip, even after the insurance was paid.

In the meantime, as the suit dragged its painful way through the courts, I was off for the Antarctic on what was to be the first of my many trips to the least known and most treacherous of the continents.

10

First Misadventures in the Antarctic

From Crete, I went back to London to wind up the business details of the England-to-Australia air race, and while there, John Cope and I went over the plans for our Antarctic expedition. Postponed to the latter half of 1920, which would be the spring and summer in Antarctica, the venture was originally conceived as the first assault on the unknown continent by plane. We planned to take twelve planes, which could be bought cheaply from the postwar stocks held by the government. With these twelve machines carrying little except our fuel supply, we would start from Graham Land (now more often called Palmer Peninsula), the great horn-shaped peninsula of Antarctica that juts north toward the southern tip of the South American continent. This was a spot where whalers passed every season in the Antarctic spring, and was therefore the logical point to be put ashore from a ship.

The plan was to ferry our planes and fuel forward down the coastline toward the main body of Antarctica and to establish a base several hundred miles within the Antarctic Circle. As our gas would be used up, we would shift cargoes from time to time, and send an empty plane back to the base with one pilot, while the other planes would carry men instead of the fuel load. As I calculated it, the squadron would be finally reduced to two planes, with which we could fly to the South Pole and back.

This closely resembled the plan that Robert E. Peary had used with dog teams in his successful assault on the North Pole eleven years earlier—except we would be moving much faster, in longer leaps toward our objective. I believed that we could thus cover a much larger area of unknown territory than by other means of transportation, and I would have my chance to test my theories of the feasibility of flight in the polar regions.

John L. Cope, the expedition organizer, was a physician and biologist. About a year and a half younger than I, he had been surgeon with the detachment of Shackleton's 1914–1917 expedition that was sent to the Ross Sea, on the far side of Antarctica, to await his chief's arrival after his planned transcontinental trip by dog team. As the whole world knew, the trans-Antarctica journey had been frustrated by the wrecking of Shackleton's ship, *Endurance*. Cope returned home to serve in the wartime Royal Navy with little to show for his long wait at the other end of the world. Quite naturally, he was keen to accomplish something spectacular in exploration after the 1914–1917 fiasco.

An enthusiast for both biology and physical science, member of several learned societies in England by the time he was thirty, Cope was, however, just about the poorest executive in the world. I got my first sign of this some months after leaving him in England with all our plans agreed on—or so I thought.

I had returned to Australia and was engaged in some final work on the war history, when I received a cable from Cope, sent from Norway where he was negotiating for passage for the expedition aboard a whaling vessel outbound for Montevideo, Uruguay. To my amazement, Cope wanted me to go at once to Canada and buy dogs and meet him in Montreal! On inquiry I learned that my plan of using planes had been abandoned, because Cope had spent all the money on other affairs. In reply, I cabled that under the circumstances I did not care to go on with the expedition, and instead was taking an excellent job I had been offered to do civil engineering in Australia.

Cope cabled frantically that he was depending on me, that he had organized the expedition with the understanding that I was a part of it, that none of the other men had any experience in polar conditions. He begged me not to let him down.

The whole thing was a hard blow. I really had no desire at all to go along with the expedition if we could not use planes. The

Australia offer was an important one, and under the circumstances it was a sacrifice to give it up. However, I agreed that I would meet Cope and his party in Montevideo, stipulating that he would have to arrange for the dogs himself. This was the inauspicious start of perhaps the most mismanaged Antarctic expedition in history, one from which I was to learn, by horrible example, all about how *not* to direct an expedition into the unknown.

Arriving in Montevideo, I was chagrined to find Cope stranded for debt. Furthermore, instead of the promised scientific party, there were only two other men, one nominally a topographer, the other a geologist. The three had come out together from Norway on a whaling ship; the other two, Lester and Bagshawe, had gone on south with it while Cope was held up in Montevideo. He could produce no money, and the whalers had attached all the expedition equipment, including the moving-picture outfit I was to use. To top it all, they refused to take Cope any farther south.

All the whaling ships had gone on toward the coast we wanted to reach except one that was delayed for repairs, and these ships were the only vessels that went to the Antarctic. There was one lone mail and supply ship a year that went as far as the Falkland Islands, but it had already gone.

When I appeared on the scene and argued the case, the whaling company spokesman relented and said that if Cope would turn over control of the expedition to me, they would take us south. In return, I agreed to take a series of pictures of their whaling work to be used in publicity. In addition, I was to leave my motion-picture camera as partial security. So Cope and I went south on the whaling vessel that had been delayed, and after passing the Falklands and making our way southward through 600 miles of pack ice, they landed us on Deception Island, which lies slightly northwest of the tip of Graham Land. Here we met the other two members of the expedition.

M.C. Lester was supposed to be the topographer, and W.T. Bagshawe the geologist. Actually, Lester had been second mate on a tramp steamer, and Bagshawe had no real knowledge of geology. They were fine young lads, eager to do all they could, but it

was unfortunate they were not really equipped for their assignments.

It was a disheartening situation. Obviously there was nothing
to do but make the films of whaling as I had agreed, and then try
to include as much work of exploration as possible in the little
time that would be left. It had long since been decided that I
would spend only the summer with Cope, since the grand plan
we had evolved back in England had been reduced to almost
nothing. Our objective now would be simply to gather as much
topographical knowledge of nearby Graham Land as we could
until the whalers should leave these waters. The large whale-oil
factories on Deception Island, 800 miles from the nearest inhabited
land, were open only during the whaling season. No one lived
there in the winter, and there had never been a woman on the island. The factories operated when the whaling ships came in,
from November until March or April.

Throughout the season, while the catchers were out, the factories
on shore were running day and night, trying to handle each whale
as soon as it was brought in. At that time, it used to take two days
to cut up one of the hundred-ton creatures, but with modern
methods and machinery a factory can now handle eight or nine
a day. Whales must be got into the pot as quickly as possible;
otherwise they cook themselves. This occurs because as soon as
a whale is dead the icy water chills the outside fat, which then
holds in the animal heat, and within three hours the fat inside
the body is beginning to cook.

I was able to make a most interesting film for the whalers. Then
I asked them to take us farther south to a point where the expedition could begin work. They obligingly sailed for Graham
Land, which was then marked on maps as a big peninsula extending from the south polar continent. The land was a magnificent
sight as we slowly approached it through drifting ice and icebergs,
the dark green and black heights of rock protruding here and
there from the ice and glittering snow, looming far above us against
the sky.

The whaler landed the four of us with our equipment and a

whale boat on the Graham Land coast. It was not the introduction to Antarctica I had dreamed about for years, since well before that day back in 1913 when my hasty reading of a cable had made me think that I was about to join Sir Ernest Shackleton. I was really not with much of an expedition at all—just four fellows camping in the Antarctic for a few months of summer. Anyhow, I was here, and Cope and I set out to explore the area after we'd got our camp in order. Turning inland, we soon found our way blocked by an almost perpendicular cliff, with no apparent way around. We saw that the only way to surmount it would be to cut steps for several hundred feet in the steep-walled snow surface. Neither of us particularly liked this sort of Alpinism, but there was no escaping it, so, roped together, up we went. To make matters worse, a storm came up and our hand and toe holes were filled with drifting snow almost as soon as we made them, which meant that each man had to cut the holes anew. Movement upward was slow. It was as well for us that the wind was at our backs, making it easier to hang on to that near-sheer cliff of ice and packed snow. The cold was numbing. By the time we had climbed halfway to the top our fingers and our toes were frostbitten. Yet we had to go on because to return down that side would have been more difficult than to ascend.

At last, after about a four-hour climb, resting occasionally where we thought we had a sure foothold, we reached the crest and lay there not at all happy at the sight before us. The far side of the mountain was just about as sheer as the one we had climbed. A treacherous cornice, newly formed by the drifting snow, hung over the ledge, and on the leeward slope the snow was whirling so thick we couldn't see what lay at the bottom of the descent. We had climbed to a narrow col that would have been almost a knife-edge if it hadn't been for that overhang, the cornice. We discussed the terrifying situation. Would we try to back-cut our steps? This would be extremely dangerous and would still leave us in a quandary as to where to find an easier way over the mountain. Would we try and edge along the knife-edge col to the right or the left? There seemed to be no advantage on either side. Or, would we take a chance and make our way down the far slope and hope for the best? It looked impossible to cut steps on the way down that far side for the whirling snow would blind us and fill up our toe holds as we made them.

It was too cold to stay long up there on that ridge, so something had to be done. We decided to try edging along the ridge to the right to a higher part of the mountain in order to scout for an easier descent, or maybe to find a sheltered spot where we could dig in until the storm cleared. I led as we set forth, straddling the ridge. If all of it had been narrow, we might have succeeded in crossing it. But the surface broadened and became too wide to straddle, and it seemed that we should have to crawl. In doing so I found it impossible to see just where the snow cornice began and ended. In the lead, I had crawled only a few yards when I fell headlong through an overhanging part. Cope had no firm foothold or place to thrust his ice ax to hold my weight and was instantly jerked from his position. Down we went at great speed, first on our faces, then on our sides and on our backs—over and over, trying our utmost to control our downward slide with our ice axes. But our pace was too fast, and the slope was rough.

At last, I bumped into a sitting position. Clasping my arms around my knees and holding my ice ax across them, I gained still more speed. Cope was less fortunate, being less under control than I was. My weight dragged him down at the end of the rope which bound us together. We careened on for what seemed an endless time. When our speed slackened somewhat, I gathered that we were either coming to the bottom or—and my heart almost stopped beating at the thought—we might be coming to a slight rise on the other side of which there could be a crevasse. A moment later, I swept over a rise and felt myself in the air. Then I landed with a terrific bump, slid on for a moment, and came to a full stop that caused the rope around my chest to squash the breath out of me. I collapsed, unconscious.

When I came to I could hear Cope yelling for help at the top of his voice: "Are you there? What's happened? Come and help me! Pull me out of here!"

For some moments I was too helpless to reply, but at last I managed to call feebly, "Hang on. I'm okay. I'll get to you in a minute."

The time I took to get my breath and plant my ice ax firmly in the snow must have seemed hours to Cope, but at last I had one end of the rope fast to the ax. Now, as I looked through the swirling snow, I saw that we were by no means at the end of the slope. From there on, the grade, although not so steep, was dangerously crevassed. I struggled upward a few feet to where the rope had cut through the crusted snow, looked over, and saw him hanging several feet below, upside down. His rope had slipped to about his hips, and it was a miracle he had not slipped out of the loop and vanished into the deep, blue crevasse, the bottom of which I couldn't see. It must have been down a hundred feet or more.

Cope's ice ax had been lost while he was being dragged down the steep slope, and he dared not try to right himself without it. It was going to be difficult to rescue him, for I couldn't haul him up hand over hand, and I couldn't be sure that my ice ax had sufficient hold for me to haul him up by using it as a purchase. There seemed only one possible way out—my heavy sheath knife. If I could drop it, if he could catch it, and then cut hand holes and gradually bring himself to an upright position, that would help. But if I dropped it to him as he hung there upside down, he might not catch it and down it would go into the crevasse.

We had no other rope or string. I could not use my belt; I would need that to keep my trousers up. My heart was sinking as I hastily ripped off the tail of my shirt, slipped the piece through the loop on the knife sheath and tying it loosely around the rope, let it slide down to Cope's waist, where he could reach it.

It seemed like a long, long time before he could get himself right side up. Then with me pulling at the rope and holding fast while he cut step by step, he managed to reach the top of the crevasse and haul himself out, utterly exhausted.

"Thank God, we've made it," he gasped, and seemed almost happy until he looked down and saw all the crevasses between us and the smoother slopes beneath. The sight was almost too much for him.

We rested for several hours, or tried to. Shivering and chilled to the bone, we had to make a move or freeze to death. Edging our way cautiously through the maze of crevasses—our fear of them helped keep us warm—we came to a place where we could edge off the top of the glacier to solid ground and then follow it in the direction of the harbor. We had many a narrow squeak before we made it. But finally we were safe, and went around the coast to our camp.

I've never really enjoyed mountain climbing since that first experience on the edge of the Antarctic continent. Every time I see a sharp-ridged col, or a glacier with a steep descent, I'm reminded of our slide and its near fatal ending.

We spent four months on Graham Land, doing as much work as we could without the help of trained men or even proper equipment. At any rate, during those four months we did succeed in mapping some thirty miles of the coast, and many times we attempted to climb to the Antarctic plateau, which had never been explored at that point. Always we met a sheer cliff some 500 feet high. It appeared to me the only practical way of exploring the top of the continental plateau would be by airplane.

At the end of four months, knowing the close of the whaling season was upon us, we left Bagshawe in camp with our equipment while Cope, Lester, and I set out in a small open boat to search for a home-going vessel. We sailed 40 miles along the coast, through drifting ice and among some big icebergs. It was on this trip that I had another of the more hairy scares of my life.

During my watch a school of killer whales rose suddenly around the boat, blowing and puffing. One came so close that it touched my hand, over the stern. Instantly the killer whirled, and all but upset the boat, rocking it so violently the sea poured in over both sides. I yelled to wake up the other two, who were asleep on the thwarts, but there was nothing we could do about the killers. For twenty minutes or so they circled all around us, churning up the water and blowing clouds of steam in our faces. Luckily for us, they were not too set on an explorer dinner, for they could have stove us in with a swish of the tail. Eventually, to our vast relief, they swam away.

After making our way along the coast for 40 miles, we found a whaling ship and eagerly climbed aboard. The captain, however, refused to welcome Cope. He said Lester and I were welcome, but he wouldn't have Cope at his table. Cope's irresponsibility of months before still rankled. He grudgingly said Cope could bunk with the men in the fo'c's'le as far as Montevideo. But he said he wouldn't speak to him and would have nothing to do with him.

At heart, Cope wasn't a half bad chap and he was an amusing companion. But he was immature, and the whalers had no use for him because of an incident some months before. While we were at Deception Island, Cope had gone aboard this same ship to call on the captain, and not finding the captain on board he had ordered the steward to cook him a meal and, in the meantime, to fetch him a bottle of whisky! The captain, a straightforward Norwegian sailor, felt that Cope should not order his people about in his absence. On that previous visit, Cope would have been offered all the hospitality in the world if he had only waited a few minutes.

When the captain was adamant and wouldn't treat Cope with any respect at all, Cope refused to stay on the ship, and that meant Lester and I couldn't remain either. The only course open to us was to go in search of the whaler that had brought us south. So in our 20-foot boat we started out again.

By now there was a heavy fog with a choppy sea running, and we could all observe that a storm was coming up. The captain urged me to wait at least until the weather was not so threatening, but I decided it was best to leave. At least we could take advantage of the rising wind and sail before the storm. We knew other whalers were somewhere along the coast, anchored in the bays and channels between the rocky mainland and the island cliffs. But we didn't know where they were, and we hadn't been here before. Cope and Lester took turns, one at the bow watching for icebergs and pack ice, the other watching the sail, while I handled the tiller. All day we sailed, and all night, without sighting a whaler.

Just before dawn, Cope and Lester fell asleep in the bow. The wind was increasing, and I realized now was the time to put on all sail if we were to keep ahead of the storm. So I lashed the tiller, and hauled up the rest of the canvas. Suddenly a "willy" of wind came down, almost capsized us, and the strain sprung the tiller.

I leaped astern and cut the lashings. Instantly the boat came broad to, half full of water. I shouted to the others. Cope and Lester staggered up, dull with fatigue, and began to bail. I had to hold the tiller on and managed to steer around the projecting end of a glacier, but I could scarcely see ahead in the dim light, and before I realized our danger, I had run the boat full speed onto some submerged rocks half a mile from shore. The side of the boat was stove in just at the waterline and it filled quickly. In no time, we were standing in icy water nearly to our waists, putting as much of our heavy supplies as possible on a rock above water. We managed in this way to lighten the boat just enough so we could bail it out and get it off the rocks. After making hasty repairs with canvas and some strips of wood, we pushed the boat into deeper water and sailed out into the wind—the only thing we could do. There was no hope of help or rescue on that coast.

While one of us bailed constantly, we averaged 17 knots for 70 miles, running before the storm, all the while on the anxious lookout for the whalers. Our only chance was to find one, for without supplies and in that weather we couldn't survive for long.

Sailing at this terrific speed, we shot past a point of the deeply indented coast and, looking back, we saw a whaling boat anchored about two miles behind us in a cove. But we couldn't turn back, for with that badly leaking boat we couldn't sail against the wind. The high cliffs cut off our glimpse of the whaler almost immediately. There was a steep ice cliff to our windward side against which the waves were breaking in tremendous fury, sending spray shooting into the air. We saw we were going to smash against the cliff in spite of all we could do, and we even forgot the whaler in our anxiety to keep off that cliff.

As we drove closer and closer to the ice wall, I could see no way to escape it, but I also saw no use sailing into it at high speed. Releasing the tiller for a moment I moved forward and with my sheath knife slashed the falls. The sail came down on top of me and I was half-smothered for a moment. I don't know why the boat didn't capsize in the waves, but a well built whale boat is about the steadiest craft in a heavy sea. Our boat, even without the sail, rolled and twisted like a thing alive. I think sometimes as I look back on it, that the boat must have been alive, or else some mysterious hand was guiding it, but I realize that the guiding physical influence actually was the current. When we were within a few yards of the ice cliffs, amid the deafening roar of the crashing waves, I was amazed to see that we were making some headway past them, not drifting directly broadside toward them.

Fortunately, the watchman on the whaler had seen us flash past the point and, calling up the crew of the ship's motor launch, he sent it after us. Never have I seen a more welcome sight. That motor boat crew reached us not a minute too soon. When they towed us back to the whaler, the captain willingly agreed to pick up Bagshawe and our equipment and take us all to Montevideo. Then it developed that Cope wanted to leave the other two lads and me on Graham Land all winter while he went to London to raise money. Having an expedition in the field would help him get it, he thought.

So far as I was concerned, the idea ended right there. But when we stopped to pick up Bagshawe, both the others said they wanted to stay. The captain, the ship's doctors and I did our best to persuade them to return with us. I thought they would only waste their time, since they had no instruments with which to take observations or do any work through the winter. But Cope kept urging them to stay, and they wanted to do so.

I finally compromised by saying they might remain two weeks and see how they liked it. I wanted to give them a chance to change their minds, which I thought they might do if they were left alone on the Antarctic continent without Cope's persuasions. I said that after those two weeks, if they still wanted to remain, then I would withdraw my objections. We left them there on shore, with supplies and seven dogs, and after arranging for a whale-catcher to call for them, Cope and I went on with the ship to the whaling station. All the ships would come in to the whaling station, and the whole fleet would leave those seas together for the voyage home to Norway.

On the morning of the fleet's departure, I was amazed when I found that the last whaler arrived without bringing the pair. Then I found out that no other ship had called for them. It turned out that Cope was so determined they be left behind that he had gone to the captain of the whaling station and threatened that if a boat went near their camp he would use influence with the Colonial Office to prevent a renewal of the Norwegians' whaling licenses in these British waters. The captain, impressed by this threat, had sent out orders that the whalers must stay away from the camp.

To insist on returning would have more than taxed the patience and hospitality of the whalers. I realized Lester and Bagshawe would be quite safe, since they had plenty of food, a comfortable hut, warm clothes and a Victrola with records. They had made their camp in the midst of a penguin rookery, which would furnish them endless amusement, and they also had the dogs. If they had been boon companions, with never a cross word between them, I would have brought them away at whatever cost. But they got along well together, quarreling bitterly yet never bearing any malice a few hours later. Any two men who can have an angry row in the morning and forget all about it by afternoon can get along together anywhere for any length of time. So I sailed away with the whaling fleet, and we left young Bagshawe and Lester where they were.

When we reached the Falklands, the affair became most unpleasant. I was taken before the Governor, virtually under arrest, and charged with abandoning these two. A fuss was made about their being "boys," when actually they were young men. The father of one of them had consented to his coming with Cope only with the understanding that I assumed full responsibility and would take his son in hand. Although I had never heard of this until we were in the Falklands, the father held me responsible, and so did the British Governor and the Royal Geographical Society. Although Cope was nominally the expedition leader, the officials knew I had had more experience than Cope and was of a different temperament, so I should bear the blame. I tried to convince them that the two lads were safe enough, because they were within 30 miles of one whaling station and 110 miles of another, where any of the whalers could pick them up next year. Nevertheless, the whole affair was most disagreeable for me.

In Montevideo, I booked passage for America, determined to buy airplanes and return to do some useful Antarctic work the following year. Cope decided to go to England, get a steamer, and reorganize the expedition. What he actually did was to hang around the Falklands until the British authorities grew impatient, got him a job peeling potatoes on a Scottish steamer, and sent him home. His later career was in medicine, not exploring.

Bagshawe and Lester remained all winter quite alone in the Antarctic. Next year the whalers found them comfortable and happy, and they refused to leave until the end of the next whaling season. Thus they were able to say that they had lived a full year in the Antarctic. At any rate, they had done what they wanted to do.

11

Death Pays Two Close Calls

Three days after I reached New York from Montevideo I had two German airplanes, made by the Junkers Company, to fly in the Antarctic. I had met the United States agent for Junkers, a man named Larsen, who said he would lend me the planes if I would fly them to the Antarctic. I told him I would not only fly them there, I would fly them back again.

This was in May of 1921, the beginning of the Antarctic winter, and I could not start until the Antarctic spring, in September. So we planned to fly, meantime, to the Arctic, while it was summer in the northern hemisphere. Larsen had become interested in Eskimos and wanted to fly north and see them, whereas I wanted the flight experience. We began to get our supplies together and, without asking me, Larsen went out and bought quantities of canned bacon, and beads, as presents for the Eskimos. He meant well, but he knew nothing at all about Eskimo life, and naively assumed that all "primitive" people would react alike to simple gifts. Eskimos and Africans were all the same to him. The bacon would have been all right except that Eskimos don't need any more fat in their diet, for that is about all they eat as it is. But Eskimos would not give ten cents for all the beads in Christendom.

Just as we were all ready to start, Sir Ernest Shackleton sent me a long cable saying I could not afford, for my own good reputation, to be associated with an agent for German machines so soon after the war, and that I would be ruined for life in the British Empire if I used German money. He declared he was starting a new expedition to the Antarctic and would get me a British plane if I would join him. At the same time, he cabled another man in New York to help persuade me to give up my plans for my own venture. The simple truth was that Shackleton didn't want anyone else working in the Antarctic while he was in the field.

Just as I was considering what I should do, Larsen called me up to say the Arctic trip was off because he had to go to Europe. When I told him Shackleton wanted me to go with him, and that I thought it might be a good idea for me to spend that year with Shackleton and get more experience before taking the Junkers planes south, Larsen told me to go ahead. He assured me I could have the Junkers in 1922.

I cabled Shackleton in reply that I would go with him on one consideration: that he would regard me as an apprentice learning how to direct an expedition. He could try me and if he decided I had possibilities in that line, he was to take me in hand and teach me. He agreed to this, so I joined him in London.

Sir Ernest Shackleton was the most beloved leader of men I ever knew. Even his enemies couldn't help liking him. He was of English and Irish descent; a powerful man with massive shoulders and a cheerful, breezy manner. He wrote good poetry, and knew by heart many great poems, and for hours on end would quote Keats and Shelley, Wordsworth and Kipling. No title ever stuck to Shackleton. Even when he was an officer in the Naval Reserve, no one ever thought of calling him Lieutenant Shackleton. After he was knighted, no one ever called him Sir Ernest. Other explorers had titles—General Greely, Admiral Peary, and Captains Scott and Roald Amundsen—but Shackleton was always simply Shackleton, or "the Boss."

The wisest thing he ever did was to turn back from the South Pole in 1907 when he was within 90 miles of it. At that point, he found he had just food enough to provide for the trip to the Pole and back, but no more—nothing to allow for delays by accident or storm. The other men wanted to go on and tried to persuade him to do so, but Shackleton said the risk was too great. With luck they could have nipped through and got back, but Shackleton never trusted to luck. It was his lifelong ambition to reach the

South Pole, but he also felt it his duty as a responsible leader to bring his men through safely.

When I joined Shackleton in London he had little for me to do, because the work of organizing and outfitting the expedition was in other hands, and we would not sail until September. Fortunately, a well-to-do manufacturer keenly interested in science, John Quiller Rowett, had assured Shackleton of all the financial backing necessary, and as a consequence the expedition was called the Shackleton-Rowett Expedition.

Having a little time on my hands, I asked the British Air Ministry to allow me to pass an air-navigator test. At that time, in 1921, there were only a handful of qualified air-navigators. Navigation in the air was a new thing; and nobody knew much about it. The same methods of navigation used on the sea were being used both for airplanes and for the lighter-than-air gas-filled ships that Britain was building in imitation of the German Zeppelins. Still, airmen were feeling their way toward the new branch of navigational science that made handling ships in the air significantly different from those at sea.

The Ministry gave me permission, and I made a number of flights in the airships R-32, R-33, and R-34, usually in company with Air Commodore Edward M. Maitland, Britain's top air commander. One day, I set out with the American Navy Commander Louis H. Maxfield to shift the R-34 from Pullen to Howden. The Americans were buying airships built in Britain, and Maxfield was in charge of the crew that had come to England to train for the flight home. It was a short, easy trip and nothing happened until we tried to come in for a landing at Howden, the airport near Hull. Clouds had come up and their shadows made the temperature drop rapidly, thus cooling the gas and taking buoyancy from the ship. Whereupon, in order to lighten the ship the officer pulled all the water ballast, and then we quickly became so light at the bow that we dragged away from the ground crew who were trying to pull us in by long ropes. At that sharp angle there was no way we could shift ballast from stern to bow, so we had to trim ship by going up and then pulling the gas-bags, so as to release just enough to level us off. We circled and tried again to land, but came in too high. We circled a third time and nearly smashed on the ground. Fortunately the sun came out just in time and we were buoyed up and could drag away.

Before we made a fourth attempt, the commander on the ground ordered us by wireless to remain in the air until the weather steadied. So off we went around the north of England, waiting for the weather to clear. For eight or ten hours, as long as daylight lasted, it was a pleasant trip, during which Maxfield and I practiced observing from the air, picking out a certain area and each trying to see more than the other saw, within a given time. This is good training for quick and accurate observation, for objects do not look the same from above and airmen have to train their eyes to different perspectives. When we tired of this, we amused ourselves by betting on the chickens that raced across the fields, running away from our shadow. It was sixteen hours before the changeable weather settled so we could get the ship to the ground.

The R-38 was under construction at this time, destined for sale to America. She was an all-metal ship, long and thin but not very strong. I was invited to be a guest on the trial trip and went down to the field from London for it. We made two false starts, then the weather changed for the worse. Finally Air Commodore Maitland said to me, "I don't think it will be possible to get off before Tuesday or Wednesday, so go on up to London in the meantime, if you want to. I'll send you a wire in the morning."

The next day, Saturday, the telegram did not come in the morning, and I waited for it until one o'clock. Then, deciding Maitland had found we couldn't get off till next week, I went to spend the weekend with some friends. Only a few minutes after I left, the telegram came. Had it reached me in time, of course I would have been on the R-38. On my way back to London on Monday morning, August 25, I saw in the papers the news of the terrible disaster. The R-38 had cracked in two over the Humber River, and forty-four of the forty-nine men aboard were killed, including Air Commodore Maitland and Commander Maxfield.

It was, until then, the greatest loss of life in the history of aeronautics, and a nerve-shattering experience to all those who put their faith in airships.

Soon after this catastrophe, I sailed with Shackleton, England's cheers ringing in our ears. The King and Queen had given him a personal farewell, and everyone expected big things from us. But Shackleton was then forty-seven years old and was getting tired. He must not have been his normal self when he organized this expedition, for he had left most of the actual work and supervision to other men. He had never done this before. After a man has lived furiously for a good many years, there comes a time when he has less stamina and vim and his mental energy begins to flag. I suppose it happened earlier with him than with many others.

We sailed on the *Quest* in September, 1921. She was a small wooden vessel of only 125 tons, built in Norway for sealing. The ship had been bought and outfitted by an agent, who was not going on the expedition, and I believe he must have been drunk and seeing double when he bought her. Although he said she would steam at 7 knots, the utmost she could do was 4½. He outfitted her with extra-heavy yards and masts, and built a deckhouse and superstructure on the bridge, in which he installed a big gyrocompass and range-finder, making her so top-heavy she could hardly stay right side up. She had been built of green timber, and the agent had her hauled into drydock and let her lie there two months before calling in engineers to overhaul her. Then they were stupid enough to load her in the drydock before they let the water in. Naturally, she swelled when she entered the water. Then they started out with her and wondered why the engine was always burning out the bearings, both the main shaft and the crankshaft bearings. We struggled down the Thames and were towed into two or three ports in England because the engine was breaking down. Every time we came in for repair, the bearings were tightened till the engine could hardly turn the tail shaft.

Some thought the trouble was with our inexperienced crew. Except for the chief engineer, we had a lot of amateurs and all the scientists were supposed to turn to and be stokers and oilers and what not. My assignment was to handle all dredging and sounding, and do specimen collecting work with birds and fishes. I also stood my watch of eight hours a day, and on top of that I was made official photographer because our man for this job was seasick all the way and finally quit and returned home.

Engine trouble forced us to run into St. Vincent in the Azores under sail. After staying there a week for repairs we started out again, but could get no speed out of the engine. The engineer thought the trouble was too much dust in the coal, so they got out my biological sieve which was to be used for fish and seaweed, and we sifted I don't know how many tons of coal on deck. In this crazy manner we staggered on across the sea, all of us on deck busily sifting coal in clouds of coal dust. We were coated black with it, inside and out, and still we could get no speed. Then the bearings burned out.

Through all this trouble Shackleton kept our spirits up. He had the faculty of always being liked by everyone, and was always the good fellow. He would sit around singing songs and telling stories, keeping everyone amused and entertained. No matter how things were going, he always came along with a cheerful word. When any difficulty arose, he would go to each man individually and take him aside and say, "We're up against it. Now, you're the one man I think has some real ideas about this job, and I wish you would tell me how to go about it."

The fellow would be pleased, and would give his ideas, and Shackleton would say, "Good! That's a splendid idea and I'll use it. Thanks a lot."

Then he would go on to the next fellow and tell him the same story. Each man thought he was the one upon whom Shackleton depended for advice and help. After I had seen him do this a few times, it began to amuse me. The next time he came around to me I told him I was familiar with the scheme and probably it wouldn't work quite so well this time.

He replied, "My boy, don't you make that mistake again! I'm going to tell you something. Remember this: There's an effect in the spoken word. You may think you won't be flattered, but you're wrong. Even though you know why I'm doing this, you will be flattered, because there's magic in the spoken word."

He was right. In a little while we all knew that Shackleton was flattering us, but we were influenced by it just the same. You can't get away from the fact that a word well spoken does have great influence.

We staggered into Rio de Janeiro under sail, helped out by an occasional kick from the propeller. In Rio, they found at last that the tail shaft was out of alignment, and the keel was warped and buckled like a snake. It would take at least six weeks to straighten that keel and otherwise put the *Quest* in condition.

I didn't want to spend six weeks in Rio; there was nothing to do there but go to parties and sit around drinking with the English colony. George Douglas, the geologist, felt the same way. So the two of us wired Montevideo and learned that a whaler was leaving for South Georgia, where Shackleton was planning to call for supplies before going on. With the Boss's blessing, Douglas and I sailed to Montevideo in late November and on south with the whaler. We reached South Georgia and had been working there six weeks, with me at one end of the island and Douglas at the other, when the *Quest* pulled in. Douglas and I had arranged with the whaling station to send a boat to pick us up the moment Shackleton arrived, and I was looking forward to seeing him and the rest of the expedition, after six weeks of working alone.

When we sailed into Grytviken Harbor in our small boat and saw flags half high on every mast, we wondered which of the whalers had died. We drew up beside the *Quest* and shouted: "Hey, there, on board! You all dead, or asleep?"

The ship was then at anchor and everyone was ashore. We climbed aboard, wondering why the ship was deserted, then we put off again and rowed to the pier. It was Sunday and none of the whalers were at work, but we could see an unusual number of people standing at the church which had been erected at this little outpost by the Norwegians. It was there we first learned the sad news from some of our expedition companions. Sir Ernest Shackleton, our leader and the hero of a generation of Britons who loved adventure for its own sake, was dead! With hearts heavy at the sudden news of our loss, we listened to their account.

The *Quest* had gone through such terrific storms on the way down from Rio that the men had no chance to celebrate Christmas aboard. So they agreed to have a big feast as soon after New Year's Day as possible, when Douglas and I would be there and we could all have our holiday celebrations together. They reached the island on January 4. Shackleton, who went ashore for dinner, came back to the ship and said he was going to bed early. He wanted to get a good night's sleep in order to be ready for the fun next day.

The *Quest* was at anchor and had only one man on watch. There were doctors on board, and it happened that one of them, Dr. Macklin, was standing watch from two o'clock to four in the morning. When he passed Shackleton's cabin he saw the light burning. Knowing that Shackleton had gone to bed early to get a good sleep, he paused at the door, and Shackleton called out and asked him to come in. Shackleton said he had not been able to get to sleep. He said, "I have a bit of a pain in my left shoulder. I think you'd better give me a sleeping potion."

Macklin had been with Shackleton on the *Endurance* and knew him well. He said, half joking, "You can't take sleeping powders. Give up good living and you'll sleep."

Shackleton asked for the powder anyway, so the doctor went to his cabin and mixed the medicine. When he came back, Shackleton took the glass in his hand and said, smiling, "You're always telling me to give up something. First you made me give up drink, and now—what will I have to give up next?"

He lifted the glass to his lips, and it fell out of his hand. He collapsed on his pillow. The doctor felt Shackleton's pulse and listened to his heart. He was dead.

After arousing the others, Dr. Macklin hurried to his cabin to see what mistake he might have made in the medicine. He found there had been no mistake. That morning they took the body ashore, where a postmortem examination determined that the cause of Shackleton's death was a coronary attack. It was characteristic of the man that he died joking, with those last words, "What will I have to give up next?" He was not yet forty-eight.

We buried him at the foot of the tremendous mountains of South Georgia, and quarried rocks out of the frozen soil with our own hands to build his monument. Every one of us felt his death as a personal loss. All over the world there were men who mourned Shackleton. England, especially, looked to him for great deeds since, after centuries of English leadership in polar exploration, the Americans had first conquered the North Pole, and Amundson of Norway had reached the South Pole.

When they heard the news the people who were financing the expedition cabled us to go ahead with the work. Frank Wild, the second in command, took charge, and out of respect for Shackleton he tried to carry out the original plan. Shackleton's object had been to circumnavigate the earth at the highest latitudes possible —to skirt the edge of the ice and follow it all the way around the Antarctic continent. This had never yet been done, though the *Norwega*, a Norwegian vessel, nearly did it.

We had been hoping to discover many miles of new coast and to investigate Dougherty Island, the existence of which had been reported and disproved half a dozen times by ships sailing the South Pacific Ocean between Australia and Cape Horn. We also expected to look for shipwrecked sailors thought to be marooned in that vicinity. Many vessels had been lost there, and it was possible that shipwrecked men had been living there for years.

But these plans had been made for a faster ship than the *Quest* and one in these waters two months earlier than we were. Shackleton had also intended to pick up an airplane and our winter equipment and stores at Cape Town, but he had been so delayed that he had had no time to stop at Cape Town and had left them there. So we were really trying to carry out his original plans without the equipment we needed. The *Quest* was too slow, and we were working at the wrong time of the year when the weather was against us. As a result, we accomplished little on an expedition budgeted to cost $75,000, that ended costing $375,000. However, I derived great personal satisfaction from having obtained some excellent photographs of bird life on South Georgia, of the rugged, snow-covered mountains, and of the tiny fishing settlements nestled on the narrow strip of shoreline between them and the sea.

I know that Frank Wild acted from motives of sincere respect for Shackleton's memory in trying to carry on, not realizing until too late that he was attempting the impossible. It would have been better to aim at making only a partial success instead of trying to carry out the original plans which Shackleton himself would have altered had he lived.

We managed to journey a scant 70 degrees around the Atlantic side of Antarctica, and finally had to abandon our efforts when the ice in the Weddell Sea proved too much for our inadequate vessel. Inevitably, we had to accept failure and make the long voyage home.

12

Interlude in Russia

Back in London once again, I put the finishing touches on my scientific work as naturalist with the *Quest* expedition, and wrote a detailed article on my collection of birds at South Georgia and the other islands we had touched. This article was published the following year, 1923, in *The Ibis,* the principal magazine of ornithology published in Britain. I suppose it must have attracted some attention at the British Museum, to which Mr. Rowett presented the specimens brought back aboard the *Quest,* because, as we shall see later, the museum people must have begun to look on me as primarily a natural history man rather than just an adventurous photographer.

One day in November I was doing nothing in particular when a friend called me on the phone. "Would you do a substantial favor for me, Wilkins?" he asked.

"Any time," I replied. "What is it?"

"I want you to go to Russia for me."

I must have gulped in surprise, because Russia seemed to me like another world. In the aftermath of the World War, the revolution, civil war, famine, and disease sweeping, one after the other, over that unhappy land, it hardly seemed to me like a place to visit. Still, it was intriguing to think of going somewhere not open to the ordinary tourist.

"I ... I'll consider it," I said. "Can't you tell me more? Why do you want ... ?"

"I want you there for six months," he said crisply. "Pack a bag and come over to see me tomorrow. I want you to take pictures, of course. You'll be off in no time."

Here I was—in for another adventure about which I knew absolutely nothing! When I saw him the next day, my friend explained that he had been all set to make a trip through Central Europe and then into Russia, but his wife was suddenly taken seriously ill and he could not leave her. His chief, a man high in the government, had asked him to nominate a substitute, so he had thought of me. He said he knew I was unattached, and that I was keen on expeditions and adventures in remote places.

My stated task, it turned out, was to travel across France to Austria, Germany, Czechoslovakia, Poland, and Russia, to photograph and write reports on the work of the Society of Friends' Emergency and War Victims' Relief Committee. This was a highly respected charitable organization of dedicated people, the Quakers, whose aim was the alleviation of human suffering. In order to raise money to carry on their good work, they wanted both written reports and a graphic pictorial record of the misery in which the people of Central and Eastern Europe were living— especially the children. Meanwhile, someone quite different, unknown to the Quaker organization, asked me to make confidential reports of another nature for the government—to which I agreed. I had just about gotten used to the idea of being a secret agent on short notice when my friend gave me a new jolt. "You'll be taking a lady mission worker with you."

Oh, Lord! I thought. Six months carting a Quaker lady in unsettled Eastern Europe! I had visions of a helpless, angular female in high-button shoes, having to be taken care of at every turn.

My friend could read my thoughts. "She'll just be a blind, Bert," he said, smiling, as if to put my fears to rest.

I argued that it would be far better if I carried a camera. I had found back in the Balkan War that a writer can be set down in a corner on a bench and told what is happening by a spokesman, but a man with a camera must be on the spot, and therefore has a better chance to see what is going on. I had often carried a camera when I never took a picture just for that reason. I further argued that I didn't need a blind, but if I had to have one, it should be someone besides a lady mission worker. But my arguments got me nowhere. The lady was to go with me.

I was catching the ten o'clock train the next morning, November 7, and at nine o'clock I was to stop at my friend's office and pick up my companion. You can imagine my qualms when I walked into his office. In passing through the anteroom, I noticed a beautiful young woman with dark hair and olive complexion, of the Latin type. Glancing at her as I passed didn't make me feel any happier about having to travel for six months with a lady mission worker. My friend seemed to enjoy my obvious nervousness.

After giving me my instructions, he took me back to the anteroom. "This," he said, "is your companion." I fear I gulped.

She went under the name of Lucita Squier—an odd combination of the romantic Spanish and commonplace English. She was so petite and looked so fragile, I thought she would never last out the trip, but just looking at her made me feel anything but unhappy. Later, when we were on our way to France, she told me she was an American of Spanish descent, that she hailed from San Diego and had been in the movies as a stand-in for Mary Pickford. At least, that is what she said.

Much as she liked the moving-picture work, she told me she had given up the job and come to Europe because she "wanted to do something new." She was writing articles for American women's magazines, and doing a small job for the Quaker unit as well. It didn't seem to me she had made a wise move, because I was confident that the motion-picture industry was bound to prosper and by staying with it she might have had a promising future. But, I thought, women are unreasonable and apt to go off on tangents, especially when they are beautiful and charming. She didn't know precisely what I was going to be doing on this trip, and she wasn't supposed to know.

We traveled together across France, then through Switzerland, Austria, and Czechoslovakia and on to Poland. We went all over Poland in our own car, out in war-devastated areas, taking notes and pictures under all kinds of conditions and in all weathers. Lucita was as game as she was good-looking—never a whine from her no matter what happened. She was supposed to write articles and reports from a feminine point of view, while I was writing from a man's point of view on such questions as finance and food supplies. There was no professional rivalry between us.

At that time, it was next to impossible to get into Russia without a very special reason. Conditions there were terrible, and the people in London for a time had second thoughts about sending a girl into such an area. But then, the London office decided that since I had gotten her through difficulties in Poland all right, I might do as well in Russia. Eventually we got the necessary permission from the Russian Government to cross the border, although by this time the letters, cards, and permits I had to carry—in half a dozen languages—just to make sure I would not be stopped by some petty officer, made my coat pockets bulge like a brief case. We boarded the train, crossed the frontier, and rattled on to Moscow.

Our tour of Russia was soon outlined between the Quaker officials and those of the revolutionary government. Joined by another girl, Miss Laurette Citroën, daughter of the French auto magnate, we started out across the country, with no guide or interpreter. Since we knew practically nothing of the language, we were supposed to be furnished with interpreters in each district as we proceeded. There was no interpreter in Moscow who knew all the dialects in all the districts we were to visit.

So long as we could travel by train we were fairly comfortable, in what were termed "soft" accommodations—"soft" meaning first class, with cushions and fold-up berths for sleeping, instead of the open carriages designated as "hard." The girls seemed no more embarrassed than I was that we were always allotted a four-berth compartment for the three of us.

When we had to leave the railway and travel through more remote areas, we used whatever mode of travel we could find—droshky, horseback, or rickety peasant cart. At times we walked.

The girls were marvelous travelers. No hardship fazed them, and no matter what the difficulty, they always managed to look fresh and neat, while I let my beard grow in order to look as much like a Russian as I could. The best way to carry on our work was to attract as little attention as possible by an appearance strange to the local people.

Once we were caught on the road by an early fall blizzard. The wet, wind-driven snow penetrated our clothes and soaked us. We could find no stopping place in the next village we came to. Though we had no interpreter to help us, we got over the idea that we wanted to find a stable where we could set up our portable stove and dry our clothes. We were directed to one half a mile beyond the village. The peasants told us there was room for us and plenty of hay for bedding, but we were warned not to go there, or, if we did, not to wander from the building because many wolves had been seen around that district during the preceding winter.

We had no choice, and agreed we'd rather face the wolves than stay the night under our cart in the village or risk typhus in an overcrowded home. When we came to the barn in the darkness, we could see with our flashlights that it was a wreck. There were gaping cracks in the sides, and a little loft with room in it for only the two girls, but not for me. There were a couple of old horses in the barn, and some goats in a broken-down pen in one corner. However, it would at least give us shelter from the snow. So we got our stove going, prepared our supper, tried to dry our clothes, and then hoped to get some sleep.

It was not long before we were awakened by the restlessness of the horses and the goats. At first we could not understand what was frightening them. Then we heard the crunch of many feet, for the snow by this time had ceased to fall and the surface had crusted. We knew at once that there were wolves outside.

We lay there under our robes hoping they wouldn't discover us, and that the doors were firm. Then, after a few minutes of waiting, we heard the animals break into an uproar. The wolves had seized a goat and were hauling it out of the barn. The girls, although safe in the loft, kept shouting anxiously down at me, while the snarling wolves outside were either fighting each other or devouring the unfortunate goat. Through the cracks we could dimly make out the surging mass against the snow. After what seemed hours, although it was possibly only fifteen minutes, the wolves made off with their prey and the only thing to be heard was the wind sighing through the trees and whistling through the chinks in the barn, while the horses whinnied and stomped nervously over their recent fright. At dawn, after a long and almost sleepless night, we harnessed our three horses to our cart and drove on.

Our jaunt took us through the country between Petrograd and Orenburg, and on east of Moscow as far as Siberia, camping out in haystacks, sleeping in the woods, traveling through storms and across rivers. Once the horses fell through the ice and we had to drag them out of the water. Everything we had with us was dripping wet and freezing, but somehow we survived without catching pneumonia.

Although Soviet authorities had given me all kinds of permits, I found that the more permits I had, the less I could see. Few of the guards could read, and when they saw an official paper they were afraid to take the risk of letting me pass. However, because of my beard and my peasant's blouse and old hat, I was often able to pass for a Russian as long as I kept still.

Just after New Year's, 1923, at a place called Buzuluk, not far from the Siberian border, I received a cable from the British Museum, saying:

ALL ARRANGEMENTS MADE FOR FINANCING YOUR AUSTRALIAN
EXPEDITION.

This I could not understand at all, for I hadn't even planned an expedition to Australia. Had someone in authority at the British Museum taken seriously something I might have said in jest? I had spoken lightly about hoping to lead an expedition in

the wilds of North Australia, where few white men had penetrated more than a few miles from the coast. I really was confused over the entire business—and quite curious.

It did not take me long in those first few weeks of 1923 to wind
up my interlude in Russia (about which I am bound even today
to remain somewhat cryptic), to leave my two traveling companions in the safety of Moscow, and catch the train for London.

13

In the Wilds of North Australia

In London when I went to see the directors of the natural history division of the British Museum, they told me they had all the money I wanted for my Australian expedition.

"But I haven't any Australian expedition!" I protested.

"Oh, yes, you have," the director replied. "You promised to do anything possible to help us build up our collections of Australian specimens, and we have used your name to get the money from the treasury."

I remembered that some months previous, when I had turned in the results of my work with the Shackleton expedition, the directors of the natural history division of the British Museum had told me they had been trying for years to get material from Australia. They had asked if I could help them and, thinking they merely wanted a few letters, I had said I knew a number of the government officials and some of the scientific men of Australia, and would be glad to help arouse their interest in the project. While I was in Russia they had got the idea, I suppose from my work as a naturalist aboard the *Quest*, that I should lead it. So they won a grant of funds from Parliament, for a "Wilkins Island and Australian Expedition" into the bush country of North Australia and the islands dotting the coast of Queensland and the Northern Territory.

"You must go," they said emphatically. "Now that we have the grant, the whole thing will be a bad show if you don't go."

The job was to make a biological survey of both sides of the Great Dividing Range of Northeastern Australia, that on the map resembles a giant snake, winding from southeast to northwest a

hundred or more miles in from the coast. I was also to cover both
sides of the sea-front, along the littoral from Sydney to Cape
York, and along the Great Barrier Reef as well. The expedition
was to make only a general survey and collect specimens for
actual study, not for the show cases. I knew the trip would be
fascinating, though of course it would delay the meteorological
work I had planned doing in the polar regions. However, it was
an honor to be selected by a scientific group of such importance,
and I knew the experience of acting as expedition leader would
stand me well for my later work.

When the directors of the museum asked me to make an estimate of the cost of this survey in Australia, I gave them one
covering a specified amount of collecting to be done in two years.
To my surprise, they did not question it at all, but simply said,
"Here is the money."

I quickly lined up a number of competent men to help me:
J.E. Young, of Brisbane, for botany and ornithology, Vladimir
Kotoff, a Russian, for mammals, and Oscar G. Cornwell for birds.
As it turned out, I myself worked in every field. All this aroused
a great deal of interest in Australia by the time we reached there
in the spring of 1923 and set up headquarters in Brisbane. I wrote
articles for the papers and gave lectures in schools; hundreds of
school children helped us with their observations of animal life,
and even the natives brought in specimens.

Although there is probably not an area in Australia 100 miles
square that has not been visited by white men, there are many
thousands of square miles in which no one but the aborigines
live, and at that time much of the area in inland northern Queensland where we first penetrated in automobiles was covered with a
kind of cactus that grew so thick it was impossible for a man to
pass through it. This barrier of cactus is unbelievable until it has
been seen. The plants grow together, and the long thorns tear
the flesh. Once lodged in it, they continue to work their way
through the muscles, causing an irritation that is well nigh un-
bearable.

In full daylight it was here and there possible to find one's way through the cactus growth on foot, along narrow paths that had been broken by the wild cattle roaming the area. But once headed on a path, even the cattle found it impossible to turn around, and many times we were confronted with these untamed creatures and had to lie down with our faces buried in our arms until the cattle lost their fear and finally rushed past us. We carried sharp machetes strapped to our belts, but since the cactus plants grew to a height of 30 feet, and their thorny leaf points spread outward from the stem close to the ground, it was almost impossible to clear a way in daylight, and absolutely impossible even with headlights to chop one's way through at night.

Aside from the scientific work, which was fascinating in its own way, my most notable experience during the expedition was with the cannibals in the northeastern part of Northern Territory, in Arnhem Land.

Two months before I went into that country, a boat had been wrecked on the west coast of the Gulf of Carpenteria. Sixteen men, two women, and a child made their way ashore and lived for a few days with the natives. Then the natives killed and ate the men. It was not known what had become of the two women and the child. The government was sending in a police expedition to punish the natives, and I asked permission to go along. My idea was to go into this country to complete our work, but I did not want to take my companions because of the risk.

I was given permission by the ministry officials to go with the punitive expedition, and the Government had actually provided one of their coastal boats to take me. However, the police in charge of the party had refused to let me go, not wanting to proceed into that dangerous country with an extra man on their hands who, to them, was just another butterfly collector. All I could do then was to make arrangements with the missionaries. I started with a missionary from Port Darwin, and we went overland with pack horses, a trek of 800 miles through wild country, to the missionary station near the Katherine River.

The police expedition had gone through the country before us, shooting every native on sight, exterminating them indiscriminately, like wild animals. On our way, we came upon a native from the coast who had been acting as a tracker for the police; he had got lost from the expedition, and the other natives had nearly killed him. He managed to escape from them, but he was in bad shape when we found him.

The missionary and I did not agree about the natives. From my early boyhood experience with the Australian aborigines, I believed that they were a kindly people, and would not harm anyone who did not molest or offend them. My companion, however, insisted that the natives in this region were treacherous and cruel cannibals. He told a harrowing experience of his own, of how he had gone among these savages and they had surrounded him and begun to pinch him. He had struck out against them and escaped, convinced that they had been sampling him for the pot.

I still did not believe I would have any trouble. In any case, we needed specimens from this little-known country to complete our collection. So, after a day's rest in the mission station, I persuaded the missionary to take me in his little schooner to the mouth of the Katherine River. From there, in a flat-bottomed rowboat, I set off alone up the river, camping at night on the bank, and living on fish and such game as I could catch. For supplies, I had with me six cans of bully-beef, six cans of condensed milk, a rifle, a knife to be used in collecting specimens, mosquito net, and sleeping equipment.

I was really quite comfortable. Though the country is in the tropical belt, the vegetation is not at all tropical because of the dryness. There was no great thickness of decayed vegetable matter, none of the pungent odor and excessive humidity of the African tropics. Beyond the river forest belt the land is undulating, with deep escarpments—a roll, then a sheer drop. Much of it is covered with coarse wild grass. My only trouble was with swarms of mosquitoes, both the harmless variety and the malaria-carrying anopheles.

At night, I turned my boat upside down on some convenient support, spread my mosquito net over it, unrolled my bedding beneath it, and was quite snug. I had an acetylene bicycle lamp for hunting animals at night, and at other times I used it for reading. I had brought a few books.

After the third day, I could hear the natives moving all around me among the trees, and in the mornings I found their tracks about my camp. At night when I was asleep, they came in to steal whatever they could find. I could never see one, but sometimes in the daytime I heard them shouting.

I had been out a week or more when one night I was lying on my back under the boat reading, and was quite lost in my book. After some time, the light grew dim on the page; the lamp was giving out. I looked up and standing right over me, close enough to reach out and touch, were two figures, one on either side, pointing spears directly at my stomach.

They were chocolate-colored, naked, and decorated with smears of red and yellow clay. I was so paralyzed with surprise and fright, I couldn't move. But I was sure if I did move they would jab those spears into me. I pretended to go on reading, but I didn't miss a move they made. One of them would make a short jab with the spear, and nod to the other; then the other made a short jab, and nodded to the first. They seemed to be urging each other to go ahead and do the job. Then they would back off a little, pause and come back again.

Finally, they backed so far away that I could not see them without moving. But I didn't move. I was wondering what to do, whether to call out to them or to try to get my boat into the water and escape. Yet, I was too scared to do anything. Then the lamp went out, and in the dark I saw them come back. I didn't make a sound to let them know I was awake. They prowled about for some time, and at last went to the fire, took some hot ashes, then went away.

I knew that some natives had a taboo against killing anything between sunset and dawn, and I thought perhaps these savages had this belief and for that reason had not killed me. If this guess were right, then they would return at dawn.

On second thought, I saw nothing to be gained by taking to the river. If the savages wanted to kill me, I was too far into their country to escape. I decided to try to sleep, in order to be ready for the morning. I finally calmed down and forced myself to go to sleep. Just before dawn I woke, turned over on my stomach, and got my rifle under me.

When dawn broke I could see the spears rising in front of me —points of spears above the brush, and legs below the brush. It looked as though I could lie there and take what was coming, or get up and face it fighting. One fellow, whose face was decorated with weird smears of clay, was a little ahead of the others. He would look over the bushes, duck out of sight, creep up a little closer and then peer out again. He was carrying a spear ready to throw, and I couldn't take my eyes off him. Suddenly, I saw some little movement on my left. Another fellow was there in the open, kneeling, ready to throw his spear. I couldn't help letting out a yell, and as I did so he let drive hastily with the spear. It struck in the sand beside me, and the whole lot of them turned and ran.

It seemed they were nearly as frightened as I was. I yelled out a few words of native language, saying I wanted to talk with them, and I got up and went after them. They didn't throw any more spears, but they wouldn't let me come near. Every time I drew close, they fled.

This went on for about two miles, till we came to a high cliff beside the river. I kept telling them that I had no weapons and held up my empty hands, repeating every word I knew of native language, whether it made sense or not, and approaching slowly, closer and closer. I don't know which was more frightened, the savages or I, but I had one advantage—I could see their knees shaking. Mine were inside my trousers.

We stood looking at each other for at least a quarter of an hour. There were ten or twelve of them. They didn't run, and I didn't go nearer because of the spears. I kept trying to tell them with gestures to put the spears down.

At last one fellow laid down his spear and came toward me. In his nervousness, he caught the spear between his toes and came dragging it behind him awkwardly. I pointed it out to him, and he grinned a sickly grin. Then I laughed; all the others laughed, and that cleared up the situation. They came up and began feeling me over for weapons. They were curious about my clothes and pinched up and down my arms and legs, feeling the cloth. I was talking all the time, using all the native words I knew, but they didn't understand. Finally, I beckoned to them to come back with me to my camp.

Both white men and natives had warned me never to turn my back on an Australian aborigine. It is his instinct to kill when a back is turned. When I was a boy, an old native whom we had fed for years told me that. I was leaning over with my back turned to him and, looking around suddenly, I saw him poised as if to kill me. He told me then, "Don't ever do that with a black man. We have to kill you when you do. I don't want to kill you."

So while I was coaxing these natives back to my camp, I walked a pace or two, then turned toward them, walked a few steps and turned again. In this way, it took us four or five hours to reach camp. They had been stealing raisins on previous nights. I had brought some with me, as bait to catch rodents, and the natives had stolen some of them. So now I took my supply of raisins and shared them around. I set my rifle against a tree to convince them I wouldn't use it.

After this there wasn't much more to do. I couldn't talk to them; the few words I knew of native language were of no use. They began to get bored and restless, and when I saw they were going away I decided to abandon the boat and everything else that I couldn't carry, and join them. The biological specimens could wait, but here was a chance to observe the ways of one of the least-known people on the face of the globe. How many white men, after all, had ever lived among these cannibals?

For four days and nights they tried to get away from me, and I stuck right with them. When they ran, I ran. I would sleep a nod or two, wake up to see them sneaking away, and I would be right after them. For some reason they made no effort to harm me. They only tried to get away.

Finally they gave it up, and we came to their camp. Some of the men from camp ran out brandishing their spears, and I tried to look pleasant, because I thought that if I looked scared they would kill me. The others probably explained that I was alone and harmless and had been following them around for four days and nights. Anyway, they let me come along into their camp. The camp was nothing more than a place where they were staying, but there were no women or children in it. The men had no clothes and no huts and few belongings—nothing they could not carry. There were numbers of dogs, some wallabies, and a few kangaroos wandering about among them. The women's camp was at a little distance, and I knew better than to go near it or even look that way.

Two fellows in the camp spoke a little pidgin English they had learned while working for the Australian police at one time. I told the two that I was making a collection of insects and plants. This amused them all. They decided at once that I was crazy, because I was going around getting things I could not eat and putting them in cans. They would not harm anyone who was not right in the head, so I had no further uneasiness about them.

I stayed with these natives for two months, traveling with them wherever they went and camping with them at night. During this time I went on with my work, and they never ceased to laugh at it. They would watch me catching specimens and go off into gales of laughter. Whenever I needed help, they helped me in an amused, superior way. Altogether I found they were a kindly people. Some of them were fine-looking men. Three or four were young dandies, taking great care of their beards and curls, and very proud of their handsome bodies. I obtained a number of excellent photographs of them, which illustrate how carefully they decorate themselves with colored clay and with deep scars.

This was a small, isolated tribe, superior to many. It numbered about forty men in all. They are said to be part Malay, and the Malay blood is supposed to account for their being wild, cruel, and treacherous. The two who had been with the police were bitter against white men. They had been badly treated and beaten. At first, these two were less friendly than the others, but in a little while the whole tribe was trying to make me comfortable. They told me how they had been forced to carry white men across rivers, build shelters for them, and how they had been terrorized and beaten when they made mistakes. They offered to carry me across the rivers, and to build me a white man's shelter. But I told them I would live as they did. When I made myself as inconspicuous as possible, they gradually accepted me and went about as usual, so that I was able to observe their ways and customs.

When I was in a group and had to turn my back on some of them, I remembered what I had been taught and remained always on the alert, not staying long in one position. In leaning down at a stream to drink, I would be glancing over my shoulder constantly. Because these natives were accustomed to killing animals at the water hole when they were drinking, it was their instinct to kill any living creature different from themselves caught in that position.

In the daytime, we moved across country; at night we slept wherever we were. Sometimes we went into caves and slept on the sand. The natives made drawings on the walls of the caves, and for amusement decorated themselves with the colored clays. All of them plucked out the hairs of their bodies, wrapping a little beeswax around each hair so they could get hold of it. A few had pieces of glass bottles, with which they tried to shave; they would hold the hair over the edge of the glass and cut it off with a stick.

They had a game of making their joints crack. One of them would crack his own joints, or a group would get one fellow down with two others on his chest, and crack every joint in his body. First, every joint of the fingers, the wrists, the elbows, the shoulders, then every toe, then the ankles, then the knees, and lastly the hips. When they crawled on hands and knees, they always crawled on the knuckles, as apes do, trailing the fingers behind.

These people were cannibals, but while I was among them we lived on honey and hearts of palms. In the mornings when we set out to look for wild bees, they wouldn't bother to follow a honey-carrying bee, but would go through the forest glancing up at the trees. A hole no larger than my finger, 20 or 30 feet up, would catch their eye. They would tap the tree with their fingers and listen for the bees' buzzing. Upon finding a good bee-tree, they would cut the tree down and eat honey, comb, and bees all together. It all tasted alike to them.

In many ways they were a moral people. Every particle of honey was equally divided, and nobody touched any part of the booty till it was all spread out on green leaves. From a certain kind of bush, they took twigs of suitable size and chewed them to shreds at one end so as to spread them out flat. Each man sat down with his share of honey on a leaf and scooped it up with his little serving stick. When there was not enough honey in one tree, they found another. If there was any honey left over, they made a basket of twigs and leaves to carry the honey in.

I had thought that perhaps I might find the shipwrecked women and the child with these people, but when I saw nothing of them I did not ask questions. I knew their women had seen me from a distance, and I thought if these two were in the women's camp they would find some way to let me know they were there.

Then one day, the men took me to a place in the forest and showed me a heap of ashes and charred human bones. They told me how the shipwrecked people had come and that they wanted to help them and had given them food. But the men had molested their women, so they had killed them. They meant to keep the women and the child, but the police had come killing through the country, and they were afraid they would come and find these women. So they had brought the women and the child to this place in the woods, had killed them, and burned the evidence.

Their women were always kept at a distance, and even the unmarried men of the tribe were not allowed to go within 300 yards of the women's camp. Naturally, I never went near this boundary line. But one day after I had been living with the tribe for a month or more, one of the married men called to me from the women's camp and held up his baby for me to admire. It struck me that this was perhaps a chance to get a picture of the women.

I was well beyond the prescribed distance, so I waved to the man and walked a little way toward him. He waved to me, so then I went a little nearer, and he beckoned. A little at a time, stopping every few paces and waiting till he beckoned again, I slowly approached the camp. The dogs came rushing out, sniffed around me but didn't growl. These people are strongly influenced by dogs; if a dog snaps at anyone, they think he is evil.

I took the baby. He was about three months old, laughing and crowing. The women had all walked away when I came. I saw them peeping at me, and I went on admiring the baby and playing with him.

The women carry a piece of bark as large as an American newspaper, which folds in the middle like a newspaper. When they are traveling on the trails and are warned of the approach of a stranger, they go to a little distance, sit down, and put up these pieces of bark in front of them. They had done this now, and were peeping at me above their screens of bark. They seemed to think it strange that the baby was not afraid of me, and evidently they decided that if I did not harm the baby, I would not harm them. All at once they folded up the pieces of bark and came walking, naked, toward me. Not only did I get the first pictures ever taken of the women of this tribe, but I was probably the first white man who had ever seen them and lived to tell about it.

There were only a few natives in this whole Northern Territory, and the tribe was small, yet their system of marriage was for prevention of the growth of the tribe. No young man was allowed to have a wife. The wives were given to the oldest men, and there were consequently few children.

When I left that country, I found my boat still lying on the river bank where I had abandoned it to follow the natives. The men of the tribe carried all my specimens down to within a short distance of the mission station—a journey of about 30 miles. The mission station was a school for half-caste children. Pure-bred natives rarely went near it, and only one or two men of this tribe had ever ventured in. After I had left it, the tribe had made a raid on the station and carried away a number of the half-caste girls.

All told, my work for the natural history division of the British Museum took nearly two and a half years, extending from early 1923 well into 1925. During the six-weeks' return to London, I wrote a general report of the work we had accomplished, which included collecting specimens of many hundreds of species of mammals, reptiles, birds, plants, fish, and insects. We also carted along box after box of fossils and mineral samples, really a by-product of our endeavors and not one of the main objects of the expedition.

The museum experts later reported, after studying our findings, that nine of the mammal forms were new to science, and one of them, a kind of rock wallaby, was named *Petrogale wilkinsi* after me. One of the bird specimens, the cuckoo-shrike from Mt. Driven in Queensland, was an unknown variety at the time, and four of our reptile species proved new "finds." The directors were very much pleased over the enormous mass of new material we turned over to them.

On my arrival, I handed a copy of my report to the museum secretary. When he said he wanted me to publish it, I told him this manuscript was only an outline of the material for a book, and that if I could find time I would try to write it. I never had time to write the book, but while I was in the Arctic a bit later, the secretary sent this manuscript to Benn Brothers in England, and they published it under the title, *Undiscovered Australia.* Putnam published it under the same title in America. I told the museum to put the proceeds toward further exploration in Australia.

When all my specimens and material had been delivered to the museum, I handed in my expense account. It amounted to exactly ten pounds more than I had estimated. Two weeks later, I was asked to attend a formal afternoon tea with the museum officials, who said they were amazed by the economy of the expedition. Though I had given them an estimate, they had assumed that, as usual, the actual cost would amount at least to 50 per cent more than estimated cost, and they had made provision to pay that sum. They asked me to accept this extra 50 per cent as a grant.

This they gave me in cash—3,000 pounds. And that grant, which amounted to $15,000 in American money, was to finance the Detroit Arctic Expedition of 1926.

14

Flying the Arctic

For many years before 1925, a number of somewhat shadowy reports of solid land in the Arctic Ocean north of the Alaska coast had led the map makers to sketch dotted lines and question marks in this area. A whaler, about fifty years earlier, had insisted he had made out a shoreline, and this had become known as "Keenan Land," and the renowned Robert E. Peary had returned from the north to announce he had named "Crocker Land" in this part of the ocean. But others were skeptical of the existence of any land here. Stefansson in his journey over the ice to Banks Land in the spring of 1914 had not come upon it. In fact, most of us doubted both Keenan and Crocker Land. Still, proof either way was lacking.

I was particularly anxious to explore this region because any point of solid ground this far north would be an excellent spot for the kind of Arctic weather station I had long ago set my mind on, with the advantage that now it could be kept in contact with the outside by radio at all seasons. When I heard in 1925 that Roald Amundsen, the discover of the South Pole, had tried Arctic flying with Lincoln Ellsworth and had given it up as a bad job, I attempted to obtain the planes he had been using. At the last minute, however, the deal fell through, so I decided to go to America, buy a machine there, fly to Point Barrow, and explore the Arctic ice between Point Barrow and the Pole.

I heard that Loring Pickering of the North American Newspaper Alliance was in Paris, and it occurred to me that I might get some money from his organization for exclusive news and pictures of the work. I telephoned the N.A.N.A. London agent,

John Balderson, to ask if I might see Pickering, and was told that
Pickering was on his way to London to see me. When I met Picker-
ing, he said, "I have been wanting to see you about flying in the
Arctic."

"That is just what I want to talk with you about," I replied.

He told me that the N.A.N.A. would be willing to pay well
for news of the flight, and this was exactly what I wanted to get
from him. He said he could not make a definite offer until he
reached America, but he was sailing that night. I told him that I
was going to America to make the flight whether N.A.N.A. bought
the news or not, and I might as well go on the same ship. In
four hours, I had packed my stuff and joined Pickering on the
boat-train, and we crossed the Atlantic together.

It wasn't until we had almost reached America that I discovered
that Pickering really thought he had first planted the idea of an
Arctic flight in my mind. It turned out that N.A.N.A. had approached Stefansson in New York and asked if he would lead an
Arctic expedition that year. Stefansson had suggested that they
get in touch with me, and Pickering had come to persuade me to
make the flight, not knowing that I had already planned one.
I never experienced a more remarkable coincidence. Anyone who
believed in luck would have said that it was coming my way, at
last.

Within a few days after we arrived in America, the Detroit
Aviation Society agreed to support the expedition. Thousands of
school children chipped into a fund for us, sponsored by the
Detroit *News*, and a board of control was appointed to handle the
finances. Two planes were bought from Anthony Fokker, a friend
and supporter of mine, and were shipped to Seward, Alaska.

At this point, it was my old friend and Arctic mentor, Vilhjalmur
Stefansson, who put me in contact with Carl Ben Eielson, the
man destined to be my pilot and comrade of many an adventure
during the coming years. I shall never be able to put in words the
debt I owe Stef for seeing that Ben Eielson was exactly the man
I needed as pilot on my first expedition to fly in the Arctic.

Nine years younger than I, but with more of his hair up front missing at twenty-eight than I had yet lost, Ben was broad-shouldered and lean, about 5 feet 10 inches in height. He was born in North Dakota, had studied some law, learned flying in World War I, taught school, and had come out to Alaska to grow up with the country and to fly. He piloted the first plane out of Fairbanks, which lies near the center of Alaska, and in his old Jenny he carried mail, supplies, sick miners, and expectant mothers to hospitals, and brought doctors to isolated patients. In two years of this bush piloting, Ben became so admired and beloved that the Indians along the Yukon River called him "Brother-to-the-Eagle," and a tribe at McGrath requested that the United States Government make him their chief.

When I met Ben, he was trying to persuade the Post Office Department to set up an air mail route in Alaska. Fortunately for me he failed, so was free to come with me. I found, as I got to know Ben, that he never had much to say. You could tell quickly, however, that he had a cool head and could be relied on to the limit.

We sailed up to Seward, Alaska, through the beautiful Inside Passage I had traveled back in 1913, and planned to establish a base at Fairbanks, which lay on the Alaska Railroad line. From there we would ferry our gasoline by plane to Point Barrow on the edge of the Arctic Ocean, and from Barrow fly fanwise over the Arctic ice, looking for islands between Point Barrow and the Pole. After we had explored this unknown area, we intended to end the work by flying from Alaska all the way across the top of the world to Spitsbergen, the island group lying far north of Finland. No one had attempted to cross the polar regions from one side of the Arctic Circle to the other by air, and nearly everyone declared that it could not be done. This was the flight I had wanted to make as far back as 1919; now, more than ever, I felt it could be done.

It was a brisk and snappy morning when we began unloading our crated planes in Fairbanks, and while we were working somebody happened to look at the thermometer. It registered 20 degrees below zero! Immediately everybody said it was too cold to work, although no one had thought of that till they saw the thermometer.

Eielson was so well liked and respected in Alaska that when people heard that he wanted their help, we got more assistance than we could use. Hundreds of gold miners flocked out to welcome him and help us with the planes. They knew how many times he had flown through storms to carry help to lost or injured miners. With many willing hands we hauled the yet wingless planes through cheering crowds along the streets of Fairbanks to the hangar. The Fairbanks Airplane Corporation, which Eielson had organized, already had the hangar and landing field in shape. Our next task was only to assemble the planes and take off for Point Barrow.

Palmer Hall Hutchinson, the N.A.N.A. correspondent, insisted that we must have a christening as soon as the planes were ready. I didn't care much for the idea because it seemed like forced publicity to me, but I let him go ahead. He went all out with enthusiasm, and on March 11, 1926, he got the mayor, two Catholic priests, the Church of England minister, the Methodist minister, the Salvation Army representative, and even the leaders of the Theosophists and the Free Thought group in Fairbanks to take part in the ceremony. They each said a few words, then two ladies of Fairbanks christened the three-engine machine, the *Detroiter,* and the single-engined plane, the *Alaskan,* by cracking a bottle of gasoline across each propeller.

When the ceremony ended we dispersed the big crowds, telling them that everything was over for the day. Even the newspapermen left, but privately I told Hutchinson to get away from the others and come back to the field alone. I intended to make a short test flight and he could scoop his competitors.

Hutchinson got back to the field while we were warming up the engines, and stood watching while the mechanics began rolling the big *Detroiter* out to the starting point. This was our first experience with a three-engined machine. Hutchinson knew nothing of aviation, so I had told him not to come too near the planes while they were warming up.

The *Detroiter* had gone only a little way when it stuck in a snowdrift. Forgetting my instructions in his eagerness to help, Hutchinson rushed forward to push alongside the mechanics. I was in the plane looking out at the men who were pushing on the other side, and the others were thinking only of the job and paid no attention to Hutchinson.

The other men were pushing on the tail and undercarriage, and the plane began to move forward a little. Hutchinson evidently forgot all about the steel propeller whirling at 2,000 revolutions a minute, so fast that it couldn't be seen. He stepped in front of the wheel and began to pull instead of push. It was almost a miracle that he could get between the whirling propeller and the wheel. Several men saw his danger, but before they could move or speak the plane moved quickly forward. Hutchinson stepped out of the way of the wheel, straight into the invisible blade of the propeller, and was killed instantly.

Hutchinson was a most congenial, energetic, and obliging young fellow, always the first to lend a hand in any difficulty, and it was his enthusiastic eagerness to help us that had caused his untimely death at only twenty-eight. No one felt quite the same about the *Detroiter* after that, regarding it as a dangerous machine to handle. The very next day it narrowly missed killing Major Tom Lanphier, a crack United States Army pilot, who was with me as an official observer and second-in-command of the expedition. None of us dreamed that a man of Tom Lanphier's experience would ever walk into danger. When we saw him close to the invisible propeller we didn't dare shout a warning to him over the roar of the engines, for the slightest startled movement would have killed him. We all kept silent, watching. He walked on, not suspecting his danger, and the tip of the propeller just nicked through his fur parka before he got clear of its path.

After Hutchinson was killed, I decided to leave the *Detroiter* on the ground until we had taken the *Alaskan* on a trial flight. This was the first time Eielson and I had been in the air together. We took off without trouble and circled for twenty minutes, as Eielson gave it full throttle. But the engine didn't respond and carry us any higher. I was itching to grab the controls, but kept my hands off them. Finally we lost altitude and crashed into the ground at full speed. Fortunately neither of us was hurt; the plane, however, was a wreck. The undercarriage was smashed clean off, the propeller twisted like a ram's horn, and the engine was a total loss.

This was a bad start for Eielson, but I knew his reputation as a wonderful pilot and I did not lose one bit of confidence in him. The *Alaskan* was hauled back into the hangar, but we still had the big *Detroiter* with which I expected to do most of the work. The *Detroiter* had never been in the air. It was the largest plane Fokker had built up to that time—75 feet long—and was considered something of an experimental job.

Next morning we lined it up on the field, and Major Lanphier and I took off in it. As soon as it got up speed we knew we were in for trouble. The controls were not quite correctly centered on the dashboard; one engine was given more throttle than the other two. This swung the machine sidewise, and we were racing straight to a crash on the snowbank beside the runway. We narrowly missed killing a bystander, and zoomed back into the air again just in time to skim over the snowbank.

It was obvious to us that we could not stay up, because there was so much vibration in one engine that it was shaking us to pieces, so Lanphier circled and came in for a landing. Just at the edge of the field the machine stalled and we crashed within a few feet of the spot where the *Alaskan* had crashed the day before. Lanphier and I got out and looked at the plane. The undercarriage and all three engine mounts were completely smashed.

Our two planes, worth more than $100,000, had been wrecked within twenty-four hours. This meant that the expedition's work could not be done that year. The season of good weather was too short. Before the two planes could be repaired and our base established at Point Barrow, fogs would settle over the Arctic ice and no exploring could be done from the air. All we could hope to do that year was to ferry our gasoline to the edge of the Arctic Ocean, so that we would be ready to begin explorations the following season.

Deeply disappointed in the bad turn in our luck, I decided we could at least clear the snow from the field while the planes were being repaired. The narrowness of the runway, dug through deep snow, increased our difficulties in taking off and landing. The weather was getting warmer, the snow was wet and heavy, and there were thousands of tons of it to be moved. We worked on the job with every kind of machine available in Fairbanks. Major Lanphier drove a road scraper and I handled a grader.

Meantime, I dispatched a party to Point Barrow with dog teams and snow-motors, vehicles with a caterpillar tread for negotiating deep snow. Sandy Smith, an old Alaska prospector, was in charge of the party; Earl Rossman, who was the Pathé cameraman, a wireless operator, and several Indians went with him. They took a radio set, hoping to reach Point Barrow in time to send us weather reports before we started with the planes. The snow-motors carried loads of gasoline.

It took four weeks to repair the *Alaskan* and install a new engine in it. The *Detroiter* would not be ready for another three weeks at least. So without delaying for further tests, we loaded the *Alaskan* and started to Point Barrow. The plane was built to carry 300 gallons of gasoline, but in order to make the round trip of 1,400 miles and be able to leave some gasoline at Point Barrow, we loaded her with 750 gallons. She was so heavy we could just barely get her off the ground.

Eielson very skillfully pulled her into the air and climbed to a safe altitude. Then we started north. We had no weather reports, and it was a 700-mile trip to the Arctic Ocean, up the valley of the Yukon and over the unexplored Endicott Mountains, some of the wildest country in the world. Within an hour we were flying above a terrific blizzard that covered the whole earth as far as we could see. We had to fly blind, relying on instruments and navigation alone. Fortunately, the force of the blizzard was with us, and from experience, I believed we would find clear weather when we reached the Arctic Ocean. We had expected to make the trip in about eight hours if we had no accidents. The instruments were registering 90 miles an hour, and the storm gave us the help of a tail wind. I kept a close watch on the storm below, hoping to pick up a landmark by which to check our course.

Suddenly through a hole in the clouds I saw ice—the frozen Arctic Ocean stretching before us. We were less than five hours out of Fairbanks, but already we had covered more than 700 miles and crossed the shoreline, with our instruments recording a speed of 90 miles an hour. The blizzard had blown us north at what then seemed a terrific speed.

It was still impossible to see any land behind us because the whole coast was hidden by the blizzard. With sextant and charts I could find the location of the shore, but if we tried to land on it through that storm, heavily loaded as we were, we would probably crash.

Roald Amundsen and Richard E. Byrd had both declared that there was not even one safe landing place for an airplane anywhere on the Arctic ice. I believed I could find many places on which a plane might land safely, but that remained to be proved. Nobody had ever landed an airplane on Arctic ice. So I decided to fly on, out over the unknown area, in order to do at least a little exploring before risking a crash. A landing could be attempted more safely with a lighter load, so we used up gasoline by flying on toward the Pole.

Over the ice the sky was clear and the sun shining. We could plainly see the rough ice below us, and the leads of open water. In a little while by my calculation we had passed the outer edge of known areas on the map, and began to penetrate into the unknown.

Keenan Land was the last northward island marked on my map. We flew above the place where it was supposed to be and there was no trace of an island. The existence of Keenan Land had been doubted, and our flight proved positively that it did not exist. We flew on, 100 miles farther north than anyone had ever been before in that longitude, and nowhere was there any trace of land. At this point, we turned about, retracing our course until we estimated that we were above the mainland. It was covered to an altitude of 3,000 feet by dense clouds and driving snow. To be quite sure that we were above land, we went well to the eastward. Then Eielson slowly spiraled down, out of the clear weather into the blizzard, and on down through it.

As soon as we entered the clouds, we could see nothing outside the cabin. When the instruments showed that we were only a hundred feet or so above the surface, Eielson turned to the west and flew straight, keeping low, while I searched for a landmark beneath us. From my previous visits there between 1913 and 1916 I knew there were no hills ahead into which we might crash without seeing them.

We kept within 50 feet of the ground until, through the driving snow, I caught a glimpse of the coast. After we had picked up the coast line, we knew it was only a matter of following it until we reached Point Barrow. The first point I recognized was within 15 miles of the village. In a matter of minutes after that, Eielson skillfully brought the *Alaskan* down on the frozen lagoon at Point Barrow, and we had made our first flight in the Arctic.

In that one flight, on March 31, 1926, we had covered more than 600 miles of unknown area, beyond the edge of the maps, and we had proved that one reported island did not exist. It is a 60-day trip overland from Fairbanks to Point Barrow with dog teams, and even longer by way of the Yukon. We had made the distance in less than five hours, and conditions had been as bad as we were ever likely to find them. Making allowance for the advantage given us by the tail wind, I figured our plane could cover in just one hour the distance the average dog team covers in a full week.

The storm was so fierce that even the Eskimos had not left shelter to look after their traps. We learned later, however, that one Eskimo had seen us through the clouds when we were going north and, from this man's evidence, we realized that on the outward journey we had passed directly over Point Barrow. We had come straight from Fairbanks to our target, flown over the Arctic Ocean and returned, without the aid of landmarks.

Our landing with wheels on the snow was a triumph for Eielson, and another demonstration that our ideas were sound. The final criticism we had received from Arctic explorers was their opinion that even if we could find our way over the uncharted areas, and even if there existed a possible landing place on Arctic ice, we could never land with wheels on Arctic snow. We had landed on the smooth, frozen lagoon, which is divided from the pack ice by a sandspit. The little village of Point Barrow, low and bleak, was almost hidden in the blizzard, and only a few Eskimo boys saw our arrival. They rushed down to see the strange thing that had come down from the sky, and the old people came out at the sound of our engine.

Its noise seemed to bewilder them, but they did not appear at all surprised. It takes a great deal to surprise an Eskimo. They had never seen an airplane, though they had heard of them. They stood around us, looked carefully at the plane and asked, "How can it fly? It has no feathers."

Later I heard some of the Eskimos declare that our plane resembled a huge duck when in the air overhead, but when on the ground it looked like a whale with wings. One old woman poked the fabric with her finger and said that she could sew an airplane herself, out of sealskins!

Very little had changed at the Point Barrow trading station since I had been there twelve years before. Charley Brower was still on the scene, and still had the same cook, Fred Hopson. Mrs. Brower and Mrs. Hopson were still smiling their placid smiles, and there were several more little Browers and Hopsons. They all welcomed us hospitably. Eielson and I put our sleeping bags in the corners of the store, and when we woke in the morning the chairs around the stove were filled with Eskimos intently watching us.

The Eskimos had acquired some new ideas about business since my last visit to Barrow. They were writing down to civilization for fur catalogues, and were demanding from Brower in Point Barrow the same prices for furs that were quoted on the New York and Berlin markets. Brower didn't mind and paid the prices. It made no difference to him, because he simply charged the Eskimos proportionately more for all the goods they took in trade. They had not yet thought of getting price lists of his goods.

While the blizzard kept up we put a tent over the *Alaskan*'s engine and kept it warm with an oil stove, with a fat, old Eskimo named Panuzak hired to watch it. The engine was a water-cooled Liberty, but we never had the slightest trouble from freezing.

I had brought in a radio. No one else had ever tried to use radio on long-distance flights at that time, but I had installed a light, wind-driven, short-wave set on each plane. We had tried to get the United States Government to put in a radio station at Point Barrow, only to be told that radio communication from that point was impossible. Ships' operators passing the place had reported it to be a wireless blind spot. With the short-wave set from the *Alaskan*, however, we sent to civilization the first wireless message from Point Barrow. We had only the light set, turned by hand, but we established two-way communication.

To our suprise, during the three days we were marooned by the blizzard, we were drawn into a veritable social whirl. There were four white men and six white women in the village. Miss Edna Claire Wallace, a writer, was spending a year there to gather material for a novel about the Arctic. The school-teacher's wife was there with her sister, and there were two nurses, plus the wife of the missionary doctor. These women gave bridge parties, teas, and dinner-dances. We turned on the phonograph, or danced to the music of an accordion played by one of the Brower or Hopson children, while the blizzard howled outside.

By the time the weather cleared, we found that snow had drifted around the plane and the wings were covered with ice. We had expected this and thought it would happen often, but as a matter of fact this was the only time it was to occur during our several years in the Arctic. We dug away the snow, knocked off the ice, told our kind hosts at Barrow we would see them soon again, and took off for Fairbanks. On this trip, our engine began to miss, and we felt sure we were in for a forced landing. Eielson kept the plane in the air until we had almost reached Circle City, on the Yukon, and brought it down safely on a river bar.

While we were examining the engine, we looked up to see a lone white woman running frantically toward us along the frozen river.

She ran up to us, stopped suddenly and exclaimed, "Goodness! The dinner!"

Then she turned around and ran away as fast as she had come. After a while she came running back again, carrying a pail. She lived half a mile away and had never seen an airplane before. Forgetting her husband's dinner cooking on the stove, she had run the half-mile on the frozen river to see our plane. Then she ran all the way back to save the dinner, and, thinking that anyone in an airplane must be exhausted and starving, she had packed the hot food in a pail and run the half-mile once more to bring it to us. We thought that was the height of hospitality.

That night we slept in the cabin of the plane. After making minor repairs we took off next morning and reached Fairbanks. We settled down after that to the job of ferrying gasoline. Meanwhile, nothing had been heard of the snow-motor party. When they were overdue at Point Barrow and we still had no news of them, we began to spend some time looking for them from the air. We carried extra food, to drop to them if we could find them, because they had been out longer than their food supplies would last. But in that waste of tens of thousands of square miles we had no idea where they were.

One morning, on the take-off from Point Barrow, my right mitten caught in the wheel and I felt a sharp pain in my wrist. I thought it was nothing but a slight sprain, so I climbed into the machine and gave Eielson the signal to start. In the air I found I could not use my right arm, which bothered me more as time went on—so much so that I carried out my duties left-handed. Of course, I was always constantly busy during a flight—recording instrument readings, checking our course by maps and by dead reckoning, making notes of geographical and geological observations, working out mathematical computations, writing notes to Eielson since the noise of the engine made speaking difficult. As the throbbing pain in my right wrist grew steadily worse and it became discolored, I suspected that I had broken a bone.

We got lost in clouds over wild, unexplored country; the elevations were not marked on our maps and we didn't dare fly low enough to see the ground below for fear of crashing on a mountain-side. When we climbed above the clouds we found they covered the country, including the highest peaks, so that we couldn't find a landmark. However, flying by compass alone we finally came to a stretch of clear weather and saw a village below that we didn't recognize. Eielson circled while I wrote a note with my left hand, and dropped it to the staring people, asking them to write the name of the village on the snow. They did this, but the name was on none of our maps. I wrote another note asking them to mark an arrow pointing toward Fairbanks. Quickly they formed them-selves into an arrow to guide us.

We were some distance off our course and the gasoline supply was running low. I knew my useless right arm would cause trouble if we had a forced landing, because we carried only a few days' emergency rations and Eielson was not a hunter. Anyhow, luck was with us and we got into Fairbanks that day with less than half a gallon of gasoline to spare. I lost no time getting to a doctor, who found my wrist was broken and put it in a splint.

The Endicott Mountains of Northern Alaska were marked on the maps as ranging only up to 5,000 feet. We had crossed them at fairly high altitudes on previous trips, and they had been covered with clouds. On my next gasoline-ferrying trip the altim-eter was registering 9,000 feet when we reached them, and even then we were below some of the summits. With our extra-heavy load of gasoline it looked as if we could not climb high enough to clear them. So, of course, the maps were all wrong, and we could now at least supply geographers with new data—if we got out of our present predicament.

Eielson was flying through the edges of the clouds that hung on the summits and we were searching for a pass that would let us through when suddenly I saw in the fog on my side a towering mass of rock. It seemed only a few yards away, and rushing at us.

I yelled at Eielson, "Keep over! Rocks on this side!"

"Can't!" he yelled back. "Rocks on my side, too!"

He tried to pull the nose up and climb, but the plane hardly lifted at all. There was no time or room to turn. As Ben steered between the cliffs we stopped breathing. I was watching my wing-tip. It barely missed. Then as I looked down, I saw the wheels of the plane spinning as swiftly as if we had just left the ground. We had squeaked over a saddle ridge by a matter of inches, and had actually dragged the wheels through the snow when flying at 9,000 feet above sea level!

The unexpected height of the range had forced us far off our intended route and we crossed much new territory. As we flew I made notes and sketches, and later we were able to add to the maps many thousand square miles of Alaskan territory. Among our discoveries was a lake more than 30 miles long and 10 miles wide, in the higher mountains, a lake that was probably icebound throughout the year. This was a welcome sight to us because it meant a landing field in case of emergency—probably the only safe place to land in the Endicott range. Another happy discovery was thousands of head of caribou, feeding in the foothills to the north. This meant we would know where to find food if we were ever forced down.

This trip ended safely at Point Barrow, but next morning when we were ready to take off the engine was too cold to start. The weather was bitter, and Eielson and I worked with that stubborn motor till our hands were numb. Before we went indoors to warm them and get a cup of hot coffee, I scolded old Panuzak for not tending the oil stove properly and keeping the engine warm.

While we were at the trading station, Panuzak started to stoke the stove with seal blubber, and kept right on stoking it. Suddenly we heard wild yells. Somebody shouted that the plane was on fire! We ran out to see that the tent over the motor and stove was burning. Eielson, Brower and I tore it down, put out the fire, and found the propeller so hot that it was smoking. Although otherwise the plane was not harmed, we knew we couldn't take off with a propeller in that condition.

I radioed Fairbanks and ordered the *Detroiter* sent north with a load of gasoline and a new propeller. Lanphier radioed back that the big plane at Fairbanks couldn't fly to Barrow. This seemed strange, because it should have been repaired by that time, and it was the plane bought purposely to do our long-distance flying. However, since the pilots at Fairbanks wouldn't bring the *Detroiter* north, it was up to us to go on flying with the *Alaskan*, even though it was risky to trust our lives to that one prop that had been dangerously overheated. We tested it cautiously, found it would do, and with good luck managed to fly back to Fairbanks safely.

By the time we got back to Fairbanks, the field there was a sea of mud. Although we managed to land, we couldn't take off again until the field was drained. Under Lanphier's direction, all hands set to work digging deep ditches across the field. Major Lanphier was a fine leader of men. He was always out early in the morning and always last to leave the job at night. He was good-natured no matter how things were going—always singing songs, telling stories, keeping everyone in good humor. He could hold more whisky than any other man I ever knew except Eielson, and everybody liked him.

Eielson was another type entirely. He liked to sit around and listen, but took no part in the jollity. As a general rule, I like to select quiet men for an expedition. After a month or so the most entertaining fellow runs through his repertoire and begins to repeat, and by that time you begin to wish he wouldn't because you've got to put up with each other for another twenty or thirty months.

At last the field was drained and we were ready to take the *Alaskan* north with another load of gasoline. Early in the morning when we took off, this time with a new propeller, it failed to lift the loaded plane. We hit the brush beyond the field, tore through it, smashing and bounding and bouncing, and stopped short of some stumps. Eielson and I were thrown headlong against the front of the cabin. We got out, to find we had stopped just at the edge of a deep ditch. It was a miracle we were alive.

We began to unload the plane in order to drag it free of the stumps. At the rear of the cabin was a case of eggs that I was taking to Edna Wallace, the writer, at Point Barrow. Eielson moved the case and thought he saw something move behind it.

He gave it a kick, then put his hand down and got hold of some long, black hair. To his amazement, he found a girl who at once began swearing at him and imploring him not to tell me. Eielson began to laugh. I stuck my head into the rear of the cabin and saw this furious girl. People were flocking around, so I warned her to stay there quietly and not say a word. Then I shut the door so that no one would see her and told Eielson to stop grinning. I figured we had better get the plane back to the hangar with her inside it, and not let anyone know.

The people of Fairbanks had given a dance for us the night before, and I had been dancing with this girl. She was a gypsy, both by blood and by nature, and had been roaming about the world. She was striking, in a dark way, a talented musician and artist, with the roving disposition of the gypsy people. Wherever she wanted to go, she went, and if she couldn't get a job as a musician or artist or stenographer, then she'd dye her face, dress as an Indian, and sell souvenirs on street corners. While we were dancing she told me she had twice stowed away on my plane in order to get to Point Barrow and write a thrilling, illustrated account of life among the Eskimos. But each morning before I came out she thought how stern I looked and was afraid of what I might do to her, so she had sneaked out again.

I remarked to her, "Well, probably I'd have admired your nerve. If you managed to get away with it, I wouldn't have minded. But it's just as well you didn't, because there's a girl in Point Barrow who thinks she's getting an exclusive story of her life among the Eskimos at Point Barrow. The perils of flying over the Endicott Range are nothing compared to what you'd face when she finds you are trying to beat her out of an exclusive."

Encouraged by my attitude toward her stowaway attempt, and despite my warning, she had climbed out of her window at the hotel wearing riding trousers and equipped with her feminine face make-up, water colors, drawing paper, and a pair of woolen stockings. She had crawled into my sleeping bag stowed in the rear and, but for the smash-up, we wouldn't have found her. Probably her hundred-plus pounds made just the vital difference between take-off and our crash. She stayed in the plane until we got it down to the end of the field. Meantime, I sent for a friend to come with his closed car, which I had him drive close to the plane. Then she slipped into it with only a few people suspecting that anyone had been there.

It seemed incredible that the *Alaskan* had not smashed to pieces on those stumps, but we went over it carefully and found no damage. We decided, therefore, to put on another type of propeller and try to take off with the load—minus our gypsy girl. Taxiing down the runway, this time we were just getting up flying speed when the right wing flew clean off and we crashed again. Fifty 5-gallon cans of gasoline were in the cabin. I had been standing in the doorway of the pilot's cockpit and those fifty cans of gasoline piled onto me and blocked the door. Some of the gasoline was pouring down on the hot engine exhaust.

Eielson yelled, "Get out quick! She's catching fire!"

But I was pinned under the heavy gasoline cans and couldn't move. Ben himself was penned in the cockpit and couldn't budge. Luckily, the plane didn't catch fire. Our friends rushed in and dragged away the cans of gasoline and freed us.

When we climbed out and inspected the wreckage, we decided there was no hope whatever of repairing the *Alaskan* that year. The *Detroiter* had been repaired, but none of the pilots liked the big machine. They had tested it and declared it would never fly to Point Barrow. With the *Alaskan* gone, however, there was nothing else for it, so we transferred gasoline and our equipment to the *Detroiter* and within six hours after the wreck of the *Alaskan*, we were in the air with the big *Detroiter*.

Just for extra measure Tom Lanphier, who was at the controls, pulled off a stunt or two over the field. It was probably the first time a machine of that size had been looped, but we weren't in the Arctic to do fancy flying, so I vetoed any more tricks. Already the season for successful flying over the ice had passed, since in early May the Arctic was covered with low clouds and fog, and very few observations could be made from a plane. Nevertheless, when we got to Point Barrow with the *Detroiter* we waited there hoping for even a few hours of clear weather in which to explore.

While we were waiting, I experienced one of the greatest thrills of my life. On the morning of May 13, at about 7:30, a shout from someone brought us all tumbling outdoors, and there in the sky, floating majestically above the scattered puffs of thick, white clouds, was the silver-gray dirigible, *Norge*. We had heard by radio that this airship had taken off from Spitsbergen two days before, in man's first attempt to fly an airship over the North Pole, from one hemisphere to the other. Aboard was a distinguished international group, including my personal friends, Roald Amundsen of Norway, Umberto Nobile of Italy, and Lincoln Ellsworth of the United States. We waved and cheered until she glided out of sight to the southwest, following the shoreline.

In 1919, when I had tried to persuade the British Air Ministry and the builders of Zeppelins that an airship could fly the Arctic, they had said I was crazy. When I saw the *Norge* flying over Barrow, I knew my friends' flight was a complete vindication of our estimate of conditions and possibilities. It was a tremendous moment for me.

Although the *Norge* passed within a few miles of us, those aboard later stated that they couldn't see the village. With better visibility from the ground, we watched them feeling their way and finally saw them pass over a cliff some 15 miles from us and, evidently using it as a landmark, make a turn and then sail on out of sight.

Two days later the *London Times* correspondent, a man named Lyons, came into the village, nearly worn out after a 900-mile trip with dog teams. He had made the journey to Point Barrow partly to see our work but largely to cover the flight of the *Norge,* and he had expected the *Norge* to pick him up as it passed. When he was still 30 miles south of Point Barrow he saw the airship coming. It turned and flew toward him while he stood watching it, and he believed the men in it had seen and recognized him. Leaving the dog team, he rushed far out on the ice to be picked up, but the *Norge* sailed over him and went on out of sight, without a sign of recognition. We found out later that the men in it had not seen him at all.

After this disappointment, he came on to Barrow, only to find that he could not even notify his paper of his safety. He had brought radio equipment, complete—except for the motor. In Seattle, he had been told that the missionaries at Point Barrow had bought a motor two years before, but this motor had broken down long ago. So, after making that difficult journey of more than 900 miles with dog teams, he couldn't get his message out. I would have been glad to give him the facilities of our radio station for sending his story, but the N.A.N.A. vetoed that, and the *Times* did not request it. By this time, the story of the *Norge* was already old, for we had sent it out forty-eight hours before Lyons reached the scene, scooping the world on the news of the successful flight. In fact, my report was so far in advance that some people would not believe it.

Our lost party that had left Fairbanks with the snow-motors finally reached help, but all the men were in serious condition. The snow-motors, built in Michigan, worked well in the wet, soft snow of Michigan winters, but were not equal to the dry snow of Alaska. When they stalled, the men abandoned them and went on with the dog teams, making painfully slow progress because of the deep snows of that season. By the time they were 150 miles from Point Barrow, they had eaten all their food. There were millions of fish to be caught through the ice or in the open whirl-pools of the river on which they were traveling, and there were reindeer, caribou, and ptarmigan on the tundra, but these men did not know how to live on the country. Eskimos finally rescued them. In Fairbanks it had been estimated the trip would take thirty days and cost $3,000, but it actually took more than sixty days, the bill was $5,000, and the men got through more dead than alive, and without their equipment. In the meantime, we had made fourteen airplane trips between Fairbanks and Point Barrow, carrying tons of supplies, and I had hardly missed a regular meal.

After the *Norge* passed we waited two weeks longer, but the weather was never suitable for exploring. We could have flown easily through the clouds or above them, but by now it was not possible to search for land in the unmapped region between Point Barrow and the Pole. Nor had the *Norge* been any more successful, because clouds had hidden the whole area. We had to leave its secrets unknown for another year.

15

Alone on the Frozen Sea

Ben Eielson and I returned to Fairbanks with two new Stinson planes in February, 1927. This time as our second pilot we took along Alger Graham, a flier of long experience with Stinson Aircraft, who came primarily to fly the plane turned over to me by the *Detroit News*. By cannibalizing our two wrecked Fokkers, we assembled a third, single-engine plane equipped with skis in place of wheels. Our hope was to fly all three together to Point Barrow, loaded with all the additional supplies we needed for the year's work. However, the composite Fokker smashed a ski in the attempt to take off, so I didn't bother any more with it. This left us with the two Stinsons.

When the Fokker failed, a young Fairbanks pilot, Joe Crosson, rolled his own open cockpit machine out of the hangar and carried our North American Newspaper Alliance correspondent to Barrow. This, by the way, was the first time anyone had dared fly north to the Arctic Ocean in an open cockpit plane. Joe Crosson already had won quite a reputation as an Alaska bush pilot. Like Ben Eielson, he had made many ticklish flights, taking help to men in remote camps and bringing in hospital cases. He made such an impression on me at this time that I marked him as a pilot I would like to have join me. Later, as we shall see, he went with me to the Antarctic.

At Barrow, we now had enough gasoline for the aerial exploration I had planned, and on March 29 we were all set to resume where we had been forced to leave off in 1926. Our main intent was still to explore the unknown region north of Alaska, and then make the flight all the way across the Polar Sea to Spitsbergen.

The weather seemed perfect for our plan, because a furious blizzard was raging on land—a storm that would give us a tail wind on leaving Alaska. We hoped the storm would move southeastward and again help us with a favorable wind on our return. I decided first to fly north about 600 miles; then, if we failed to discover land, we would come down on the ice and make soundings. Contrary to what some experts believed, I was certain I could find plenty of landing places on the ice. At that time, Eielson knew nothing of conditions on the ice of the Arctic Ocean but was willing to try an ice-floe landing on the strength of my confidence. As usual he said nothing—just took the controls and off we went. He was that way.

The tail wind gave us the great speed we had hoped for, and by 7 A.M., as soon as we had left land well behind, the sky was clear and we could easily observe the icefields below. In a matter of minutes, we were beyond the edge of the mapped areas and I was charting a course into the unknown. Nor was there any indication of land. When our instruments indicated we were 600 miles north of Point Barrow and I could see below us no place to come down—nothing but rough ice, which would mean a crash—I told Eielson to continue on northward.

We had gone less than 50 miles farther when the engine began to stutter. Eielson tried to nurse it along, but in a moment we both saw we would have to descend. We did not know the thickness of the ice, but to keep up Ben's courage I shouted, "There, that's right. Keep her on that course! This ice is thick . . . enough to hold a hundred tons!"

I went on to say that if he could get the engine started again, he should kick her over and keep up speed when we landed. I told him there was plenty of room. When the skis touched the ice he was not to stop until I gave the word. Ben dived in order to swing the propeller faster. The engine spluttered, then took hold.

"She's okay now. Let's keep going!" Ben shouted.

But I shouted back, "No, no! Let's land. We'd better check the engine, and I want to land anyway!"

I could see that Ben was reluctant, but he brought her gracefully down—and a good thing he did, because even before we hit the ice the engine had stopped again. We glided to a landing, skidding along for several yards. When the plane came quietly to rest, I was rather exultant. Looking through my window, I could see by the tracks the skis made that the ice was firm and strong.

Again we had made history! Ours was the first landing ever made by an airplane on the Arctic ice! When Amundsen had landed with his flying boats in a lane of water, one of them had been wrecked, and he had taken the two crews off in the other and returned safely to the land. Both he and Byrd had insisted that there was not a safe landing anywhere on the Arctic Ocean, for a land plane. I had stoutly disagreed with them, and now we had proved it. It was just our good fortune that day to be not too far from a firm, smooth landing area when the engine went out.

While Eielson examined the engine, I cut a hole through the ice and prepared to take soundings with a dynamite explosion and a listening instrument. When I was ready, I asked Eielson to shut off the engine so I could be sure of hearing the echo from which to make the depth calculation. He shut it off without a protest. Later he told me he thought, "All right, go ahead and take your sounding. But if I stop this engine I may never get it going again, and then nobody but us and God will ever know what the sounding is."

The ocean floor at that point proved to be about 18,000 feet down—well over three miles. Such a depth made the presence of other islands in that vicinity unlikely. I decided we would explore no farther in that region, but return to Point Barrow. After working on the engine for some time, we got it running smoothly, took off without difficulty, circled, and started south. But within two minutes she failed us again, and we were forced to come down once more.

This time we worked for several hours making repairs. With the temperature at 15 to 20 below zero and growing colder, we had difficulty keeping from freezing. In fact, Ben's fingers were already badly frostbitten.

While we were working we saw the storm that had helped us along on the outward journey was moving toward the southeast as we had hoped it would. But by the time we had repaired the engine and got into the air again, the wind had swung around and we had to fly toward land against a fierce head wind, through dense, dark clouds. We left the visible ice behind us and climbed above the clouds, struggling against the terrific wind. Although we were using power enough to give us a speed of at least 90 miles an hour, we were making headway at only half that rate.

A good deal of gas already had been burned up while we were working on the engine, and now the fight against the wind was fast consuming the rest of it. We watched the failing supply, hoping it would hold out until we could reach land, but we were still 70 miles from the coast according to my reckoning when the quivering needle of our gas indicator showed that the last of our fuel was gone.

The hour was near midnight. There was daylight in the sky above us, but among the clouds below there was total darkness. Our altitude was 5,000 feet. We were alone over the Arctic Ocean with no hope now of reaching land before we would be forced down.

The engine cut out suddenly as if the switch had been snapped. There was no sputter from the starved carburetor, but a sudden silence—an intense stillness after the roar of the engine died. In a few seconds our ears were filled with the hum of the wind in the wires. Ben put the plane into a smooth glide and snapped the switch right and left. There was no response from the engine.

We could feel the sag of the falling plane, and the last thing we saw was a bit of pale blue sky as we plunged down into the dark of the cloudbank. After we entered the clouds it was impossible to see anything outside the lighted cabin. With great coolness and skill Eielson steadied the machine, righting her to an even keel and a steady downward glide as she entered the heavier atmosphere near the ice. His eyes were glued to the turn and bank indicator; my hands were ready to guide and keep the compass course.

Near sea level, the air was rough and the plane swerved and pitched, but Ben calmly corrected with the controls each unsteady move. The altimeter indicated 100 feet, then 50, then 25. Bracing ourselves against the empty gasoline tanks we waited for the crash. Eielson flattened her out, and as he did so the left wing-tip violently struck something. The plane jerked around in a half-circle, and came to rest in a snowdrift.

We were both so astonished to find ourselves still alive that we burst into hysterical laughter. There was nothing but darkness outside. When we could stop laughing, I climbed out and found that we were on ice thick enough to support us. Except for the twisted skis, the plane was undamaged. So for a third time, we had landed safely on the Arctic ice, but this time we were faced with a situation entirely new. We were the first men ever to land on the sea with an opportunity to walk home.

Nothing could be done until daylight, so we had supper and turned to in the cabin. When daylight came we found that as we had glided down, a rough ice-ridge had caught the left wing and swung us onto a smooth patch of ice with not more than 60 feet to spare ahead of us. It appeared to be the only patch of smooth ice anywhere around. But for that helpful collision with the ridge of ice, we would certainly have wrecked the plane and been badly injured, if not killed. It seemed as though a hand had reached out in the dark that night to save us from destruction.

The blizzard that had brought us down was still raging so hard that it was useless to try to travel, so we stayed in the cabin of the plane. I tried to radio a report of our accident, but found the instrument had gone dead.

The storm continued furiously for five days and nights. The first day it broke up the ice and set us drifting farther from shore and to the westward. We slept most of the five days and nights and were glad of the opportunity, for we seldom got more than four hours of sleep a day while on an expedition. Seasons for work are so short in the polar regions that little time can be wasted in sleep, and on this occasion we had been under such pressure that forced repose was a blessed thing. We slept like the dead, while the storm howled outside the cabin windows.

In our sleeping bags we were quite comfortable, and whenever

either of us was hungry he helped himself to food from his own
bag of supplies. Our emergency rations could all be eaten cold—
pemmican, biscuits, chocolate and nuts, raisins, and malted milk
tablets. We had no need to cook, and so were spared the annoyance
of hoarfrost collecting inside the cabin, as it would have done had
we tried any cooking. When we emptied our thermos bottles we
easily melted enough snow in the warmth of the sleeping bags to
give us water to drink.

On the sixth day, the blizzard cleared and we could see broken
ice stretching around us in all directions. Refreshed by so much
sleep, we made preparations to walk to land. With our instruments, we determined that the storm had drifted us a little more
than 100 miles out from shore and toward the west.

Since we never knew when we might be forced down, the planes
always carried equipment for such an emergency. We had snowshoes and skis, both useful under different conditions in the Arctic
and Antarctic. If the snow is deep and soft then snowshoes are
best, and with your supplies lashed on the skis, you can drag them
behind you like a sled. When the surface is hard and smooth, you
strap the pack to the snowshoes, step into the skis, and carry the
pack on your back.

Eielson and I had to cross rough and broken ice, irregularly
covered with varying depths of snow, both hard-packed and loose.
For this, skis would be useless, so we decided to abandon them
and make small sleds from the tail skid and the metal sheeting
under the plane. We hated to leave that beautiful plane which
was quite undamaged except for the slightly twisted skis. Conditions were perfect for flying, and if we had not run out of fuel we
could have reached Barrow in less than an hour.

Packing our supplies on the sleds, we set out on snowshoes, but
almost at once found the ice too rough even for snowshoes. We
also discovered that we could hardly manage the sleds, because
they continually stuck between jagged pieces of hard ice, or they
capsized. Traveling this way was so slow, that on the third day we
discarded the sleds.

From the supplies, we kept only the scientific instruments, our sleeping bags and rifles, and 30 pounds of food. We packed instruments and food in the sleeping bags and carried them on our backs. This was much easier than dragging the sleds, though my pack seemed to me to weigh about 90 pounds, most of which was the weight of the scientific instruments that I had to carry all the way.

We also found it was not safe to hurry on the ice, for it was so rough under the snow that we could not find firm footing. Walking on it at all was dangerous. We slipped and stumbled and fell so often with the packs that we decided, frequently, at the roughest spots, to go down on our hands and knees. In a space of 50 miles, there were many places where we literally crawled. Eielson's fingers had been so badly frozen while repairing the engine that both his hands were useless. However, despite the pain, he was a good sport about it and said that he preferred losing a few fingers to losing both arms and legs and what they were fastened to!

Not only was Ben unable to help in building the snow houses, but he couldn't even look after his own clothes. We would have made better time if these tasks had not taken so long, but that couldn't be helped. At best, it took me about two hours every night to build a snow house for shelter while we rested, and another two hours to take care of our boots and clothing.

Caring for Eskimo clothing while traveling in cold weather is a complicated business. First, the boots and stockings and outer clothing must be taken off and thoroughly beaten to remove snow and frost. Then boots and stockings must be turned inside out and all frost carefully scraped from the inside. After this, they are turned right side out again, shaped to the foot, filled with some soft substance to hold the shape, and put out to freeze.

We ate from our stores of concentrated foods, not stinting ourselves, but at the same time realizing we must not overeat. In the open water every day we saw seals, and on the ice we saw bears. But to get these animals meant a delay for hunting and cooking, so we determined to live on our condensed food as long as possible.

The leads of open water constantly forced us to make long detours, and often the only way across was on thin, young ice.

Once when I was crossing a lead with the heavy pack on my back, the ice gave way beneath me. I floundered forward over the rapidly sinking ice until I crawled out on the firm floe on the other side of the lead. The icy water bit my skin like fire, and when I crawled out, every garment I had on was soaked and freezing. I knew there was only one thing to do. Throwing off my pack as quickly as I could, I took off all my clothes and began rubbing them in the soft, dry snow to blot up the water, at the same time dancing around and flailing my arms to keep up the circulation.

Afterward, Eielson told me that at that moment he felt certain there was no hope for either of us. When he looked across the lead and saw me stripping stark naked and dancing about like a madman, he thought I had gone crazy from the shock of falling into the water. If that had been true, he would have been done for because with his frozen hands he was helpless, and he was on the wrong side of the lead. Nor could he get across until I had got dressed again and found a safer route for him, thrown him a rope and pulled his pack across the thin ice.

When we reached ice on which it was safe to walk erect for some time, we made better progress. On the thirteenth day away from the plane we came up over the ice-ridge formed by the pressure of the outer floe against the ice attached to the coast, and 3 miles away we saw the chimneys of the trader's house on Beechey Point. After thirteen days of zigzagging across the icefields, finding our course by the aid of the pocket compass and the two watches I carried around my neck, we had come out within three miles of our intended destination. By this time, we had less than three pounds of food, but our packs were still heavy because we were carrying the scientific instruments that were indispensable to the continuance of our work.

We walked two miles more, and then saw Eskimos rushing to meet us with dog teams and sleds.

Following the instructions I had left before we took off from Point Barrow on March 29, Alger Graham had been flying up and down the coast, dropping messages to the Eskimos and to this trader at Beechey Point, telling them we had disappeared and

asking them to keep a lookout for us, in case we should show up
on foot. He had also made several attempts to find us by flying
out over the ice. After the five-day blizzard it was impossible to
know where we might have drifted, even if we were still alive, and
there was not a chance in a million of finding us from the air on
thousands of square miles of rough ice covered with moving animals and shadows. Nevertheless he had not hesitated to risk his
life in trying.

The Eskimos and the trader were surprised to see us because
we had been missing then for eighteen days, and all hope of our return had been abandoned. One old Eskimo at once volunteered
to travel the 120 miles east to Point Barrow to tell Graham we
had come ashore, and to ask him to fly to Beechey Point and pick
us up.

In the trader's house both Eielson and I suffered a strange kind
of relapse, though we had not been at all exhausted when we
arrived. Our muscles had served us as long as there was need, but
as soon as the danger was over we could hardly move.

Eielson's frozen fingers were in such condition that we knew
they must be amputated by crude layman's surgery. The only other
thing that could save his life was immediate medical help. But
there was no doctor nearer than Point Barrow, and a dog team
couldn't possibly make that distance in less than three days, in
good weather. Eielson might have risked the trip rather than lose
both hands, but a blizzard was blowing up the coast and that
settled the matter—he could not possibly reach a doctor in time.
We had no proper surgical instruments and no anesthetics. There
was nothing to do, we decided, but fill him up with whiskey and
do the best we could. He took the idea standing up, though it
would mean the end of him as a pilot.

His ordeal, and ours, was about to take place when we were
astounded to hear the noise of an airplane motor overhead. Because of the howling wind, we thought at first we had imagined
it, but then we rushed outside to see Alger Graham's plane come
in for a landing.

Graham was bowled over when he saw us, because he hadn't

heard we were alive. He'd been down to Fairbanks to get help
to look for us, and on his way back to Barrow he had been forced
out of his way by the storm and had landed here at Beechey Point.
Now without delay, we got Eielson into the plane and in less than
an hour we were flying high above the storm to Barrow. There
we hustled him to the tiny hospital, where Dr. Newhall amputated only one finger, the fifth one on the right hand. Under his
expert medical care, all the other fingers were saved.

Eielson wasn't in shape to make any more flights that season,
but in spite of his condition he volunteered to stay at Barrow and
take care of things there while Graham and I again flew north
over the ice. During the next few weeks, we made three flights
northward, but each time found low, thick clouds and could not
determine whether there was land below them. The clouds also
prevented our finding and bringing back the plane we had abandoned. I like to think it may still be floating somewhere on the
Arctic ice—that first plane to make a landing on the floes hundreds
of miles from the shore.

We decided to fly Eielson back to Fairbanks, fit the big Fokker
with wheels, and if the weather were at all favorable, fly it from
Barrow across the Arctic to Greenland, a trip that would enable
us to explore a vast, unknown part of the polar region. My plan
was to land on the Greenland icecap and walk out to some Eskimo
encampment on Davis Strait, between Greenland and Ellesmere
or Baffin Island.

On the way to Fairbanks, we were forced down once by engine
trouble and three times by storms, in a distance we should have
covered in a few hours. This trip took us more than a week.

We got the Fokker ready, but after trying it out, Graham felt
no confidence in it and preferred to take a chance with the Stinson.
So we transferred our load to the Stinson, flew again to Barrow,
and twice set out on the flight to Greenland. Each time we returned after flying a few hundred miles, because clouds hid the
ice and made the trip valueless for exploring.

By this time, the open season was at an end and we could do no
more work that year. We had now been working two years and

still hadn't succeeded in carrying out our original plan for the first season's work. But the time had not been wasted. In our forced landings, deep-sea soundings, and during our thirteen-day walk we had covered a large unknown area, and had collected a great deal of information.

I did not believe that any land existed in this part of the Arctic Ocean. The islands earlier explorers had reported would have served admirably for meteorological stations, but our work had just about proved they didn't exist. If, as I believed, there was no land in that region, then we must establish stations on floating ice. But in order to know whether the ice would support a permanent station, we would have to explore the area in midsummer, when an airplane would be useless because of the fog. More than ever, I realized that the one way to explore the Arctic in summer would be by submarine.

But there was still the area to the northeast in which Peary believed land might be found, and we hadn't yet actually flown over it. So I determined to make one long flight to the northeast the next year. If we found no land, I would continue on to Spitsbergen.

16

Winging over the Top of the World

Almost without exception, the experts declared that the trans-Arctic flight I planned for April, 1928, was impossible. Not only was it a very long way by air from Point Barrow to the Norwegian archipelago of Spitsbergen—some 2,000 miles—but a route over the Arctic Ocean would provide no check-point on land by which to verify our navigation. This in itself would be difficult in the extreme, because we would have to adjust our compass course perhaps twenty times during the flight so that in effect our route, if drawn on a chart, would resemble twenty short lines bending in a great curve. Should we miscalculate by a degree or two, we'd never hit Spitsbergen and end up somewhere on the Arctic ice.

"What you are trying to do is beyond the possibility of human endeavor," Roald Amundsen told me.

Amundsen's opinion, of course, carried great weight, not only because he was the veteran explorer who had been the first to reach the South Pole, but also had been the first to bring true man's long dream of making the Northwest Passage voyage around the top of North America. Furthermore, he had tried airplanes in the Arctic and had given them up. This, quite naturally, impressed many serious men engaged in scientific work who objected to what they thought was a risk of life that would serve no useful purpose. Almost to a man, they were convinced I could not succeed, and that failure would only advertise the dangers and difficulties of polar exploration, thus making it even harder to get financial support for their work.

Right at that time I, too, had my own problems of financing. Though I had the two big Fokkers in storage in Seattle, I couldn't afford to fly either of them because five or six men were required to handle these large planes, and the expense for gas and oil and transport to Alaska was more than I could manage. I had only 500 gallons of gasoline at Point Barrow, barely enough for one small plane. I had to find some way of unloading the old Fokkers, and turn them into cash with which to buy one small plane.

One day late in 1927, while sitting in a room in the Hotel St. Francis in San Francisco thinking this over, I saw a small monoplane fly past the window. At first I hardly noticed it, just absent-mindedly watched it sailing by as though it were coming in for a landing at nearby Crissy Field, Oakland, Hamilton, or somewhere. Suddenly I realized how beautifully streamlined it was and how gracefully it flew. I had never seen that model before. I jumped to the window just in time to see it go out of sight.

Right away I began telephoning airfields, one after another, describing this plane "with full cantilever wing, without struts on the wing, and flying over 120 miles an hour." I wanted to know its name, where it was built. Every airport replied that as far as they knew no such machine existed in America, and that furthermore no such plane had ever been built. I insisted there was such an airplane because I had just seen it.

When no information could be got by telephone, I drove from one Bay Area flying field to another with my old friend Ray Shreck, and sure enough we found my plane at the Oakland airport. It was a beauty, a bird of paradise compared to the clumsy-looking planes I had flown up to that time. It had no flying wires or exposed controls to offer wind resistance—simply a sleek, shiny, bullet-shaped body coming to a sharp point at the nose, with a trim radial engine, and a shimmering wing extending outward from the top of the fuselage like the wings of a soaring sea gull riding the air currents. There was a cabin with space for two. This was the plane for Ben Eielson and me!

On the tail were the markings "Lockheed Aircraft Co., Los Angeles," and the model marking was a dark star marked "Vega," the distant star toward which astronomers say our solar system is rushing steadily through celestial space. Lockheed-Vega! I rushed toward Los Angeles with the eagerness of a young swain to the side of his beloved, and looked up Mr. Allan Loughead of Lockheed Aircraft at Rogers Airport. He introduced me to his principal designer, Jack Northrup. Both of these names, long since household words in the aircraft industry, were not well known in 1927. Together we went out to inspect the very aircraft I had seen in Oakland.

The plane had been completed only the day before, and had made the one test flight to San Francisco and back. It was the only one of its kind. I liked the plane so much, after looking at the blueprints and data of tests and trials, that I wanted to have one for my Arctic flight. Telling Loughead to go ahead and build me one, I set out to find some means of paying for it. Two or three days later that original Vega took off for Honolulu on the Dole Prize flight and was never seen again.

Eielson, meanwhile had taken a job with the Department of Commerce, in order to earn his living while waiting for me to get the expedition ready. He had already heard unfavorable reports about the Vega, and just about the time the Pacific flyers were lost, he got my letter telling him I was trying to buy one. We exchanged letters. I assured him that in my judgment it was the best one ever designed for our purposes. Ben replied at once saying he would leave it all up to me—if I got the Lockheed-Vega, he would fly it.

That was the wonderful thing about Ben Eielson. I had absolute faith in him, and he seemed to have the same faith in me, even to the point of letting me select the plane we would fly in the Arctic.

I was at my wit's end trying to find a buyer for my two Fokkers in order to purchase the Lockheed-Vega when I ran across a couple of young Australian flyers, Charles Kingsford-Smith and Charles Ulm, who were looking for a ship in which to fly the Pacific, from America to Australia. There was a great deal of negotiation between these two, me, and the various potential backers of my two countrymen, but eventually one man advanced them all the money they needed. They were then able to pay me for the big trimotor Fokker, and I in turn could pay the Lockheed Company. I at once wired Ben Eielson that we were all set for the Arctic, to leave for Fairbanks early in 1928.

It is part of aviation history now, the story of how Kingsford-Smith and Ulm flew from Oakland, California, to Australia in three long jumps, setting a new world record for long-distance flying—3,138 miles from Hawaii to Fiji nonstop. Later they flew that plane around the world, including a hop across the Atlantic from Ireland to Newfoundland. The *Southern Cross,* their big Fokker plane which is now among the immortals, was the same three-engined plane I had used in the Arctic.

Ben Eielson had to stick to his job till the last minute without even seeing the new plane until we were practically ready to push off for Alaska. Lockheed made two planes this time. The test pilot who took mine up came down pleased with its performance, but I had no time to talk with him because I had to rush to meet Eielson at the train. I drove him out to the field, and we reached it just in time to see the other Vega crash. It happened that the pilot who was testing it for the Department of Commerce to decide whether or not it was safe to license was one of Eielson's friends. He took it up and found it so fast that he thought he must make a fast landing. He came racing down, smashed into the runway, broke the landing gear, and flopped on one wheel. Feeling the wheel smash, he flopped her over on the other wheel and ground looped.

I could see her marvelous quality despite the crash, but Eielson didn't say anything.

His friend got out of the machine and said, "It's no good. It flies fast and tricky. It's unreliable, and you can't land it."

But I thought Ben could handle it much better on the landing, and in fact, I had more confidence in it than ever. When I asked Eielson if he would like to try it, he just quietly took it up and handled it very well. A big crowd had collected to watch him, for wherever a Lockheed-Vega went it attracted hundreds who never tired looking at it. The plane was beautiful from every point of view.

Eielson kept it in the air for some time, and I thought I could tell from the way he was handling it that he was beginning to like it. Then he circled to come in and, blinded by the late afternoon sun, headed straight into some high-tension power lines. The whole crowd made the nervous, murmuring sound that crowds make when a plane falls. For a moment, in my mind's eye, I could see Eielson and everything else gone, right then. But at the last second, Ben must have caught sight of the wires, for he zoomed her up a little and went over, the wheels missing by no more than a foot.

When he came down, Eielson said he'd like to test the Vega where there was more room. We had three weeks to test it, so the next time we went up together. On the third flight, one of my friends asked to go up. They had hardly left the ground when the engine cut out. Eielson quickly made a complete turn from a scant 50-foot altitude and crashed in a plowed field, a mishap that convinced me that we had a great plane. Even at 50 feet in the air, without an engine, she had made a complete turn, crashed, and still stood up. Nothing was wrecked but the landing gear.

This time we found the trouble had been an air-lock in the gas pipes. The Lockheed people had insisted on putting in a complicated gas system, to guard against the danger of a broken pipe, but we changed this to a simpler one of my own design. I preferred to run the risk of a broken pipe rather than the chance of an air-lock. We also put on heavier landing gear with special heavy axles, and these were later added to all Lockheed planes.

Then we took our Vega up and landed her fifteen or twenty times a day, till Eielson knew her thoroughly. Fast as she was, she handled as easily as any simpler, slower plane. She was quick and flexible and light, weighing less than one ton, though she would carry more than a ton of gasoline.

Meanwhile, I went on working out the calculations for our flight, in the expectation of clear weather over the Arctic sometime in April. We would have a steady change of compass variation during the flight, and we would cover 171 degrees of longitude; the rapidity with which we would cross the lines of longitude would counteract the great change I must make in compass setting. So after all, on paper the problem was not so complicated. It was simply a matter of working out all the calculations correctly.

I worked on the flight plans and practiced the International Morse Code all the way to Fairbanks, where we arrived on February 26, 1928. Then we flew our plane around Fairbanks for two weeks, testing her under all weather conditions. We fitted her with broad skis in place of her wheels. This time, I myself took all care of the engine, because we had no mechanic. Eielson, though a wizard pilot, made no pretense of being an engine man.

Our Vega, marked with the serial number X-3903, was bright orange, and when Eielson was flying her far out between blue sky and wastes of snow, or when he brought her in through a roaring blizzard, the bright splash of her paint somehow made her look gallant. When she was so far away she was only a speck, you still could see her, and that was the reason I had her painted so vividly. If we were forced down, our lives might depend upon her attracting the attention of the Eskimos. The color somehow seemed to add to the personality of the little plane. This one always seemed willing and eager and light-hearted, with all the nerve in the world.

Late in March we flew her to Point Barrow. Although she made a perfect landing on the snow, we had to haul her seven miles with dog teams to a point on the firm ice of the lagoon suitable for a take-off. We put a tent over the engine and kept it warm with an oil-stove while we set about cutting a runway. We had to get down through the deep snow to solid ice because the heavily overloaded plane couldn't lift out of the snow. Every Eskimo we could collect at Barrow was put to work clearing the runway. It took scores of them thirty hours to clear a track 14 feet wide and a mile long, and Eskimos, contrary to what some people may think, don't work for nothing. I had to pay them $5 a day plus overtime.

They no sooner cleared the runway than the wind rose and quickly filled the track with snow to the tops of the banks on either side. Another two days of steady work cleared the runway again. This time the weather was clear and calm. We worked all that last night checking over supplies, going over the machine and getting everything ready for the take-off. Early in the morning we started.

The runway was only 14 feet across, and the tail was 11 feet, 6 inches wide. This left a clearance of about fifteen inches on either side, and that take-off was a dare-devil trick to ask any pilot to attempt. A swerve into the snowbank on either side might be fatal.

I knew she would never take off perfectly straight, but I was sure Eielson could control her within the narrow limits the pathway allowed. The runway was a straight mile across the lagoon, curving up to a steep rise on the far shore. We went roaring down it at 80 miles an hour, increasing speed to take off, but she just wouldn't rise. The Lockheed alone weighed only 2,000 pounds, we had a 2,500-pound load on her, and it was too much—Eielson couldn't get her into the air. So we sent for the dog teams, got the plane turned around and hauled her back to the starting point, where we set to work to eliminate every possible ounce of unnecessary weight.

We already had the load down to the barest necessary minimum, so I decided to sacrifice the brakes. In their place, I devised a lighter tail-skid, which would stick in the ice and help us stop if we had to make a forced landing. Eielson believed that with this reduced weight he could get her into the air by giving her full throttle on the mile run and rushing up the hill at the end. So off we went again.

I was standing in the cabin, watching the tail swaying with our speed. The faster we went the farther it swayed, and it was missing the snowbanks by the narrowest margin. We ran the mile, I felt her rise to the hill, and then came a jarring, bumping, crashing sensation, all mixed together.

At the top of the hill in the deep snow, my tail skid had tripped of its own accord. We went lickity-split down the far side of the hill and crashed into rough ice. Still, that marvelous plane stood up, with nothing damaged but the skis, which were twisted clean off. We had to repair these, fetch out the dog teams again, and haul her back to the starting point. We now knew that we couldn't possibly take off without a wind to help us.

Our plan had been to make the flight during the first two weeks of April, when the weather was clear and we would have a better chance for observation. The two weeks were now gone; every day made the weather more uncertain, decreasing our chances of being able to do useful exploring. Besides, expenses were mounting so high that I couldn't even meet another payroll for clearing that runway and have enough left to pay for breakfast in Spitsbergen —if we should ever get there.

Eielson and I worked Friday night, all day Saturday, and Saturday night, bossing the Eskimos, checking up everything and going over the machine for the last time, and watching the wind. It was slowly shifting; by early morning on April 15, at long last, it was blowing from the right quarter.

The runway was clear; we had everything ready; and we had the wind. But not one of the Eskimos who had been engaged to help us would lift a hand. It was Sunday morning, and they had learned just enough from the missionaries to know that they should not work on Sunday.

Eielson and I set to work, got the Lockheed in place and squared away by ourselves. Before we could get it done the wind was shifting against us. We knew that if we didn't get away at once, the chances were we couldn't make a useful flight that season and we would have to wait still another year.

We climbed in and started up the engine. The Eskimos had piled up the snow till the banks were 3 to 4 feet high on either side. As we rushed down the runway, gathering speed, the snow flying into a cloud from the prop-wash, we could see the tail was swinging farther and farther every second, missing the banks on each side by inches. We had 25 pounds load to the square foot of wing surface, and it was asking a pilot to be a superhuman to hold her on that icy track with the wind changing from one gust to another.

Eielson held her against the wind and against the torque in the engine for almost the whole mile, keeping her steady until he got up full speed and thought he could whip her up the instant he felt her swaying too far. At the last instant, when I felt we were going into the bank, he pulled her back, and she lifted smoothly into the air. This time we were really on our way over the top of the globe.

Once aloft, we both settled down to work. I had all my calculations already worked out for every hour from six o'clock to twelve noon—the compass course, altitude of the sun, all necessary facts ready for quick reference. This gave me more time to plot our actual course, make observations and records, use the camera and wireless, and so on.

A navigator and explorer in a plane have no time to waste. Navigating alone means plotting on the charts and working out mathematically the swiftly changing position of the plane; taking sights of the sun with a sextant—six observations, each accurately timed, then working out calculations based on them; checking the drift of the plane by means of the instruments and calculating it mathematically; studying weather conditions ahead, and of course recording velocity and altitude of the plane, while constantly keeping in mind possible changes of course to avoid storms, and scanning the surface below for safe landing places in case of sudden trouble.

I was also taking moving and still pictures, sending and receiving wireless messages, observing and recording the character of the icefields below, and in the unknown area, searching intently for any indications of land anywhere within the circle of the horizon.

There were two windows of curved plate-glass in the bottom of the plane, each 15 inches square. I took pictures through the flat side windows, giving more exposure to allow for the glass. The plane was practically airtight, and we were quite comfortable inside at temperatures ranging between 15 degrees and 0 degrees Fahrenheit, while it was around 30 below outside, but the slightest opening of a window would have let out the warm air. We took no heater because it would have added unnecessary weight for which gasoline would have had to be sacrificed, and I figured that

we had just enough fuel to take us to Spitsbergen. The light wooden
frame of the Lockheed had the great advantage of softening the
noise of the engine. It was scarcely louder than the sound made
by a moving-picture projector.

For the first 50 miles after we left Point Barrow and flew a
few points east of north, we found the ice was so badly broken
that we could not have made a successful forced landing anywhere
on it. Then we came to the wider, older floes and flew on for 700
miles, never crossing a floe more than 25 miles wide. The ice now
was not badly ridged, and apparently was not thick. There were
no indications of land.

After 700 miles, just at the point where there might have been
some possibility of discovering new islands, we ran into dark
clouds, so thick that even though we flew down through them and
ventured as near the ice as we dared, we could get no visibility.
For more than 120 miles we were unable to see the surface.

Beyond this dark spot we emerged into gloriously bright, clear
weather, which extended for another 700 miles, over nothing but
floes. Already we had added 1,400 miles of new area to the map of
the Arctic Ocean, in that we could say definitely that it *was* ocean,
with none of the fabled islands in view. Then we ran into another
storm. In the distance through the clouds ahead and slightly to
the right, we sighted the mountain peaks of Grant Land, the northern part of Ellesmere Island, from which Peary had made his dash
to the North Pole across the ice. This glimpse of land gave me the
first check on our position. We knew then that we had accurately
crossed fifty degrees of longitude. The landfall was quickly lost
in the storm, and we headed out toward the northern tip of Greenland.

Both Ben and I were feeling the effects of sleeplessness, unre-
laxing concentration, and the ceaseless sound of the engine. We
were not at all sleepy or tired—rather, we felt abnormally keyed
up and alert. It was a hot, sandy, dried-up sensation physically,
combined with perfect mental clarity and precision.

We flew toward Greenland through a thick snow that made it
impossible to see outside the cabin. From this storm we emerged

briefly into clear weather, but ahead of us we could see another tremendous storm developing across the entire horizon. I asked Eielson if he wanted to come down on the smooth ice below us and rest in the cabin until this one was over, or would he prefer to stay in the air and take the chance of finding Spitsbergen through the storm. Neither of us was a flying fool, but both of us wanted to accomplish what we had set out to do—fly across the polar ice-cap in one big hop. I was proud of Ben and happy when he replied that as long as I would chart the course, he would fly. The storm might last five or six days, even fourteen or fifteen, so in going on we were taking the chance of relying on blind navigation, but avoiding the danger of perhaps being snowed in on the ice and having to walk several hundred miles down the Greenland coast to a settlement.

We had a glimpse of the mountain tops of Greenland, giving me another quick check on our position. When we soon lost sight of them, I thought it best to circle a particularly threatening disturbance, and swinging far north, we flew within 300 miles of the Pole. We had not followed the direct route across the Pole, although that would have saved us at least 300 miles in distance and gasoline, because our object was to search for land in regions that had never been seen before. From this point, we turned slightly southward and crossed another 40 degrees of longitude, all in clear weather. Then a bearing on our wind-drive generator gave out, and the wireless failed.

Up to this time, I had been sending frequent wireless messages. We had a splendid outfit, capable of carrying on a two-way conversation over 8,000 miles or more, and for nineteen hours, over a distance of 2,000 miles, our messages had been heard at Point Barrow. The one most talked about later was the wireless I flashed to Dr. Isaiah Bowman, President of the American Geographical Society: "No foxes seen." This was my code message to him that no land had been sighted along our route over the Arctic Ocean.

Three hundred miles northwest of Spitsbergen we ran into another storm centering on those islands. We flew on through clouds, sleet, and snow which covered ice and land to an altitude of 15,000 feet. Now and then we were able to dodge between the clouds long enough to get an observation of the sun with my sextant, and fix our position. From the formation of the cloud tops, I could judge where they covered mountains and where they lay over the ocean ice. This enabled us to steer for the western side of Spitsbergen but, being unable to see land or ice, we doubted whether we could come down through the clouds to a safe landing.

It was impossible to locate King's Bay or Green Harbor, for which we had been heading, because I had no large-scale map of Spitsbergen by which to chart a course, and we couldn't see more than a hundred yards at best. Nevertheless we had to land somewhere. We had calculated our gasoline supply with care, and the Vega had accurately consumed just about her whole load on the flight, with barely enough left to reach a landing on Spitsbergen. Our only possible course was to dive through the clouds and fly low over the sea, in the hope of picking up the line of the coast and follow it until we could find a landing place. We thought we might get beneath the storm, and in any case, an altitude of a couple of hundred feet might give us visibility enough to see the coast.

Eielson nosed her over and we dived through the clouds. Part of the time we could see nothing, then again we could see for a few yards. I had the sensation of flying down into a deep cleft in the mountains, and I was afraid we would crash against a mountain wall on one side or the other.

Looking ahead, keeping a sharp watch, I suddenly saw the surface of the sea. We were diving straight down into gigantic waves! At that moment, Eielson pulled quickly out of the dive and lifted the shuddering plane through a welter of spray as the wind whipped the tops of the waves and drenched us. For a minute we saw nothing but swirling water against the glass. Then we came up out of it, with the windshield coated with icy spray frozen on it so we could see nothing at all.

I had to look out into the driving snow and guide Eielson by shouting directions and frantic hand signals. Suddenly I saw a little neck of smooth ice a short way ahead. In the noise of the wind Eielson could hardly hear my shouting, so I directed him

with my hand as he circled and brought her in against the wind.
She settled down like a tired bird onto the soft, snowy surface, and
the wind was blowing so terrifically that we hardly traveled 30 feet
after the skis touched the snow.

Eielson cut off the engine to save what little gas we had left, and
characteristically for him, he did not say a word. We must have
sat there quietly for some while, breathing heavily in our relief to be once more on terra firma—God knew exactly where!
—somewhere in the Spitsbergen group of islands with our mission accomplished. We looked at each other and smiled our satisfaction as I made a record of the exact time.

In twenty hours and twenty minutes, since take-off at 10:15 A.M.
on Sunday morning, we had crossed 171 degrees of longitude. Including the curve of the earth and the zigzagging on our course,
we had flown more than 2,500 miles. But in flying nearly halfway
around the world, we had flown away nearly a half-day of our
lives, since it was now late on Monday afternoon, Spitsbergen
time.

Ben and I were too exhilarated to be tired. Outside the cabin
the snowstorm howled, registering over 70 miles an hour on our
instruments, and we couldn't see more than 50 yards, nor talk
without shouting. I knew we must be within a few miles of King's
Bay, the point where we had intended to land, although we could
not take observations or fix our position with accuracy. Neither
was it possible to observe the contour of the coast. We were storm-
bound, with nothing to do but stay in the cabin of the plane until
the weather cleared. As we had done on the ice off point Barrow,
we ate a few nuts and raisins, crawled into our sleeping bags and
went to sleep.

For five days and nights while the storm raged we slept comfortably most of the time. Meanwhile, there was quite a bit of
excitement about us back in civilization, because we had been
far out over the Arctic ice when our wireless signals abruptly
ceased; we were not reported from Spitsbergen; and people quite
naturally filled in the five-day silence with their imaginations.

When the storm finally blew over, we cleaned out the cabin and got the engine ready to start again. So much snow had drifted around the plane that we practically had to dig it out, but fortunately the wind had kept the little neck of ice fairly clear of snow ahead of us. There were a couple of false starts when I tried pushing the plane to break her clear of the friction of the broad skis on the unpacked snow—and Ben suddenly found himself roaring down the ice and pulling lightly into the air, leaving me shouting forlornly at him from the ground. It was easy now, without either my weight or that of the ton of gas we had burned! The third and final time, however, I managed to start us forward with a mighty push from a safe position in the doorway, using a long piece of driftwood much as a Venetian gondolier uses his pole, and in this manner we got safely off. No sooner were we in the air than we saw, just a few miles off, the masts of a wireless station that had been hidden from our view when we were on the ground. I recognized it at once as Green Harbor, of which I had seen photographs. We turned toward it and landed at the foot of the bay, near the home of the official Norwegian wireless operator, a man named Ihlen, who rushed out to meet us along with his four colleagues. To them it seemed incredible that we had crossed the Arctic in such a small plane and so quickly. They told us that the place where we had slept through the days of the storm was named Dead Man's Island. I at once radioed out the story of our trip and our safe arrival on Dead Man's Island.

There was no gasoline at the wireless station, so we moored the plane to the ice, and waited two weeks before we got word that a small steamer was coming to the edge of the icepack. Then we set out on foot and traveled 20 miles across the pack to find the steamer, the *Hobby*, and ask the captain to take us to Norway. He not only agreed to take us to Norway, but lent us a dog team with which to return to the plane. By this time the little Lockheed was again buried in snow and we had a hard time digging it out, but eventually we got a runway cleared.

On the evening of May 9, just before we left for the ship, the men at the wireless station threw a gala farewell dinner party for us, and a number of Norwegians, Danes, Dutch, and Germans came in for it from the coal-mining community near the station. The costumes varied from regular outdoor Arctic wear to dinner jackets. We wound up the evening having a grand exhibition of dancing, which they induced me to lead in my flying suit.

We were up only a few minutes in bright sunshine the next morning and for 20 miles we flew alongside the rugged mountains we had barely missed when we came down through the clouds. That wild coast was a marvelous, unforgettable sight. As Eielson brought the Lockheed in for a perfect landing only a few yards from the steamer, our tanks were only a few cupfuls from being bone dry. So handy was that little plane that we did not have to dismantle it; we simply ran it up beside the boat, swung the boom over the side, and lifted it easily aboard.

The *Hobby* pushed through 100 miles of pack ice and early on May 15, at 3:00 A.M., we came into the port of Tromsö, Norway. Tromsö had been used as a base by Nansen, Andrée, Sverdrup, and Amundsen, so the local people understood what Arctic explorers were trying to do, and it didn't surprise us that they gave us a tremendous welcome. We felt like cheering too, for over 1,400 miles of the previously unexplored Arctic had now been wrenched out of the unknown.

Down the coast at Trongjem we were indeed surprised by another, and bigger ovation. The whole town turned out in a pouring rain, and muffled in raincoats we had to march, streaming, at the head of all the people in procession through the downpour. At Bergen, a few days later, we had to buy dinner clothes in haste for a party given in our honor by King Haakon VII of Norway, and at Oslo, the capital, all the official dignitaries met us. It was a particularly touching moment for me when the little daughter of Hjalmar Riiser-Larsen, Amundsen's navigator in the *Norge,* presented us with huge bouquets of flowers.

Then, in the royal carriages, we were driven through the streets, while the crowds went wild with enthusiasm, cheering for us and for their own Norwegian polar heroes. They took Ben Eielson to their hearts as one of their own, because of his Norwegian family background, and because he used their language when saying a few words from the platform. The procession ended at Amundsen's house, where we were taken formally to meet him. A ceremonial welcome had been arranged for us in his garden.

Amundsen had been criticizing my ideas on polar flight severely for years, both privately and publicly. But the grand old veteran of the Arctic welcomed us now with hearty congratulations, happy that we had succeeded. He presented both Eielson and me with the Norwegian Air Club's Gold Medal of Honor. Not content with this official ceremony, Amundsen presented us with an enormous cake, decorated with a map of the Arctic on which our Vega's course was marked in red. It was brought out for the grand tea party that followed the ceremony.

For weeks after this, we were overwhelmed with all kinds of official ceremonies and festivities, as we made our way through Europe to England and finally back to New York. Germany sent its largest airplane, with an escort of two squadrons of fighting planes, to carry us from Norway to Berlin. On that leg of our journey across northern Europe, I couldn't help remembering that day some ten years before when I had dangled by my hands from that balloon basket, with a German fighter plane circling around me and letting rip with its machine gun. How long ago that seemed!

Thousands of people were at the Tempelhof airdrome in Berlin to welcome us when we roared in with our escort. The British Ambassador, the American Ambassador, and a representative of Field Marshal von Hindenberg were there to meet us, and for several days we were guests of the city of Berlin.

Paris was as enthusiastic as Berlin, but the city seemed more personal in its regard for us. At the reception there, we were talking to Ambassador Myron T. Herrick when a dapper young French officer came up and asked Ben, "You are Monsieur Eielson?" Ben said he was.

"Monsieur," said the officer, indicating a beautiful young lady, "permit me to present my wife. She wishes to kiss you." And she kissed him, right there. For some reason I was not so lucky.

When the King of England's official birthday honors were

made public on June 4, my name was included in the list of knights. I was on the Continent at the time and therefore could not be immediately present, but on June 14, I was received by George V at Buckingham Palace to be dubbed with the symbolic touch of the King's sword on my shoulder. Although some people mistakenly thought at the time that I was honored for the one flight from Alaska to Spitsbergen, actually I was knighted for my work both in science and exploration over the fifteen years since I had gone north in 1913 with Stefansson.

Within one week, from the American Geographical Society, the Royal Geographical Society of London, and from fifteen other scientific associations in many countries came their highest awards. All this notwithstanding the fact that the flight from Point Barrow to Spitsbergen, though the most spectacular, was in my opinion one of the easiest flights we had made.

17

First to Fly the Antarctic

In contrast to my difficulty a year earlier in obtaining financial backing for my aerial expedition in the Arctic, I found no trouble in the summer of 1928 in lining up help for my next venture. William Randolph Hearst, the publisher, paid me an advance of $25,000 for exclusive reports from the Antarctic, where I proposed to explore the continent in our reliable little Lockheed-Vega, now known as the *Los Angeles,* since she had become such a famous plane. No one had yet flown a plane in the Antarctic.

Fate and my own stubborn nature seemed to conspire to return me frequently to old, familiar haunts. This time my route led once again down through the South Atlantic by ship to Montevideo, the jumping-off port for the Norwegian whalers' yearly cruise in the Antarctic, and thence to Deception Island, which I had visited with Cope back in 1920. After a whirlwind tour of the United States with Ben Eielson, during which we made a number of flights and delivered lectures, we sailed on September 22 from New York for Montevideo. Not many days later we were clearing the Uruguayan port on the 16,000-ton steamer *Hektoria,* mother ship to a group of smaller whale-catchers of the N. Bugge Whaling Company, with our expedition crew and planes aboard. The *Hektoria* had started life as a White Star liner, and since some of the first-class cabins and salons had been left intact, we lived luxuriously. It was quite a contrast with the hardy life Ben Eielson and I had experienced in the Arctic a few months before.

I had planned that the entire Hearst-Wilkins Antarctic Expedition should rely on the whaling fleet, because during my unhappy experience with Cope I had recognized the value of securing their friendly cooperation. Having arranged to live on their ships from the time we left Montevideo early in the Antarctic summer until our return some four or five months later, we did not have to carry a heavy supply of food and other equipment. We had only two planes with us, both of the Lockheed-Vega model. We named the newer one *San Francisco*, and Joe Crosson, the intrepid pilot who had flown that first open cockpit plane from Fairbanks up to Barrow and back, came along as our second pilot. He had had great experience as an Arctic pilot and was a close friend of Ben Eielson's. While Ben and I had been on tour, Joe had taken delivery of the *San Francisco* and had flown it across the United States to join us in New York.

Our party was very small, but even so the payroll was $2,000 a month, in addition to travel fares, living expenses, and cost of the new equipment. I paid the pilots $500 a month and all expenses; the mechanics got $400, and the wireless operator $200. Wages were guaranteed for the season and the money deposited in banks before we left, so it would be paid for certain in case anything happened to me. In this way, I had no bother about finances after we started, but it was the whalers' help that gave me the little additional margin to make ends meet.

We called at the Falklands, and then set out for Deception Island, 800 miles farther south. In 1920 and in 1921 the sea had been open all the way, but this time we encountered heavy pack ice 300 miles north of Deception. The *Hektoria* broke the way through, followed by her five small whale-catchers, but the farther south we went, the more difficulty we had in getting through the closely packed ice. At last we saw the peaks of Deception Island in the distance, towering blue-black into the sky, and capped with clouds. After a day's struggle the *Hektoria* forced her way through the ice and steamed into the little harbor I had last visited nearly eight years before, when returning from my misadventures with Cope. The tiny cluster of buildings at the shore, overshadowed by craggy, ice-covered mountains that make them appear insignificant, looked just about as I remembered them.

Deception is a tiny dot on the Antarctic map, sheltered from

Point Barrow, April, 1928. The Lockheed-Vega, chart, and bubble sextant that enabled Wilkins and Eielson to fly halfway round the world.

(Left) *Following their historic flight, Eielson (left) and Wilkins were welcomed by New York City.*

(Right) *Aboard the press boat someone suggested that fellow Australian Suzanne Bennett greet Sir Hubert.*

(Below) *Honeymooning in Switzerland, Suzanne and Sir Hubert were guests of Lincoln Ellsworth.*

Completion of the historic first airplane flight over Antarctica: Wilkins and Eielson aboard the Lockheed-Vega.

View of Graham Land, taken during first Antarctic flight.

With Dr. Hugo Eckener during the round-the-world flight of the Graf Zeppelin.

At the christening of the Nautilus, *March 24, 1931:*
Sir Hubert, Suzanne, and Jean Jules Verne.

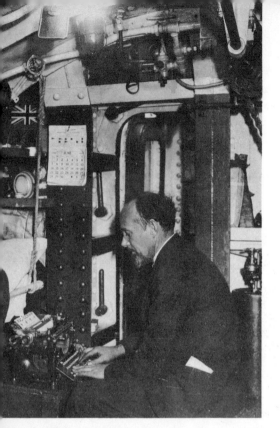

(Left) *Aboard the* Nautilus *as the Atlantic crossing began.*

(Below) *Preparing for a dive beneath the polar ice, August, 1931.*

The search for Levanevsky: refueling at Aklavik, Northwest Territories, August, 1937.

In Moscow, 1938, Wilkins discussed the Levanevsky search with Professor Komarov, president of the Soviet Academy of Sciences.

As consultant to the Quartermaster General of the U.S. Army, beginning in 1942, Sir Hubert taught survival methods to army personnel.

Flying over the North Pole, 1957: Colonel Bernt Balchen, Admiral Donald B. MacMillan, Lowell Thomas, Lowell Thomas, Jr., and Sir Hubert Wilkins.

the ocean by larger members of the South Shetland Islands group to the north and west, and by curving Palmer Peninsula (Graham Land) to the east. Geologically, the island is an extinct volcano, with the harbor lying in the ancient crater. The lofty peaks of the volcanic rim almost enclose it, like the letter C. The whalers established their station at the edge of this perfect natural harbor 120 years ago, and it has been their base of operations ever since. Deception is operated under British control by virtue of Edward Bransfield's having charted these waters and their islands as far back as 1820, and having claimed them for Great Britain.

We found little snow on the lower slopes of the island and the harbor ice was thin. In 1920 it had been 6 feet thick, but this time it was less than 3 feet thick at the same season of the year. The *Hektoria* easily broke through, and anchored so close to land that a gangway was put from her stern to the shore.

The island, deserted all winter, became a scene of bustling activity as soon as we arrived. The boarded-up factories were reopened, supplies unloaded, and boilers fired. The British magistrate, our fellow passenger, took charge of customs and opened his office on shore; the steamers and the whale-catchers went out for the whales; and we began unloading our planes and equipment. Warmer weather had set in just as we arrived, and a steady rain was falling, covering the thin harbor ice with water.

I had intended to use the harbor ice as a landing field, but had taken the precaution to bring pontoons so, if necessary, we could use the machines as seaplanes. We fitted on these pontoons, and Eielson made an attempt to take off from the water, but it soon became apparent that this was too dangerous. Hundreds of small water birds of an albatross type live on the island throughout the year, and they flocked to the water as soon as the ice was broken. They were not at all afraid of the plane, but had an immense curiosity about it. Whenever it got up speed on the water, clouds of them flew with it, dashed into the propeller, and made it impossible to take off. We had to abandon the idea of using pontoons.

There was not enough snow on shore to permit a take-off with skis, partly because of the abnormally warm weather and partly because of unusual conditions on the volcanic island. The Deception Island volcano is not yet completely cold; in fact, much of the beach is so warm that at low tide clouds of steam roll up from the edge of the water, and even the soil some distance from the beach is quite warm to touch and snow rarely stays on it.

The only thing to do was to put on wheels and take off from land. But the sides of the crater rise so steeply and are so rough that there is only one possible runway on the entire island, and this stretch is less than half a mile long. From such a short runway we could not get into the air with the heavy load of gasoline needed for a long flight. I hoped that normal cold weather would return and freeze the harbor, and in the meantime decided to clear the runway, make a few short test flights, and do a little reconnoitering around the island.

The surface of the strip was covered with boulders and lava, and we set to work with picks and shovels and wheelbarrows, trimming down rocks, carting away stones and smoothing the lava surface. The lava was almost as hard as steel and sharp-edged, with the result that we wore out many pairs of work gloves and cut our fingers often in this work.

On November 22, figuring the runway would do, we decided to try a flight, with Eielson at the controls of the same Vega in which we had crossed the Arctic. We wanted it to be the first plane ever to fly in the Antarctic. Sir Douglas Mawson, an Australian from my own city of Adelaide, had intended to take a plane to the Antarctic as early as 1912, but it had crashed beyond repair just before he was to leave Australia. So now, sixteen years later, our twin Lockheeds were to be the first. Ben took up his plane on a short flight the first day, and Joe Crosson made a brief test flight the second day. Both machines were in perfect condition.

Although there are countless thousands of penguins on Deception, they avoid the harbor when the whalers are active. The refuse of the factories pours into the water, staining it with blood and grease, and coating the birds' feathers. The factories didn't make the harbor at all unpleasant for us, living on the *Hektoria*, because in the icy water there was no noticeable odor. While waiting for the weather to change, we took a day off to visit a fairly large penguin rookery about three miles from the station. To reach it we had to climb a steep hill some 5,000 feet high, scored with deep crevasses. The danger of an accident did not keep the whalers from visiting the penguins, and every now and then a man would be missing at the end of his day off. If he didn't show up in a reasonable time, his tracks were followed and, like as not, he was hauled up from the bottom of one of the crevasses, sometimes painfully injured.

This particular rookery was really worth seeing, with about 4 square miles covered with penguins, living so close together they barely had room to move about. They were not afraid of us, though for more than a century the whalers have been taking their eggs. Indeed, they crowded around to watch us, as curious about us as we were about them. They made no objection at all to our robbing the acres of bare stone nests, and the twelve of us, in that one day, gathered hundreds of eggs.

We found them almost as good to eat as hens' eggs, but they did not look so appetizing because the white does not solidify in cooking. The penguins themselves seem far too human to make pleasant eating. Even veteran whalers did not use them for food, and I never tasted penguin meat. They are hunted for their oil, and many brands of hair tonic contain penguin oil. Also quantities of it are used for fine lubrication, especially on clocks and watches. It is especially valuable because it will not freeze but remains liquid at extremely low temperatures.

The day we visited the rookery was so hot that all the penguins stood around us panting. The temperature had risen to 50 degrees, a heat almost unheard of in that latitude. It was this heat that accounted for our having met floating ice so many hundreds of miles farther north than usual. The fringes of the great southern icecap had broken loose and drifted northward, leaving a ring of comparatively open water behind them.

This unusually warm weather was keeping us prisoners on Deception Island. We had now been there two weeks, and had not been able to get into the air with a full load of gasoline. I decided to wait one week more. If the weather continued warm we would then risk a take-off from the runway with a heavier fuel load. Fortunately, during that week there was a cold snap, and when I thought the cold had thickened the harbor ice sufficiently, I hurried out to the sea-ice and tested it until I found an area that seemed solid enough for the planes.

Eielson and Crosson skillfully managed to take off from the runway and came flying out through the gap between the mountains at the harbor mouth. When they circled for a landing, Eielson was first to come down. The ice was so slippery that he couldn't stop the plane within the limits of the area I had marked as safe. As he shot on past, he desperately tried to turn. The wheels went down through the thin ice, the plane turned up on its nose, the ice gave way beneath it, and the engine went under. Nobody dared start toward it. We stood horrified and held our breaths as we saw the plane hanging precariously over the hole in the ice. We watched Eielson climb cautiously out and get to safety. Then we ventured over the ice toward the plane and tried carefully to move it, but more ice gave way and it went down further. Now, with the undercarriage and engine under water, it still hung by one wing and the fuselage. The harbor at that point was about 1,200 feet deep.

Crosson, meanwhile, seeing the accident from the air, did not try to land on the ice but circled and went back to the runway, where he came down safely. He reported our trouble to the whalers, and they left their own work at once to hurry out to our rescue with ropes and planks.

It was risky work because the ice around the Vega was steadily sinking. Every now and then a man who ventured too close broke through into the water. We got each one out safely, and because of the thickness of the ice there was really little danger to the men. But we expected every minute that our precious plane would slip away from us and go to the bottom. The temperature was rising fast. There was no secure anchorage for the weight of the plane, even on the thickest ice. The whalers tried to get planks under the machine, but more ice gave way, letting it farther down.

At last we fastened ropes to the tail, jacked the plane up very cautiously with levers, slid planks under the skis, and managed to drag it back to solid ice. All told, it took us eighteen hours of nonstop labor to recover the plane from its perilous perch. No one had been hurt, and the plane was all right, though salt water had gotten into the cylinders. We could never have saved it but for the help of the whalers, who had promptly left their own pressing work and come out to our rescue.

The plane was hauled ashore and laid up while the mechanics went over it to clean the engine. Meanwhile, the whalers gave me the use of one of their catchers, and on it I searched all around the neighboring islands for a place we could use as a landing field —but in vain. The pack ice was thin and broken, and whenever we approached land we were confronted by sheer walls of ice, and on the islands themselves the ice was seamed with deep crevasses.

The one hope of even attempting a flight was to widen and extend our meager runway on Deception Island and try to take off from it with a heavy load. This meant running half a mile over rough surface, up over a hill, down across ditches, up another rough slope and down to the harbor. Then, if the plane didn't get into the air, it would plunge into the water and sink. The water was hundreds of feet deep at the shore line, so it would sink beyond recovery.

We got some of the whalers to help us work on the runway, and with the weather promising too clear, we worked thirty-six hours without stopping. Even then, the surface was still far too rough to satisfy me under normal conditions. But the second morning was so clear Ben Eielson and I decided to take off at once, despite the dangers.

Jolting over the rough ground, gaining speed, up the hill and

over it, racing down the slope, we hit the ditches, and the plane
leaped high in the air. For a moment I thought the landing gear
surely would smash when we hit, but fortunately it held, and on
we ran up the second slope, made a sharp turn, losing speed, then
dashed downhill to the harbor, where, just at the edge of the water,
Eielson managed to pull us up, the plane lifting just enough to
skim out over the harbor and climb to safety.

Once in the air we believed our major difficulties were over.
Eielson, without even waiting to circle, headed out through the
narrow gap between the mountains and then turned south. There
was enough gasoline on board for 1,400 miles, and in the air the
plane was not overloaded, so she climbed with ease and after
throttling down we cruised along at better than 125 miles an hour.
At last we were off to explore the Antarctic in the same Lockheed-
Vega which had carried us over the top of the Arctic a half-year
before.

We had aboard the same equipment and emergency packs with
rations for two months, so if forced down we could walk at least
500 miles. Besides these emergency rations we had a pound or
so of other food, and a quart thermos bottle full of hot, heavily-
sweetened black coffee. In the plane we carried the same fur
clothes we had worn in the Arctic, but now we were wearing light
summer clothes of camel's hair wool. The fur outfits were to be
used in case we had to come down and walk out.

We also had the same radio equipment, with a new generator.
This radio was built by Heintz and Kaufman of San Francisco,
the firm that up to that time had fitted wireless to nearly every
plane successfully making a long-distance flight. Kingsford-Smith
used it, the successful Dole fliers used it, and Byrd took it with
him to the South Pole later. The complete set weighed less than
fifty pounds, and it could establish two-way communication between any two points on the planet. It was so constructed that
when I was not sending a message, I clamped down the key and
the mechanism sent out a continuous buzzing by which the wireless operator on Deception Island could keep a continuous record
of our course. What a change this represented from the way we

had been cut off from the outside world when we sailed north with Stefansson in 1913! The difference radio had made in exploring by 1928 was certainly revolutionary.

For the first 70 miles we flew a little east of south over the waters of Bransfield Strait, which were studded with icebergs and occasional drifts of pack ice. Dead ahead was Trinity Island, with peaks rising to 6,000 feet. We flew around this, making for the big peninsula jutting from the Antarctic continent—Graham Land.

The panorama was magnificent—the jagged mountains of black and green rock and glittering snow slopes of Trinity towering beside us, above us the clear sky, below us blue-black water and icebergs—everything frozen and still, black and blue-black and black-green and glittering white.

Flying at 6,000 feet we expected to come in over Graham Land. Eight years before, I had tried to reach the top of that plateau on foot, always encountering a sheer cliff at the top of a 10,000-foot elevation. Now I hoped to discover that the near edge of the plateau itself was much lower.

This time, I had a tremendous sensation of power and freedom —I felt liberated—when we were approaching Graham Land by air. The contrast was most striking between the speed and ease of flying in by plane and the slow, blind struggles of our work along that coast a few years before. It had taken us three months, on foot, to map 40 miles; now we were covering 40 miles in twenty minutes, and I had scarce time to sketch the principal terrain and shoreline features in my notebook before the scene had entirely changed and I was drawing a crude map of the next section of this area.

No one had climbed to the Graham Land plateau summit, and I was thrilled to realize that for the first time, human eyes—our eyes—were going to see it. As we approached, I realized, first of all, that it was much higher than it had been reported. At 6,000 feet, it still rose high above us. We had to follow along the western coast, climbing until we reached an altitude of more than 9,000 feet before we could turn southward above the land. As we sailed in over the continent, Ben Eielson, I, and our little Lockheed-Vega were making another record; for the first time in history new land was being discovered from the air.*

We crossed the plateau to the far side of the narrow Palmer Peninsula, and then followed southward along the eastern coast above the shelf ice of the Weddell Sea. The area before us was blank on the charts since no one had ever visited it before. We had to make our course by dead reckoning and by the sun, and as landmarks emerged one by one before us we sketched them into our map. Then a broad bay opened before us, so broad that we had to turn westward to follow the coast. We swerved far westward and saw that the bay was not a bay after all, but a channel. It ran into the sea on the other side of the land mass, cutting Graham Land in two. The long, thin body of land to the north was therefore not really part of the Antarctic continent, and the peninsula that we had been exploring and mapping turned out to be an island.

Leaving this channel behind us, we flew on southward, mapping the coast, until we came to another channel, which meant the land immediately north of it was also an island. We therefore had not yet reached the Antarctic continent. Beyond lay a third island and we flew across still another channel. Beyond the third channel we found a group of smaller islands, while still beyond these we came to a wide strait, separating this island archipelago from what appeared to be truly a part of the Antarctic continent. Ahead of us, this land extended as far as we could see, beyond a shore line running roughly east and west.

By now we were 600 miles from Deception Island, we had used nearly half our supply of gasoline, and a dark storm was developing behind us. To go much farther would be inviting trouble. Besides crossing the Graham Land plateau and discovering the channels which apparently transformed the great peninsula into

* Among the mountains Wilkins and Eielson passed on this historic flight are the lofty peaks that were mapped and named in 1947 by a private American expedition headed by Captain Finn Ronne, United States Navy. On the latest maps one can see among them a group named for Sir Hubert Wilkins, and another for Lowell Thomas.

a chain of islands, we had discovered altogether eight new islands, three channels and a strait, as well as an unknown land which seemed to be part of the Antarctic continent. Still anxious to see more, we flew along its coast for some miles, finding no indication that it turned southward; then, with half our fuel remaining, we turned back to face the storm. We wanted to fly westward across the islands and follow their western coasts northward, but the violence of the storm and our barely sufficient supply of gasoline impelled us to take the shortest course for the return to Deception Island.

A little less than eleven hours after we left Deception, we came in, directly above a round hole in the storm, through which we caught a quick glimpse of the harbor. The air above the opening was turbulent, with all the winds of the storm trying to pull us to pieces. Nevertheless, Eielson held the plane against them and circled down. Keeping just inside the tunnel of storm clouds, he neatly spiraled through the hole and then, through the dense fog that shrouded our rough airstrip, he brought the plane to a landing.

We had left at 8:30 that morning, had covered 1,300 miles— nearly 1,000 miles of it over unknown territory—and had returned in time to cover the plane with its storm hood, go to the *Hektoria*, bathe and dress, and sit down to our eight o'clock dinner as usual.

I was truly elated. Certainly there could be no more doubt about the value of airplanes for exploration. And Lady Luck was with us that day, for within an hour after we landed the storm became so violent it would have been impossible to land on the island. Its force did not abate for days, and then bad weather continued until the last of December. Shortly before the end of the year, we flew again over a part of the newly discovered land, enlarging our maps and looking for some point at which we might establish a base for flying farther south. Everywhere we met the same conditions—sheer walls of ice fronting the sea, and deep crevasses on all level land.

I concluded we had done as much as we could for the summer of 1928–1929, and by radio chartered a boat in the Falklands to come and take us back to civilization. In preparation for further work the next season, we removed the large wheels from the planes, installed small iron wheels, and buried these and the tail skid in the gravel. Then we removed the wings and stored them in the whalers' warehouse. The fuselage and the engines were covered with tight-fitting suits of canvas, and the engines were swamped with oil in every cylinder, plus a thick coat of grease on all exposed metal parts. Then we waited for the boat to arrive from the Falklands.

On the last day of December, 1928, all the whalers came ashore for the traditional big New Year's celebration. This is the only break in the terrific work of the whaling season, and they make the most of it with games, songs, enormous eating, and plenty of drink. Most of them are so drunk from the time they come ashore until they start work again that they don't know what they are doing and have no memory of it afterward.

That afternoon a couple of them climbed up on two big sperm whales that were lying on shore waiting their turn in the factory. The whales had been cooking themselves from the heat of the blood inside the insulating layers of blubber and were swollen with gas. One of the sailors thrust his long knife into the carcass, whereupon the whale exploded and blew both men into the harbor. The few of us who were sober hauled them out before they drowned.

In the officers' mess that night there were the customary speeches and songs. All over the beach, hundreds of big, brawny Norwegian sailors and gunners and engineers were roaring drunk, bawling songs and shooting off guns. The whole place was a riot of yells and explosions.

Two of these happy sailors, not satisfied with the uproar, decided they would produce a really big noise. All the black powder and the bombs for the harpoons—70 tons of explosives—were stored in a barge moored at the beach. They got hold of a fifty-pound keg of powder and started laying a train from the barge across a gangplank to the shore and then inland.

One was still trailing out the powder when the other, growing impatient, lighted the train in the middle. The fellow at the end saw the flames pursuing him and tried to keep ahead of them, trailing the powder as he went. The fire gained on him, so he dropped the half-empty keg and went back to remonstrate with his friend. Meantime, in the other direction the flames were running toward the barge. Seeing this promising sight, the fellow forgot his grievance, embraced his friend and the two waited expectantly for the explosion. Suddenly behind them the keg blew up. The explosion flung them some distance and burned all the hair off their heads.

The fire running toward the barge went to the end of the plank that led out from shore, and there it stopped. If it had gone a few feet farther it would have wrecked everything on the island.

This was our farewell to Deception Island and the hearty whalers. A day or so later our steamer came, and in a week we reached the Falklands. As guests of the Royal Mail Steam-packet Company, we came back through the Straits of Magellan, up the west coast of South America, and through the Panama Canal to New York.

18

Around the World in Twenty-one Days

Since it would be a good half-year before I could return to the Antarctic to take up our exploration work again, I was more or less at liberty during the summer of 1929. Mr. William Randolph Hearst, who took a keen interest in the development of air transportation, proposed to me that I take this opportunity to join the *Graf Zeppelin*'s flight around the world, of which he was the sponsor and chief financial backer. The *Graf Zeppelin* was the most modern of the big German dirigibles, and had shown her sturdy dependability in the fall of 1928 by crossing the Atlantic in a smooth flight with passengers and mail. Whereas the news story of the flight was to be covered for the Hearst papers by Karl Von Wiegand, and Lady Drummond-Hay was to write the lighter, more human side of life aboard the luxurious floating air palace, Mr. Hearst wanted me to write about the trip from the technical viewpoint—the problems of navigation, meteorology, engine performance, and so forth. Needless to say, I was delighted at the prospect.

The plan of the flight was to circumnavigate the globe in four long hops, starting officially from the United States Navy air station at Lakehurst, New Jersey. The stops for refueling and delivery of mail were to be at the *Graf*'s home base at Friedrichshafen, Germany, at Tokyo, Los Angeles, and at Lakehurst once again. No airship had ever flown around the world, nor had any sustained flight been planned with such great distances between stops. Yet Dr. Hugo Eckener, the *Graf*'s commander and Germany's grand old man of the airship world, had perfect faith he could bring his craft through it with credit.

230

When I went to meet the airship at Friedrichshafen, I rather expected to get the cold shoulder from Von Wiegand because, after all, he was in charge of the story, and here I came barging in at the last moment without his approval or consent. When I explained that Mr. Hearst had sent me to report the technical side of the trip, he said in a friendly way, "All right! Come along and we'll work together." Von Wiegand proved to be a prince of a colleague. He never showed anything but a spirit of cordial good-fellowship and was always ready to help me.

At dawn on May 16 we left Friedrichshafen for Lakehurst, where our flight would officially begin. The start was delightful, as we sailed over Lake Constance, the myriad picturesque mountains and lakes of Switzerland, and then due south down the valley of the Rhone in eastern France. The strong cold north wind of that region, known in the Rhone Valley as the mistral, was blowing us along from behind and we made great speed above the valley and its clusters of little French towns, until we came out over the Mediterranean and turned southwestward toward the coast of Spain.

Just as the stewards were setting the salon tables for lunch, the first of our five engines gave out. Eckener and his officers thought the remaining engines would take us safely, but it was not long before another failed and Dr. Eckener explained to the passengers that we must turn back. We swung round and faced the wind, and the great ship fought gallantly, hour after hour, toward the coast of France and then laboriously upstream against the bitter mistral with the Rhone flowing majestically far below.

We had a cosmopolitan group of twenty passengers—Russians and Japanese, American and British, Austrians, French, and Spaniards. There was even a chimpanzee bound for the New York Zoo. We called her Susie-the-Baboon. Naturally, when our difficulties began, the passenger salon was a babel of various languages, but no one was really alarmed. The great airship gave us a sense of security, and what everyone was mainly interested in now was our fight against the wind. The first strangeness among the passengers began to wear off, just as it does during the first day on shipboard. Lady Drummond-Hay spent most of the time in her cabin, writing. Von Wiegand and I tried to send dispatches, but could not get them off because the officers were using the wireless.

The mistral was still blowing at 40 miles an hour when the third, and then the fourth motor gave out. The one remaining engine could not give us a speed of more than 25 miles, so we found ourselves being blown backward toward the French Riviera at 15 miles an hour. There was some excitement when the passengers saw our shadow flying across the farms and towns toward the sea again. Everywhere below us motor cars were tearing along the roads and people were rushing about, apparently realizing our danger. Susie-the-Baboon set up a great chattering and broke loose, dashing around on the girders and up among the gas bags. She led the crew a merry chase until she was caught and boxed up again.

Dr. Eckener and his staff handled the situation beautifully. They used every trick known to the airship commander, going low and taking advantage of every little hill that would shelter us from the wind, then trying to rise above it. But without a possibility of repairing the engines in the air, and with weather reports indicating that the wind would continue, Eckener had to give up hope of reaching Friedrichshafen, the one base properly equipped with a trained ground crew, a mooring tower and hangar to bring the ship in for repairs.

In a forced landing it would be a question as to whether or not the 780-foot ship could even be saved. Dr. Eckener announced to the passengers that we might be obliged to abandon the *Graf*, and said that stations would be assigned everyone if this had to be done. Our orders were to get out of the exposed passenger gondola and into the air space below the gas bags in the main envelope until the ship should reach the ground. Then the gas bags would be ripped, the weight would crumple the envelope down, and we could get out through doors in the fabric without any difficulty.

I did not believe there was any serious danger to the passengers because the crew had everything well in hand and knew how to land the ship. No one appeared seriously alarmed. The passengers sat around in comfortable chairs in the salon and some of them went to sleep while the ship's officers were fighting to keep the wind-blown giant of the skies under control.

Dr. Eckener radioed an appeal to the French Government for help in landing so as to save the ship, and while we were waiting for the Air Ministry to reply, he carried out a number of practice maneuvers to show us what his ship could do. Shutting off the single engine, the crew brought us down without power, riding the air currents and nipping between the hills into the narrow valleys, then rising a little and dropping eastward over into the mountains toward Italy. Once we came near crashing into a mountainside when a hill behind which we came down was not quite wide enough to give full shelter. The wind caught the tail sideways, and we escaped only by starting the single engine and turning the ship in time so that the passenger gondola missed the mountain by a few feet. It was a wonderful demonstration of the ability of the crew to handle the *Graf*, the way a skilled yachting crew control their craft in a stiff breeze.

At last the French Government radioed that we might land at Cuers, an old airship base about 50 miles east of Marseille, where there was a hangar. After the war the French had demanded an airship and a hangar as war reparations from the Germans, and got them. The airship, the *Dixmude*, was no longer there, but the hangar was still in perfect condition. It was the only thing that saved the *Graf Zeppelin* that day. Just at dark, we arrived above the Cuers landing field to find a small army of French soldiers hastily summoned to help bring us in. They had never handled a Zeppelin, but they obeyed orders with absolute precision and caught our lines, hauled us in to a perfect landing, and walked the *Graf* into the hangar.

Then began another sort of adventure. Because this was an unexpected arrival in French territory by a German ship, we found ourselves surrounded by cordons of police and suspicious customs officials determined to do their full duty. In effect, we were prisoners in a polite sort of airport-arrest. None of the correspondents on board had been allowed to send out a word to their papers. We found that there was a telegraph office 20 miles away—the closest one—but the police adamantly refused to let us go to it. A young fellow named Frank Nicholson and I decided to try to slip out. At our first attempt, the police caught us and brought us back, but the second time we got out among the soldiers and began trying to hire, beg, borrow or steal a motor car. Finally we prevailed upon a French officer to lend us his.

The police nabbed us a second time, brought us back and took our identification papers to make sure of our staying there. A few minutes later, we took advantage of the confusion around the hangar to sneak out again. We found a French Army truck and bribed the soldier who was driving it with practically all the money we had with us. Then, worse luck, the van was held up by the police at a roadblock.

We managed to get away in the dark and were trudging along the road when we met two young girls. In my best French, which, having hardly improved since my desert days, was so bad I could hardly understand it myself, I asked them where we could rent a car. One of the girls could tell our origin readily and replied, to my amazement, in perfect English—with an Australian lilt! She pointed out the tail light of a car in the distance and said that her mother was just driving it to town. We ran shouting down the road and managed to stop her. We found, by fantastic coincidence, that she, an Australian by birth, was the wife of the French telegraph operator we were seeking. We persuaded her to drive us the 20 miles to town, but she dared not take us to the telegraph station and made us promise not to let the police suspect that she had helped us.

It was eleven o'clock before we got to the telegraph office, and my story had to go before one in order to reach my papers in time for the morning editions. We went into the office without any money or identification papers—just our dispatches. It took a quarter of an hour to convince the operator that I had authority to send messages collect to London.

We watched him sit down at his instrument and begin tapping

the key, but after a time we decided to go get something to eat while he was working. We returned in a half-hour to make sure the dispatches had gone, and found the whole place locked up with the lights out. Then two gendarmes appeared out of the shadows, arrested us, and hustled us back to Cuers.

Next morning Dr. Eckener and his officers were as cold to me as an Antarctic iceberg. I did not understand why until a perfect storm of telegrams came at me from Germany, England, and America, in which people wanted to know why I had attacked the German crew, the German ship, the German people. Why had I written that I would never again step into a Zeppelin—indeed would never fly again?

I was dumbfounded. Actually, I had written about the efficiency of the Zeppelin's crew, their perfect control of the ship, and the confidence of everyone aboard. Sensing where the trouble may have originated, I returned to town, where I asked the telegraph operator if he had sent my dispatch. He swore that he had. Insisting that some other story must have been sent in my name, I got permission to search the telegraph operator's records, and found that my dispatch had not been sent until after three o'clock in the morning. Then the poor devil broke down and confessed.

The mayor of the town had telephoned him that two correspondents had escaped, and had ordered him to send nothing that was not passed by French censorship. When the operator told him that our stories praised the Germans and the German Zeppelin, the poor fellow was compelled to translate every word of the messages and read them over the telephone to the mayor, before he could send them. The mayor didn't understand English any too well and had worked until three o'clock on the translation.

In the meantime, when no dispatches reached our papers, desk men were set to work making up a story from the scattered reports, quoting the excited villagers who had watched us from the ground. All our practice maneuvers had been transformed into desperate, last-second escapes from death. Naturally, everyone supposed that the passengers on board were in a state of panic and terror, screaming, fainting, and saying their prayers. So the rewrite men had made a hair-raising tale of it, and then had the audacity to put my name on the product. A few hours later, they received my dispatch stating quite the opposite, but the damage had been done. No newspaper likes to print a retraction of its own "news," so they didn't.

I spent the next several days trying to reestablish friendly relations with Dr. Eckener and the officers of the Zeppelin company. When they finally read my original stories and understood my predicament, they sympathized with me, but still could not help being irritated by the falsehoods that had been printed.

The flight back to Friedrichshafen from the French air base after our motors were repaired was the most beautiful dirigible flight I have ever experienced. We left at night, flying low along the coast, looking down on the people dancing at the open-air beachfront pavilions, and seeing the lights of pleasure craft along the Riviera. It was a marvelous moonlit night as we flew up the valley of the Rhône and over the mountains and lakes of Switzerland. I shall never forget the snowy peaks and the shadows of clouds on the lakes, and the lights of Geneva and Zurich. We arrived at Friedrichshafen the next morning.

During the six weeks that the *Graf Zeppelin* was delayed at its home base for repairs, I went to England to see if I could induce the authorities to lend me a British dirigible for the Antarctic during the following summer season. Despite the engine trouble on its first flight this year, my brief experience with the *Graf* had convinced me of its extraordinary possibilities, and indeed the epic flight of the *Norge* had proved how easily an airship could negotiate polar winds and weather.

I got no clear answer by the time I had to return to Friedrichshafen for the second start, which proved to be serenely uneventful. The entire trip amounted to the smoothest crossing of the Atlantic I had ever experienced. The water was calm in midsummer and we flew low—at 1,500 feet or less—and could see sharks, whales, and other marine life quite easily. The crossing took 100 hours, in part because with favorable breezes Eckener cruised along at times using only three of his five motors. Before we touched down at Lakehurst, Eckener floated over New York City and Coney Island, where the people were packed like sardines on the beach in the August heat and waved at us with what seemed like a million tiny arms.

For the *Graf*'s round-the-world trip, every one of the twenty available tickets had long been claimed, even though the cost was a substantial $12,000. Actually, we had almost no private travelers among us, since just about everyone aboard was sponsored by a publisher for whom he or she was writing the story of the epochal flight. But still the *Graf Zeppelin* officials were besieged by persons offering much more than the established fare. One American woman offered me $30,000 if I would somehow fail to show up in time to start, so that she could get my place.

On the night before our departure, August 6, Eckener directed that an all-night "stowaway guard" be maintained around the ship to prevent a repetition of an embarrassing incident a few days earlier. A young baker's apprentice had hidden aboard the *Graf* in Friedrichshafen, and was not discovered until we were in flight —and Eckener did not want any more of that kind of monkey-shines.

We sailed out from Lakehurst on the morning of August 7, 1929, flew over New York to render the great city a salute, then headed out over the Atlantic. Eckener hoped to set a new speed record for circling the planet, but with his usual imperturbability he saw no reason to omit the courtesies while doing so. And the starting leg was promising, because our flight from New York to Paris, where we did not stop, required only twelve hours more than Lindbergh had taken in the *Spirit of St. Louis*, only two years before. Lindbergh, in 1927, had risked his life and strained his energies to the utmost. In contrast, we ate sumptuous meals aboard the *Graf*, slept in comfortable berths, admired the wonderful view from aloft, and took endless rolls of pictures between New York and Paris. The ship was almost noiseless. We hardly heard the engines except when we were leaning out of the windows, and the wireless machine and the electrical kitchen equipment made no more noise than the whirr of an electric fan.

In Friedrichshafen, we picked up two Japanese, a newspaper reporter and a naval officer assigned to the ship. As before, we were harried by people wanting to go with us. Anna May Wong, the Chinese actress, came down to see us off, and one of her admirers offered to pay any price for a ticket to Japan for her. There were many others, but all had to be turned down.

In Germany, several passengers asked me, as an expert on polar weather, to tell them what they should have in the way of furs and heavy clothing while crossing northern Siberia. I told them to dress as they would in New York or Berlin in the wintertime. Without exception, they decided that I was not an expert after all, so they went out and bought fur coats and the heaviest underwear available.

We left Friedrichshafen flying east and north across Germany to Berlin, where crowds went crazy with enthusiasm welcoming us from the ground. Our big ship pointed its nose out over the Baltic Sea, and then flew eastward into the U.S.S.R. Hardly had we crossed the Russian frontier when it developed that the official Russian representative on board, a man named Karklin, could speak nothing but Russian. Although we were an international group and most of us could get along in two or three languages, none of us knew Russian. Our Soviet man was supposed to translate official messages and weather reports from Moscow so as to help direct our course over Russia, yet now we found he was all but useless. Poor chap, he thought he could speak enough English for this job, since he had studied it somewhere in Russia for a while. The ship's officers would write out a message to him in English or German, but he had the greatest difficulty in reading either the English letters or the German script. He would pick out the letters one by one and transliterate them into Russian characters, and by brooding over these for a while he would emerge with some kind of meaning, though it was not always correct. Then he would write a reply and transliterate the characters into German or English script. Sometimes this was intelligible, but more often it was gibberish. Meanwhile, we were flying on, with Moscow sending out weather signals and our wireless picking them up, but our Russian was always hundreds of miles behind in translating them.

At one point, I remember we were looking down at the crowds of peasants and soldiers lined up along the river banks, when suddenly our crew fired off the echolet, a device for determining altitude. A shot is fired from it, and altitude is determined by the time between the explosion and the return of the echo from the ground. At the detonation most of the people beneath us ran wildly in all directions, while others grabbed up their rifles. I expected them to send up a volley toward us, but when we made no further warlike demonstration and, in fact, continued to wave at them from the windows they let us continue in peace.

The next day, with the weather apparently threatening in the east, Eckener decided to swing far to the north to avoid a storm and to follow the high northern circle across Russia and Siberia. We were sailing blithely along at a good speed, with everybody comfortable and interested in the villages and countryside flowing beneath us, when we saw our Russian was much perturbed. Nobody could tell at first what was the matter with him, but it was clear that he was upset. Part of the time, he tried to talk; the rest of the time he was working madly with paper and pencil. Finally he succeeded in making the officers understand that we were exceeding the orders he had been given. We were supposed to be following the Trans-Siberian Railroad eastward, but we were already far north of that landmark. On we went, in contempt of the Kremlin no doubt, but deferring to the Russian weather.

As we sailed serenely on over the vast expanses of Eastern Russia and then Soviet Asia, we noticed a peculiar change in the behavior of the people down below. All across Europe we had seen enthusiastic crowds waving flags and shouting at us as we passed above them, but in the remote parts of the Soviet east, where apparently the people had not heard of our flight and had never seen an airship, frantic mothers seized children and fled into their houses. Along the muddy roads, peasants jumped out of their ox-wagons and ran to hide behind trees. North of the steppes, we sailed over the encampments of the Mongol nomads and the villages of northern fishermen. It was strange to watch these people bolting at the approach of the Zeppelin, like the chickens and cattle in other countries.

The mighty rivers of northern Asia were wonderful to observe, broad and beautiful streams like the Ob, the Yenisey, and the Lena that very few outsiders had ever seen, and yet are among the greatest rivers on the globe, flowing northward to the ice-covered waters of the Arctic Ocean. Most of the hills and valleys were heavily timbered, mile after endless mile. We could even see indications of gold-bearing strata along the river courses.

The weather was clear and sunny, and even though we were far north, the passengers were sweltering in the heavy clothes they had put on after spurning my advice in Germany. Finally most of them broke down and took off their heavy underwear and all their furs. The Siberian cold upon which they had insisted just had not appeared.

Everyone felt quite at home in the ship by this time. The food was well cooked and served, with a special menu at each luncheon and dinner. There were four tables in the salon. The distinguished-looking Eckener with his Teutonic aristocrat's goatee presided over one; his officers had two others; and Von Wiegand and I sat at the fourth. The seating of the other passengers was changed from time to time, so that each had a turn at the captain's table. We were all more or less men of the world, plus our one lady passenger, and all had traveled widely and got along well together.

There was the rather amusing little Dr. Jeronimo Megias, personal physician to the King of Spain, who was the pink of Castilian courtesy. We liked him but we had to avoid him whenever we had work to do, because he was so excessively polite that it was impossible to have a short talk with him. It took him fifteen minutes even to get through a flowery Castilian "Good morning."

An amusing and boisterous fellow was Baron Heinz von Petrk-hammer, a dispossessed German nobleman who was now taking pictures for the German press. He wore leather knee-breeches, a colorful vest, shirt, and brogues. He was a wild, hare-brained individual who smashed and danced, shouted and howled when it pleased him. Everything he touched came to pieces. He had a whole battery of fine cameras, but whenever he tried to use them he fumbled his way into making every shot go wrong.

Our oldest passenger was Lieutenant Colonel Christophe Iselin, a Swiss Army officer who had earned the nickname "All-or-Nothing Iselin." He had led an active life, done a lot of Alpine climbing, and been a successful inventor. Now retired from the Army and getting along toward sixty, he was erect, lean, and full of nervous energy. He had never been in the air before, and he had said nothing to anyone about making this trip until just before we left. When he at last mentioned it to his wife and son, they exclaimed that he couldn't do such a thing. His reply was, "I am 'All-or-Nothing Iselin,' and my first flight will be around the world!" I found him the most interested passenger on board. Often he asked me to explain something on the technical side of aeronautics, and he was curious about everything new, so it was never a bore to tell him what he wanted to know.

Hundreds of miles from any sea, in the heart of Siberia, we passed over the town of Yakutsk. Political prisoners were exiled to Yakutsk in days of the Czar's regime, and during World War I German prisoners were sent there. Many had died in the place. In memory of these dead Germans, Dr. Eckener flew low over a church cemetery and dropped a wreath which had been made up from flowers on our dining tables. It went spinning down from the ship, and by a curious chance caught and hung on the corner-post of the fence around the German graves.

We met our first serious storm over the sea as we approached Japan from the northwest. It was a cyclone. The night was dark and we could see nothing, but messages began to come through from the Japanese meteorological stations. They reported to Eckener the enormous area covered by the storm, and Eckener immediately flew the *Graf* into the rim of the storm and followed it around. We were swept far out of our course, but the storm winds carried us half-way to Japan.

It was dawn when we came over the northern Japanese island

of Hokkaido and went sailing down toward Tokyo while the sun
was rising out of the Pacific Ocean. Flying along the coast, sometimes over land and sometimes over sea, we reached Tokyo in
the early afternoon of August 19, having flown 7,000 miles from
Friedrichshafen in 102 hours. The wind was still rather strong,
so while we waited for it to moderate we flew on south to Yoko-
hama and then back and circled Tokyo once more before going
to Kasumigaura Airfield, some miles outside of the city.

Beneath us we could see an enormous rush of traffic everywhere
on this densely populated island—bicycles, carts, horses, wheelbarrows, and cars. Hundreds of thousands of Japanese had walked
the 20-odd miles to the airport to meet the Zeppelin. Like the
French, the Japanese had taken a hangar from the Germans after
the war, and it was ready for us. The ship was walked into it, and
we alighted for only the second time since leaving Lakehurst.

The Japanese officials had put up a marquee on the landing field
where they met us with all kinds of ceremony, as well as food and
entertainment. Japanese hospitality continued with banquets, and
even a tea at the Emperor's Palace. Lady Drummond-Hay and I
gave public lectures and radio talks, as many as we possibly could,
and still we could not satisfy all the urgent requests to hear about
the *Graf*'s flight. I found the questions asked by the Japanese to
be based on sound knowledge, and I recognized they were as up
to date in aviation as the Europeans and Americans.

Bad weather delayed us several days in Tokyo. We made three
starts, but each time had to return because of storms. When at
last we left, escorted by squadrons of Japanese planes, we flew
north, skirting the edge of the Sea of Japan, directly into another
storm. Instead of going around it, Eckener took the bolder course
and flew straight through it to reach the wind he knew was on the
other side. The flying was rough for a while, and we were all so
exhausted by the lack of sleep, the crowds, formal entertainments,
and the stuffing down of enormous quantities of food in Tokyo,
that most of us were thoroughly air-sick.

On the other side of the storm we came into sullen, cloudy

weather, which continued most of the way across the Pacific. Now and then we rose above the clouds for a sun observation at about 4,000 feet. Then we would go down within 500 feet of the water and record the wind at the surface. But for the greater part of the way we saw nothing but gray fog upon our windows. The first steamer we sighted after leaving Japan was about 150 miles out from San Francisco, and more ships came into view as we neared the coast.

Gliding in over San Francisco was for me the most thrilling part of the entire trip. We arrived on August 25, just at sundown, and hundreds of planes flew out to escort us in. We crossed San Francisco Bay to Berkeley and Oakland just in time to look back to the west to see the sun sinking between the dark headlands guarding the Golden Gate. There was a splendorous haze of golden light over the mountains and the sea and the craggy piles of buildings on the hills of San Francisco. The white and orange ferryboats were plying across the darkening blue water beneath us, and the sea gulls were flying far below among the shadows of the planes.

After this evening tour of the San Francisco Bay area, Eckener pointed the *Graf* south for Los Angeles. The night was gorgeous with moonlight, clear and cold—ironically enough, the coldest part of the trip. After flying comfortably across Siberia, we got into our heaviest coats above the California coast in August.

As we flew over Mr. Hearst's ranch at San Simeon, Eckener dipped the *Graf* in a symbolic salute to the sponsor of the voyage—though in the dark of night no one below was aware of it. Then on down the coast to Los Angeles in the moonlight. Just before midnight, we saw the lights of the great, sprawling metropolis appear far ahead. As we approached, it seemed as if every light in the whole district were shining for us. As far as the eye could see along the whole horizon there was a sea of twinkling little lights, a spectacle of shiny jewels against the dark background, some in straight lines, others strung out in sweeping curves—so beautiful it didn't seem real. Back and forth we turned and circled, drinking in the incredible beauty of Los Angeles alight, until day-

break, and then came in to the mooring mast that had been erected
at the United States Naval Station.

Hundreds of thousands of people jammed the streets leading
to the airfield to greet us when we disembarked. At the hotel,
however, we were left in unsolicited solitude. Believing we were
exhausted after our long journey, and knowing that Mr. Hearst
was giving us a big, formal dinner that night at the Ambassador
Hotel, our friends in Los Angeles thought surely we would fall
into bed and sleep until we had to crawl out for the fruit compotes.

The General Pershing suite at the Ambassador was pleasant but
much too quiet for us. Finally, needing to celebrate, we sent out
for refreshments and had a small morning party all by ourselves—
the same old crowd that had been on the Zeppelin. In the afternoon
Monte Blue and Raquel Torres, the movie people, joined the
party. They seemed to be the only persons in Los Angeles who
didn't think we were asleep.

Dr. Eckener, who always declined formal entertainments if
he could, was persuaded to go to Mr. Hearst's dinner because he
had to be, quite naturally, the principal speaker. However, throughout the evening he must have been a bit apprehensive as word of
the changing weather was frequently brought to him. It had turned
quite hot during the day and was still very warm by evening. Still,
he went through his speaking performance with his usual cool
self-control and grace.

When I was called upon to say a few words, I stressed the fact
that we had been able to see from the *Graf* in the most startling
manner and great detail the tremendous contrasts in the surface
of the earth. I pointed out also that in the past three weeks we
had all come to understand the extreme importance of accurate
meteorological forecasts—for if I had known this back on the
station as a boy, if I had this lesson confirmed again and again
during my adventures in the Arctic and the Antarctic, it was driven
home even more forcibly during this flight around the world by
airship. I hoped that my appeal for intensified work on weather
problems would be a seed well planted.

We were scheduled to take off at midnight, but when we arrived at the field we found the naval officers worried about the difficulties caused by the heat. Dr. Eckener was not at first concerned, although he was warned that he would encounter a change of temperature as soon as he left the ground. The weight of the passengers and hand baggage was an unsettled question. The ship had been weighed off for ballast, our luggage had been weighed, and of course our own bodyweight was known and allowed for, but all of us boarded with souvenirs of Los Angeles—toy Zeppelins, dolls, boxes of California candied fruits, not to mention the lavish favors from Mr. Hearst's party. The added weight was not great on the ground, but it would make a difference when we were trying to get airborne.

Still, Dr. Eckener believed he could take off without trouble, and he gave orders to walk the ship all over the field, feeling for a suitable air condition. There was not a breath of wind. The character of the surface makes a great deal of difference in a windless take-off because the weight of the air is not the same above green grass as it is over dry soil. For nearly two hours we were walked around, hunting for air that would give the proper degree of lift. We were still too heavy, and in walking about we had come close to the high-tension wires of the airdrome. Two or three of us who could see this were rather anxious. Just then one of the ship's officers leaned out and shouted to the sailors, "Give her all you can! We need it!"

At this, the sailors who were leaning on the gondola handrail gave the ship a terrific push. Up we went, about 15 feet. There we struck the rebound of the cooler, heavier air at that distance above the ground, and there we hung, immobile.

Realizing the ship was too high to be pulled down and too low for safety, Dr. Eckener rang for full speed ahead on all five engines. That speed against the resistance of the air thrust her nose up, but the tail still dragged on the ground, and as the engines took hold we were drifting steadily toward the high-tension wires. The searchlights were on us so that as we leaned out of the windows we could see the wires just ahead of the rear engine car. If they should touch it, the contact would let loose a more terrific flash of lightning than ever came out of a storm. It would blow us all to pieces in a mighty explosion of hydrogen—and not only us, but the crowd on the ground below. There was no time to say or do anything. One or two let out a shout, but most of us just leaned out of the windows, looking on tensely and expecting the next moment to be in eternity.

Then Eckener, the master airship pilot, directed his crew in a marvelous bit of work. They switched off all power suddenly and bucked the rear end of the ship over the high-tension wires like a cow-pony going over a gate. The banked air pressure kicked up the tail, and the nose came down and hit the ground on the other side of the wires, the rear car missing them by inches. Then the officers eased the ship up and kept her climbing steadily till we were out of trouble.

We were now safely on the way to New York, after the one moment of great danger on the whole trip. Because Eckener, in his desperate maneuvering to clear the wires, had jettisoned our water ballast, this time we had no supply of fresh water on board, so all the way across the United States, still thirsting under its Prohibition Law, we drank champagne in lofty disdain of water and the law. We washed ourselves in eau de cologne!

Crossing Arizona and New Mexico was one of the most beautiful parts of the whole journey. We were flying in cumulous clouds, the air was hot, and there were turbulent air currents. The colors of land and sky were intense, and the shadows of flying clouds gave the whole scene an air of gaiety. That afternoon we were over a desert landscape of tawny sand and cactus, with burning, flat-topped mesas marked out by deep blue shadows, when we saw a lone cowboy galloping ahead of us across the empty land. Just as we overtook him he turned in his saddle, drew his gun and fired a couple of bullets at the ship. The gesture startled us although we knew he couldn't hit us at that range.

As we came over Chicago, Detroit, and Cleveland in the dark, these cities put on splendid displays of lighting for us. Next day, on August 29, we reached New York shortly after sun-up, then turned south to Lakehurst, ending the trip in thirteen days and a few hours' flying time—twenty-one days and some hours in all, including stop-overs. Dr. Eckener had his new world record for circumnavigating the world, and had done it while his passengers enjoyed all the comforts of an ocean liner. The whole trip had been a most enjoyable vacation for me.

19

Antarctic Reprise

I had just a few hours in New York that day after stepping from the *Graf Zeppelin* in Lakehurst, and then I was off by train the same evening for Cleveland, where I was scheduled to witness the national air races. So it was in that city on August 30, 1929, away from the publicity and crowds of New York, that I was married to Suzanne Bennett, my fiancée for the past year. Suzanne and I had first met during the New York reception given Ben Eielson and me in the summer of 1928, and throughout the past year she had given in, with great understanding and good humor, to my way of roaming from one end of the world to the other—and around it—in the course of my professional activity. An accomplished actress of the New York stage, Suzanne was Australian by birth and had studied at the University of Melbourne before coming to the United States. We hit it off together from the start, and so it had been a somewhat sad departure for me in September the year before when I had sailed to the Antarctic without her. Suzanne's words of adieu on that occasion, incidentally, were those of a farewell song which she sang over the wireless for me, and which we picked up while plowing southward in the Atlantic Ocean.

My arrangements were already well advanced for the second season's work in the Antarctic with the two planes we had left there, and it was therefore not long after Suzanne and I were married that I said the first of many good-bys to my new bride. A short while later I was off again for Montevideo to rendezvous with the whaling fleet.

When the Hearst executives had asked how much more money

I wanted for this season's work in the Antarctic which Mr. Hearst was expecting to finance for me, I told them that he had already given me all I needed. He had paid me $25,000 the year before, but now I discovered that he had supposed it would cover only one season. I said I considered he had paid me for exclusive news of my Antarctic work, no matter whether I spent one season or a dozen in the South. The British Government had lent me a ship, and with my planes already on Deception Island and my instruments and equipment remaining from previous expeditions, plus the assistance of the whalers, I believed I could work another season without additional money.

Ben Eielson, my stalwart colleague of three seasons in the Arctic and one in the Antarctic, did not go with me this year. He and Joe Crosson were both flying with the Alaskan Airways. Eielson loved the Arctic, and though he had done marvelous work in the South, he was never at home there as he was in the North.

Ben sent me a pilot named Parker Kramer to take his place. Kramer had flown in high latitudes and once, when attempting to reach Denmark from the Western Hemisphere, he had been forced down in Greenland and had to abandon the plane and walk 70 miles for help—a major feat for a man inexperienced in Arctic conditions. A year later, he again set his course for Denmark, and this time had a forced landing on the north coast of Labrador, again walking out.

Kramer was a good man and a fine pilot, but as it turned out he had very little chance to show what he could do while he was with me, because, as he was my more experienced pilot, I always left him at the base, ready to take charge in case Al Cheesman and I were lost.

It was Joe Crosson who had suggested I telegraph Cheesman, then a pilot with a commercial flying company in Canada, saying that Al Cheesman could probably recommend to me a pilot experienced in low-temperature flying. Cheesman answered that he could indeed recommend another man, but was willing to take the job himself. I looked up his record and the other man's and found they were both fine pilots. Because Cheesman was on the way to a big position with his company, I did not like to ask him to leave, so I wired him I would hire the other man. Cheesman pocketed the telegram, got a six-month's leave of absence from his company, and came down to meet me in New York. He turned out to be as fine a pilot and companion as one could wish for.

When we left Montevideo with the whalers, aboard the *Hektoria* again, I was hoping to find normal weather in the Antarctic, with ice solid enough to serve as a landing field for the planes, but as we approached Deception Island we saw no sign of ice at all. The previous year had been unaccountably warm, yet we had encountered pack ice 300 miles north of Deception. Now the sea was open, and the ice in the harbor even thinner than in 1928.

We found the planes in perfect condition, not even covered with snow. In a few days we had them ready to fly, and with a light load, Cheesman and I took off from our rough-but-ready runway and flew south to scout for sea ice. We were amazed to find the edge of the pack lay as much as 300 miles south of the island. This meant the floating icefield had receded about 600 miles since the previous year, and the weather was still inexplicably warm. In 1928 the unusual warmth had broken the ice loose from the polar icecap and sent it drifting northward. The continuing warmth had now melted the floating bits and the great mass of ice at the South Pole was still diminishing in size.

Thinking back on it later, I believed that this unusual phenomenon may have had a long-range effect on climatic conditions throughout the world, or may have been somehow related to them. This 600-mile retreat of the ice in the Antarctic summer (our winter) of 1929–1930 was followed by the memorable drought in the summer of 1930, during which many parts of the United States, for example, saw the ground turn as dry and hard as any season in memory.

The lack of ice left us unable to establish a base anywhere within flying distance of Deception Island. I had had this possibility in mind when, as a precaution, I arranged to borrow the steamer *William Scoresby* from the British Colonial Office, and we could do nothing more until she arrived.

We were in daily radio communication with San Francisco, from which point the station operators sent us the general news of the world every morning, and we sent a dispatch every night. One morning early in November, they sent us the startling news that Ben Eielson was lost in the Arctic. I had every bulletin about Eielson sent us immediately. A dispatch came every few hours, day and night, at first, then less and less frequently as the mystery of his fate deepened. Those of us who knew him tried to keep our hopes up, but as waiting days turned to weeks we were prepared for the worst. At length it came—Ben's plane was found smashed near the Siberian coast, on Bering Strait, and some days later his body was recovered.

Eielson and I together had seen, in the North and in the South, more than half a million square miles of the earth's surface that no other human eyes had ever seen. We had flown 5,000 miles on a straight line over unknown coastlines and seas and had added literally hundreds of terrain features to the charts and maps of the known world.

None of these would have been known so soon but for Ben Eielson's superb mastery of his job, his cool head, and his gallant spirit. He was a splendid companion, as well as an expert pilot, whose personality had helped me as much as his professional skill. He was a sincerely modest man who did his work for the work's sake entirely, but it made him the hero of hundreds of thousands of boys and won him the respect and admiration of older people everywhere in the world. Eielson will live in exploring history as long as men fly over the earth. Typically, he died while trying to effect the rescue of a fur-trading ship caught in the ice. His death was a great loss to aviation and to everyone who knew him. It was a great loss to me.

Al Cheesman and I continued making short flights from Deception Island, mapping the land within a radius of a few hundred miles, until the *William Scoresby* arrived in December. Then, with one plane on the steamer deck, we sailed down to Port Lockroy, on the west side of Graham Land, an Antarctic harbor well known to whalers.

We had fitted pontoons to the plane, and from this sheltered coastal indentation we made a number of flights over the mountains and along the coast, searching for a stretch of flat ice from which we could take off with a heavy load. At last, far to the south, we found a long, narrow bay where the ice seemed solid. So we came back to Port Lockroy, again put our plane on board the steamer, and set out to reach the bay.

The steamer pushed out to sea and turned south amid loose pack ice and huge bergs, many of which towered high above the steamer's masts. On the drifting floes we saw numbers of the giant Emperor penguins that live much farther south than the other species. These birds are more than 4 feet tall, weigh over a hundred pounds, and look like little men, all dressed up and somewhat pompous. It was a weird journey, southward in the Antarctic silence, with the glittering icebergs towering around us, and the multitudes of gnome-like creatures watching us from the ice floes.

Farther south, the pack ice thickened and it was difficult to work the steamer through it. Even after we reached the bay, the captain and crew worked for nearly twenty-four hours to push through the pack and gain the narrow strip of water by the land-fast ice. We reached it at midnight, and mooring the steamer to the ice, we went overboard to test the surface.

At that hour the temperature was low, and I found the ice firm though not very thick. Despite the risk, I believed that if the temperature remained down we might be able to take off, so we returned to the ship and started to get the plane ready. The pontoons were changed for skis and the plane swung over the side. To ease the task of hauling fuel from ship to plane, I had brought with us a baby Austin automobile—the first automobile ever brought to the Antarctic. We had fitted it specially for work in the snow with eight wheels, bound together by chains, so as to give it maximum traction and bearing surface. It was quite frankly an experiment, but we found it worked quite well at Deception Island, where we had used it carrying gasoline and supplies.

While Cheesman and I went over the plane, the little car was making trips back and forth between us and the steamer. The penguins flocked curiously around us in great numbers to watch us and the car, getting in the way just like a human crowd.

But to our great chagrin, the temperature began rising rapidly as we worked. The crust of snow on the ice began to melt, and the car was soon down to the axles in watery slush. Half a dozen times it had to be jacked out, and this delayed the loading. By ten o'clock the ice itself was honeycombed. Even the men were falling through it here and there, so that it was not safe to bring the Austin out again. Just as the car was swung aboard the steamer someone shouted that the ice under the plane was bending. We rushed to unload it as quickly as possible and, keeping the men away from it, we pulled it back to safety. The ice was stretching like rubber under the skis before we got the tackle fastened to hoist it aboard. By noon the temperature had risen to 51 degrees, the highest ever recorded in the Antarctic, to our knowledge. Even the penguins stood around panting.

I was greatly disappointed, because we had hoped with skis to be able to take off with a big load of gasoline and make a long flight southward. But it was fortunate that we didn't start that day, for before nightfall the astonishing warmth ended in a violent storm which lasted three days. Had we succeeded in taking off that morning we would never have been able to get safely back on board the steamer with the plane, nor could we have landed on the ice. Furthermore, I doubt if there was a safe landing place anywhere within a radius of flight, unless possibly on some unknown stretch of the Antarctic continent.

The ice around us was broken up by the storm, and the season was now so far advanced that we knew it would not freeze solidly again until April or May. So we pushed out into the pack ice once more and steamed 400 miles farther south. By this time we were far from any known territory, and our only hope was to find a stretch of solid ice or smooth water from which we could make a flight.

Eventually we came to open sea and moored to a convenient iceberg. We knew we were far from land, for our instruments showed that the water at that point was more than 6,000 feet deep, with wide ocean swells which made the use of a seaplane extremely dangerous. Kramer and Cheesman were nevertheless eager to make an attempt, though I believe that they did not fully realize how dangerous it would be. Not only was the take-off doubtful, but flying over open water and loose pack ice meant we would find no landing place in case of engine trouble. Even if by a miracle we came down in a patch of water, we could not possibly reach solid ice or return to the ship. We might find some game on the ice or contrive to exist on our emergency rations until the ice froze in the fall, but at best we would be in an extremely perilous position.

I refused to attempt a flight from that point, and the *William Scoresby* turned to the south and then westward, following the edge of the loose ice pack. After some days we had a few hours' fine weather, when we were directly north of Charcot Land, which was on the maps as part of the Antarctic continent. Here, the water conditions being somewhat safer, I decided to fly south, pick up the edge of the coastline at the point where Eielson and I had charted it the year before, then follow it westward along the south side of the Pacific Ocean.

I had my moments of doubt about that take-off from the sea, especially since a breeze picked up as we were getting ready. But I had given my assent, so Al and I took our places in the plane and shoved off from the mother ship. As we warmed up the engine, the seaplane rocked and rolled in the water, responding both to the swell beneath the pontoons and to the breeze as it caught the Vega's wings and fuselage. Al let the motor run with a roar and the plane picked up speed, springing from wave to wave like a hunted kangaroo. The pounding of the pontoons on the water sounded like artillery fire, and the light plane seemed to buck on the sea like a thing run wild. There was a shift to a rapid tattoo, as if someone were beating on giant drums beneath us—then the thrill of soaring smoothly upward, leaving the waves and the *William Scoresby* behind and below us.

Storm clouds were rising in the north behind the steamer, and we found in flying away from it that we lost sight of it almost immediately. An hour after we started, we began to encounter snow squalls coming down from the south. Though we flew around many of them, the weather closed in entirely before we reached Charcot Land.

It was impossible to see more than a few feet through the swirl of snow, so we were forced down to within a few feet of the loose ice floating on the sea, and at an altitude of perhaps 50 feet we flew against the storm for some time, trusting we would not strike an iceberg, and hoping to sight land. It was impossible to steer a straight course against the violence of the blizzard. Because we knew that Charcot Land was mountainous and even at sea-level we could not see more than a few yards, there was danger of crashing into a mountain. Reluctantly, I told Cheesman to turn back. The disappointment was painful, but just as the plane came around we caught a glimpse of a mountainside through the storm. Two or three minutes' delay in turning would have meant a crash.

I was not sure we could find the ship after leaving it several hundred miles behind and dodging so many snow squalls. If it had been within the ice pack, and therefore against a white background, it would have been easier to find. But against gray clouds and sea, it could not be seen more than six or eight miles, even when we got clear of the snowstorm. I do not know how Cheesman felt, but I was relieved when at last we saw the steamer ahead and still had gasoline enough to reach her.

With the ship, we moved farther westward, stopping from time to time to make another short flight. Often when a heavy sea was running we were able to take off from the shelter of an iceberg. In these flights we discovered that Charcot Land is not a part of the mainland, but is a small group of islands. These and other islands were located and mapped, and several hundred miles of coastline explored.

When flying over open water we often saw blue whales and killer whales beneath us. When we flew over ice we saw millions of penguins in the rookeries on the mountains and a few of them on the ice, but from the air, we never saw the front of an Emperor penguin. Long before we could see them, they had heard the roar of our engine and perhaps seen the orange plane in the sky, and were running for their lives. So far as I could see, not one ever stopped to look behind him.

After each flight, we steamed farther westward, and beyond Peter I Island we found that the edge of the ice pack turned sharply south. At about longitude 100 degrees, we were farther south than any other ship had ever been, but from this point we were able to make only one flight.

With Cheesman at the controls, we took off and came to solid ice only a few minutes before meeting a snowstorm. Flying a considerable distance into the storm, and not able to see any trace of land, with barely enough fuel to reach the ship, we were forced to turn back. From then on we were unable to get into the air again, because of storms and the tumult of the sea. Several times when a few hours of clear weather did interrupt the storms, we spent these hours trying to take off from the shelter of an iceberg. But the ocean swells never had time to subside between storms, and there was always a cross-sea running behind the berg and a choppy sea on the other side. We almost pounded the floats to pieces trying to get into the air. At such times, the sides of the wooden-framed Lockheed would heave like the ribs of a panting athlete, as the pontoons struck the waves in the attempt to take off. We would keep at it until the pontoons or bracing wires were strained, then go back to the ship, reset them, and make another attempt. But we were never able to get away before another storm came down.

At last the *William Scoresby* had barely enough fuel to reach Deception Island, so we were obliged to turn back and wind up our work for that season. Our faithful Lockheed-Vegas were brought to Buenos Aires and sold to the Argentine Government.

Returning to America, I once more turned my attention from the Antarctic to the Arctic—and also switched from planes to submarines. I was, however, happy to be able to pay my last respects to a great aviator before I began my *Nautilus* adventure. With the help of the Detroit Aviation Society, I was able to present to the Eielson Memorial Committee the fuselage and engine of the first plane in which he and I had flown together on so many historic flights—the single-engined Fokker, known as the *Alaskan*. I had kept it stored in Seattle, and now had it shipped by train to Bismarck, North Dakota, where it takes its place in the museum room that has become a monument to the memory of Carl Ben Eielson.

20

First Submarine under the Ice

I had started for the Antarctic in 1929, so soon after my marriage that upon my return, Suzanne and I decided we had a wedding trip coming to us. Appropriately enough for me, we boarded the *Graf Zeppelin* at Lakehurst on June 2, 1930, and flew as regular passengers serenely across the Atlantic to Europe, where we spent a happy month as guests of Lincoln Ellsworth at his magnificent Swiss castle, Schloss Lenzburg.

It was during this leisurely break in my accustomed hurry-up routine that Ellsworth and I planned my next project in exploration, and perhaps the most ambitiously revolutionary of all. Ellsworth was fifty years old by this time, but appeared much younger than his years. Born into a well-to-do family, he had turned his back on ease and comfort to concentrate on engineering in the wilds of Canada, Alaska, and South America. Later he had directed his energies into aviation, had flown in the Arctic with Amundsen, and in 1926, had been one of the backers of Amundsen and Nobile when they flew the *Norge* across the North Pole. When I had seen the *Norge* flying over Point Barrow, Ellsworth was aboard her. We had like interests and ambitions, and so formed a natural partnership in our scheme to carry into reality my long dream of exploring beneath the Arctic ice pack in a submarine.

I was not drawn to the idea as a stunt, but as part of my over-all plan for the advancement of scientific research in the polar regions —in particular the establishment of weather stations. It was in this light that I had discussed it with Stefansson as early as 1913.

Although it was now generally believed that there was no land in the great unexplored areas around the Pole, actually the paths taken by Peary, by the *Norge,* by Ben Eielson and myself marked out fairly narrow ribbons of known area cutting across the still, vast, unknown polar sea. Ellsworth and I planned to equip a submarine for under-the-ice travel, and criss-cross the unexplored areas of the Arctic between Spitsbergen, Northern Greenland, the Pole, the north Siberian coast, and Alaska. If we should find land, well and good; if not, we would experiment to see whether a submarine could serve as a floating weather station and keep in radio contact with nearby North America, Europe, and Asia.

Perhaps because the romantic fiction writer, Jules Verne, had written in fanciful manner about Captain Nemo sailing his submarine *Nautilus* under the Arctic ice, many otherwise open-minded people scoffed at my project as a wild dream. A conversation I engaged in one day at the Explorers Club in New York went something like this:

"Wilkins, you're daft. In the first place your men will freeze to death, or you'll run into an iceberg and knock a hole in the vessel. It will be dark beneath the ice and you'll never find your way. The ice is hundreds of feet thick and too deep in the water to let a submarine get by, and you won't be able to come up for air."

"Not quite so fast," I replied. "You say the men will freeze to death. Remember that a submarine travels in water, and so long as the medium through which you travel is water, how can it be colder than water? So how would we freeze to death?"

"Well, the icebergs?"

"Ah ... but there is not one single iceberg in the whole Arctic basin. Did you ever read about one having been seen there? To be sure there are ice floes and the Arctic ice pack. But icebergs, no!"

"Is that so?" was the reply. "I guess I haven't read about any icebergs right in the middle of the Arctic Ocean. But I thought that if they are found in the Atlantic, they naturally must have come from the Arctic Ocean."

"Your icebergs mostly come from the glaciers on the Greenland coast."

"Well, anyway, the ice is hundreds of feet thick, and you can't get beneath it!"

"Who said it's hundreds of feet thick?" I inquired. "All Arctic travelers—and I happen to be one—have reported that away from the coast the ice is rarely more than ten or twelve feet thick. And we'll not be traveling along the coast."

"But you will get lost. It will be so dark that you won't be able to navigate."

"Surely," I said, "if I could find Spitsbergen from an airplane after traveling 2,200 miles over an unmapped ocean at 100 miles an hour, I will be able to find my way if I am traveling at less than ten miles an hour and coming up often to fix my position."

"But how are you going to come up to the surface?"

"There are open leads, thousands of them, but where we find none I plan to drill a hole up through the ice and put a pipe up to bring in fresh air, or even to allow the men to get to the surface if the pipe is big enough. Men drill thousands of feet *down* to get oil; surely we can drill a mere fifteen feet *up* through the ice."

"Ah, that's all very well. To talk about it is one thing, but to do it will be a different matter."

Fortunately, my plan did not seem impractical to everyone. I managed to get the United States Navy to let me have, for the token price of $1, an old submarine that was due to be scrapped —not because it was unserviceable, but because according to the London Naval Treaty, they were pledged to dismantle some of the ones they had. I had been trying for a long time to get such a vessel, and I was elated.

I expected to spend a lot of money adapting it to our special purpose, but just to get the hull was a good start. I set about having it fixed in the Philadelphia Navy Yard, to be ready by December so that we would have about six months in which to test it and get to our jumping-off point for the Arctic. At least, that was my plan. But December came and still the most important work of outfitting the ship had only just begun. There ensued one delay after another, expense after expense, and it was March before we sailed down the Delaware River to the oil refinery at Marcus Hook, there to load our tanks with fuel. But hardly was this done when we found our engine was not in good working order, so we were dragged by the nose, a lamentable way to start, down through Delaware Bay and around the New Jersey shore up to the Brooklyn Navy Yard, where the submarine was destined for a complete overhaul and refitting.

Here beneath the shadow of the Brooklyn Bridge, on the morning of March 24, 1931, before a crowd of 800 spectators,* we christened her *Nautilus,* in memory of Captain Nemo's legendary ship. Suzanne was on hand to do the honors, but because of Prohibition we had to do without the traditional champagne. Instead, she performed the ceremony with a silver bucket of cracked ice. I had persuaded Jean Jules Verne, grandson of the great French writer, to come to America from France for the ceremony, and of course the man I had chosen as commander of the vessel, Sloan Danenhower, and the crew were there. In our honor, and symbolizing the international character of our Arctic enterprise, the Navy Yard Band played the national anthems of Britain, France, and the United States.

Two elder statesmen of the technical side of transportation were also on hand. One was my old friend Dr. Hugo Eckener, commander of the *Graf,* with whom I had tentatively discussed a rendezvous at the North Pole—the *Nautilus* to surface amid the ice and the *Graf* to be lowered to the floe, for an exchange of mail in a demonstration of man's complete mastery of the top of the world. The other old-timer was the gray-bearded naval architect, Simon Lake, now nearly sixty-five, who had designed and built the first practical submarines before the turn of the century. Many years before the christening day of our *Nautilus,* Simon Lake had smashed one of his submarines up through a foot of ice in Narragansett Bay to prove to skeptics of the United States Navy that it could be done.

Now he stood silent, too overcome with emotion to speak, but

* Of whom I was one. L. T.

I knew he took a keen pride in the accomplishments of the undersea craft of which he, more than any other man in the world, was the father.

Sloan Danenhower, who was to command the *Nautilus*, was someone quite special. A couple of years older than I, graduate of the United States Naval Academy in 1907, Sloan was the son of the heroic John Danenhower who had survived the tragic wreck of the Jeannette expedition fifty years earlier, so he had grown up in an atmosphere of Arctic lore. He had known submarine work almost from the beginning, and following World War I he had resigned from the Navy Submarine Service to join Simon Lake as a designer and builder of undersea craft. I was lucky to have him in command of my ship.

The *Nautilus* was 175 feet long, weighed 560 tons, and could travel 7,000 miles on the surface without refueling. Submerged, drawing her power from huge Exide batteries big enough to supply the entire electricity load of a small city, she could travel 125 miles before we should have to resurface to recharge the batteries with our Diesel engines. She was equipped with two 500-horsepower Diesels, and a new 15-kilowatt hand-starting Diesel generating set. Her air capacity was estimated to be adequate for supplying twenty men for five days, and her hull was designed to withstand pressure at 200 feet below sea level.

The work in Brooklyn included building a special superstructure on the vessel, with long runners to allow us to slide along the undersurface of the ice. We knew this undersurface would be rough, but no one could say exactly how rough—whether there would be bulges of a couple of feet which our runners would easily fend off from our hull, or whether perhaps there might be long solid projections into which our nose might smash with great force and possible damage. To prepare against this, we installed a pneumatic shock-absorber—but we still planned to creep along until we had the feel of the bottom of the Arctic pack.

One of our key weapons against being caught under the ice was our big ice drill, with which I planned to cut a hole upward through the ice to fresh air, and in that way obtain the ventilation so that we could run the engines to recharge our batteries. I had several sections for this drill so that the leading end of a second one could be attached to the tail end of another, and we would thus be able to reach the open air even if the ice should be considerably thicker than the 12 to 15 feet I supposed was general in heavy floe ice.

In addition we had twin 5,000-watt headlights with which to light up the underside of the ice for a look with our collapsible periscope, flexible radio antennae, a trap door in the bottom through which we could safely lower instruments to the ocean floor and recover them, and the like. With all our special gear, quarters for our volunteer crew were cramped. But they were all experienced submariners, and, after all, they did not expect the comforts of the *Graf Zeppelin*.

On a test run from the Brooklyn Navy Yard up the Hudson to Yonkers, we used our electric motors for the first time, but our Diesels got their first real test when we went farther upstream for fresh-water diving trials. In some place the water under the Arctic ice is fresh, and Captain Danenhower wanted to make sure he knew how the *Nautilus* was going to behave when submerged under such conditions.

We learned considerable from these preliminary tests, and after making a few adjustments, we steamed down the Hudson again, past the skyline of New York City, on the first leg of our great adventure. It was an unforgettable sensation to view New York's "topless towers" under such circumstances, for none of us knew for certain that we would ever see them again.

Our crew was a small one, but it had been carefully chosen from among many applicants. As is usual in such ventures, we were flooded with applications from self-servers, publicity-seekers, and cranks. One man, for instance, proposed that he be set loose from the *Nautilus* in the Arctic "in a steel cylinder with a two-year supply of food. When you are lost with the *Nautilus* I will drift with the currents until I am free from the ice and am picked up by a whaler. In that way I will be able to tell the world what happened." Others offered their services for fantastic salaries, readily admitting they had no skills to offer. To balance these, however, we had the solid backing of officials of the Carnegie Institution, the American Geographical Society, the Oceanographic Institution at Woods Hole, Massachusetts, and other responsible bodies.

One of the friendly greetings I appreciated most came from Walt Disney in Hollywood. Walt sent me a delightful colored cartoon showing Mickey Mouse waving hello from the conning tower of a watermelon-shaped midget submarine amid sugary ice floes, while astonished fish, an octopus and a walrus looked on in surprise.

The trip from New York to New London, Connecticut, went smoothly, as did the voyage from New London to Provincetown, Massachusetts, at the tip of Cape Cod. Here at the edge of the open ocean we said farewell to our friends, wives, and sweethearts and on June 4 turned the nose of our tiny ship out into the Atlantic.

Although we were well behind schedule for a summer cruise in the Arctic, our hearts beat high as we churned away from American soil and realized that at last we were on our own. As a matter of fact, the Atlantic crossing was to be the most dangerous as well as the most discouraging part of the expedition.

We were a thousand miles at sea when trouble started. The wind began to blow and the billows rose higher and higher as the *Nautilus,* true to her "pig-boat" type, simply wallowed in the waves. The indicators on our inclinometers rolled through 94 degrees, 47 degrees to one side, then 47 to the other. The oil in the tanks raced from side to side, but still flowed into the engines, which throbbed evenly for several hours more, pushing us forward at a speed of 10 knots. Then mechanical difficulties silenced one of the Diesels. On one side we still had power, but at our reduced speed we could no longer keep ahead of the storm. It nipped our heels and then swallowed us.

Still the port engine held, fed by a steady stream of oil, until one fuel tank was exhausted. When the fuel lines were switched, trouble started. Slaps and bangs in the engine room indicated erratic feed. We realized there was water in the fuel. We were puzzled for a moment, until someone remembered that in the tank we were using there was a large sea valve used for diving purposes. When the valve was tried, its control wheel spun idly on the shaft, indicating the connection with the valve had broken, thus leaving the valve partly open. So sea water had leaked in and the lower portion of the oil had been thoroughly mixed with the brine. The standpipe through which the oil was drawn reached almost to the bottom of the tank, so it was pulling up this impure mixture instead of the oil on top.

The pipe was in a position far from the manhole and only at the risk of being drowned in oil was one of the engineers able to reach the pipe and hacksaw it in two near the surface. From the top of the tank clear oil flowed, and once more the engine ran smoothly.

But our trouble was not only with the engines. Due probably to age and to crystallization of metals, the wires on the armature of the motor behind our one good engine went to pieces. Showers of sparks shot from the commutator and threatened to set fire to the ship. At that time, we were thankful for a good, reliable Diesel oil, which does not easily catch fire. Only a mixture made to its specifications prevented us from being blown sky-high.

It was then that Captain Danenhower decided to send an S.O.S. We were not entirely sure we would need assistance, and believed that with our one good engine we might complete the journey across the Atlantic, but the fact was that should our engine stop, we would have no motor with which to start it.

The American battleships *Arkansas* and *Wyoming* answered our call and came racing to our side. After some skillful maneuvering on the part of the *Wyoming*, we made our pennant fast to her tow line and she dragged us the rest of the way to Ireland, with the help of the Irish tug, *Morsecock*. At Cobh we effected temporary repairs and believing we could proceed under our own power to Plymouth, England, we refilled our fuel tanks. However, it was then discovered that our repaired motor would not start the engine, and we would have to be towed to Plymouth.

In drydock at Devonport, the big British Navy station adjoin-

ing Plymouth, we discovered and repaired the leaky valve that
had allowed the sea water to enter our fuel tanks. On July 15,
while this and other necessary repairs were being made, the Prince
of Wales stopped in at the dock on a surprise visit to the *Nautilus*,
and I took him for an inspection tour through the craft. He shook
hands all around with the crew and wished us well when he left
—though I cannot imagine his thoughts regarding our standards
of neatness. We were, after all, a scientific party in an experimental
craft equipped for our work, not the spit-and-polish type of crew
and ship I suppose the Prince had usually seen.

Our repairs finally completed, we headed out into the Channel,
and thence into the North Sea, making good time with both engines running again and fine weather. Arriving at Bergen, Norway,
on August 1, we hastened to fill our fuel tanks to the limit—and
then found a leaky hull fitting under water.

This presented a problem that was finally solved by borrowing
a barge from the Norwegian Navy. We pumped oil into this barge
until our vessel was raised enough to allow repairs, after which the
oil was repumped into our tanks.

Upon reaching Tromsö, farther north up the coast of Norway,
our tanks were again filled to the brim, but before we could leave
on the last leg of our journey to Spitsbergen there was one rather
long job in the engine room which required an uninterrupted ses-
sion. I knew that as long as we were in port among throngs of
curious onlookers, the engineers would not be able to work un-
interruptedly, so we put out to a sheltered part of the fiords and,
safe from visitors and strong currents, the engineers worked while
we drifted.

At length we were ready for the trip to Spitsbergen where we
again topped off with fuel. At last, on August 19, we were clear
of Spitsbergen and at the pearly gates of the Arctic. Out of the
fog loomed the fenders of the great pack—huge, rough lumps of
ice the size of summer cottages, and widely scattered.

Delay after delay, due entirely to mechanical breakdowns, had
so eaten into our time that even before we reached the Arctic ice
we should have been heading homeward. However, this particular

season favored us because the air temperatures were still well above the freezing point, and I was confident we stood a good chance of reaching the Pole. The temperature of the Arctic salt water, 2 degrees Fahrenheit below the freezing point of fresh water, did not affect the efficiency of our fuel or lubricants.

Upon reaching the polar ice we suffered the most crushing disappointment of this entire maddening trip, one that nearly wrecked all our hopes for penetrating beneath the pack. When Danenhower set the controls in submerging position, the ship simply did not respond properly. We came to a halt on the surface and sent our best diver overside—quite incidentally, this being the first time, to our knowledge, that a man in a diving suit had gone down in Arctic waters. He came to the surface with the heartbreaking news that somewhere in the journey our diving rudders had been lost. Now we were in a submarine that had come 5,000 miles to a point within 600 miles of the North Pole, and was no longer submersible!

My log for August 23, 1931, tells the story this way:

All set for diving as soon as conditions improved, when Danenhower, looking through clear water over the stern, noticed something missing from behind propellers. Closer inspection showed that it was the diving rudder. The vessel was put in the lee of the ice. It was late last night when diver Frank Crilley, who bravely volunteered for the job, was lowered between ice fragments to inspect the vessel's stern. He was down for several minutes. Then reported that both sides diving rudder gone. But steering rudder intact and in good order.

Is mystery what became of diving rudders and how they could have left ship without damaging steering rudder. Fact remains they are gone, but ordinary steering gear is safe. Crilley, warmly dressed, down only for a few minutes, and after stiff bracer from medical comforts, said that diving in Arctic waters was not so terrifying as it looked. But unable to see behind him through the helmet, he had not known that a huge cake of ice narrowly missed crushing him against side of deck. Meyers and Clark, who were his tenders, hauled him clear. He reached deck in safety.

After considering all factors involved, Danenhower and I decided that in spite of the lost rudders we would attempt to push
under the ice. Then it was discovered that one cell jar in the
after battery room had cracked. Fumes of acidy gas quickly filled
the boat. Blumberg, Royster, and Holland, three electricians, soon
located the trouble, drained the cell, and added chemicals to nullify
the action of the acid on the hull. This cell must have cracked
through the rapid rise in temperature, from almost freezing to
considerable heat due to rapid charging.

The dangers all around were greater than we had intended they
should be, because it was now so extremely late in the season.
Still, we were determined to carry on as best we could. Great ice
cakes were pounding all about us, so we had to make for more
open water. The wind picked up to a gale and the ice pack was
moving so fast that our passage was difficult and slow. There
were times when I could get out on the ice myself and, using a
small boat we carried aboard, row far enough off from the *Nautilus*
to get some good photographs of her lying among the ice cakes
like a peculiar kind of hump-back whale. During this waiting
period, too, Dr. Harold Sverdrup, the chief of our scientific staff
was at work with the instruments, making soundings, bringing up
samples of the ocean floor, recording the temperature of the ocean
at various depths, and so forth.

A typical day in the last week in August found me writing in
my log:

> We hove to near edge this morning hoping to submerge,
> steady our craft for gravity measurements and take deep ocean
> sounding. Water hereabouts over 2,000 meters deep but storm
> increased, drove ice down upon us. We had to move to open
> water. In freezing cold high wind, was miserable work on deck
> from which all shelter has been removed for diving. Ice clung
> to deckrunners, periscopes and tops of conning towers. Ice
> even formed on floors of living compartments and fresh-water
> pipes froze solid. To add to our discomfort, rivet started in the
> diving compartment. The icy water seeps slowly through.
> We are safe away from the edge of heaving pack ice either

at sea or if we had been further into the floes. But so far the edge has been so much in motion from wind, sea, and current it is impossible go far under. We are moving slowly up and down under power electric motors. We roll heavily in trough of sea. Uncomfortable almost as when crossing Atlantic. Fog, snowstorms, often close right down upon us, but occasionally we see edge of pack. Tomorrow we hope for better luck and weather so we can push nose once more northward under moving pack ice.

Captain Danenhower agreed that having come so far, we should at least try to get under the ice somehow and try the experiment which we had been so eagerly awaiting. The next day the Arctic sea was calm. There was a fresh northeasterly breeze blowing, but it was tranquil in the lee of the pack, the floes were quiet, and the only sounds to be heard were the mewing of the sea gulls and the occasional splash of a seal, as we lay between the floes ready for our first Arctic dive.

This was to be our test—for us and for our theories of under-ice navigation. Had the experts figured our stability correctly, or would we come up under the floes and capsize, as some wiseacres had warned? Danenhower was not sure whether the vents would freeze open and prevent our unwatering our ballast tanks. Nor did he know whether our air lines would congeal and prevent our blowing water out.

Every one of us aboard the *Nautilus* knew that owing to the loss of our diving rudder we were badly handicapped in handling the submarine. We could not control the vessel closely under way, nor could we rise quickly, "porpoise," as submariners call it. To go under the ice at all we had to depend on the inclination of the submarine by the bow and the thrust. For our initial experiment we had therefore picked a floe which was not too wide or too deep. Beneath us the bottom lay 2,000 fathoms down.

Danenhower gave the order, "Flood the main ballast." We took turns watching the water line rise up to meet our eyes through the conning tower eyeports. And what a water line! It was dotted closely with ice cakes and floes of fantastic shape and size, delineating every conceivable form—minarets, domes, majestic cathedrals, and geometrical blocks.

I could see a beautiful coloring in the crystal-clear blue water. We took our time settling down ("trimming," the old submarine hands say), and after jockeying her into what Danenhower thought was the right trim, with the bow down by two degrees and our heavy glass eyeports well away, he gave the order, "Ahead!"

All was quiet in the boat, not a sound above the steady hum of the motor and the occasional sharp click of the electric steering gear as we steadied on our course. Her bow cleaved the water like a gigantic wedge, and as we neared the floe we all unconsciously braced ourselves for a shock. Crunch! Bang! Crack! She was under! Down by the bow 3 degrees, then 4½, 6, 7½!

"Stop the motor!" Danenhower called. Silence, and she came to rest.

What a beautiful sight greeted our gaze through the eyeports! As far as one could see through the crystal blue water stretched the roughened, flat undersurface of the floe, with occasional small peaks and valleys. There was a great variety of coloring as the light changed with the passage of clouds above the floe. No human eyes had ever before looked on this sight.

At last we were under the Arctic ice, with our depth gauge reading 37 feet. Since our depth gauge before going under read 20 feet, the floe above us must be about 17 feet thick. We were under all right, for the first time in history, but could we get out again? The ice was too thick to think of breaking through it. Could we back out clear into the open water? With our periscopes frozen and fogged, and without our diving rudder, we dared not keep on going ahead because if we sank too deep for our hull strength, we could not blow our tanks and we might come up against the 17-foot thick ice in an unstable condition, which would capsize us. Nor could we rely on our ice drill, which had somehow got jammed. There was no other way than to try to back out from our present position.

"Full astern!" Danenhower ordered. We waited breathless moments, our eyes glued to the eyeports. Slowly, steadily, the fascinating undersea panorama glided by as the *Nautilus* picked up momentum and rose by the stern. 6½ degrees by the bow and 30-foot depth. Then, 5 degrees and 28 feet; 4 and 26, 3 and 24, 2 and 20, and suddenly brilliant sunlight flooded in through the dripping ports and we were up clear of the ice.

Our first Arctic dive had been accomplished. Our theory was correct—not only mine, but Danenhower's, Simon Lake's, Stefansson's, and others' who had faith in us. We had demonstrated that a submarine could operate against the surface of the ice with positive buoyancy.

Other dives were made in the next few days, and other conditions tried out with varying success, but no further dive could equal the thrill of our first Arctic plunge, which was made at about latitude 82, within 500 miles of the North Pole, and over nearly 2,000 fathoms of water at a temperature below freezing.

Nor did we spend all our time looking through the portholes. Our chief scientist, Sverdrup, collected many samples of the ocean bottom under the ice, and of the marine life at various depths. He also ascertained that there are four layers of water under the ice—a cold layer near the top, a warmer layer under that, then another cold layer, and finally another warm layer next to the surface of the earth itself.

But recognizing the lateness of the season and the fact that to do our work thoroughly and in safety we required a newly-equipped ship, we regretfully turned the *Nautilus* back toward Norway. Mechanical trouble with our engines and the loss of our diving rudders had prevented us from reaching our goal, but we had collected sufficient experience and knowledge to enable someone, some day, to complete a journey under the Arctic ice. During that first week in September, 1931, as we plowed our way back toward Norway, we speculated at length over the way it would be done, who would do it, and when. There was no doubt in my mind that ours was but the first of a great submarine fleet that would one day cruise at will beneath the Arctic ice cap, the shortest distance between the great American and Eurasian land masses.

21

The Search for Levanevsky

During the 1930's I went four times to the Antarctic with Lincoln Ellsworth, acting as his second-in-command, special press reporter, and chief of the base party aboard our ship whenever Ellsworth was off in the air with a pilot. Ellsworth had obtained a Norwegian ship, the *Fanefjord,* and rechristened her *Wyatt Earp,* after his boyhood hero. She was a small vessel but very sturdy, and proved herself a first-class ice ship in every way. In my months of duty aboard her in the frozen South, equipped with short-wave radio, a wonderfully adaptable seaplane and other equipment that had been developed in the twenty-odd years since I had sailed north with Stefansson aboard the *Karluk,* I saw telling evidence of the progress polar science had made in my own adult lifetime.

The *Wyatt Earp* was only 135 feet long, displacing 400 tons. She had a single deck, three masts and a cruising range of 900 miles. Built originally of pine and oak and launched in 1919, we had her sheathed with extra layers of oak and ¾ inch of armor plate. Her semi-Diesel engine gave her the power to break through many ice floes that would have stopped the *Karluk* and the *Hektoria.*

One reason why our work was so successful in these years, during which we mapped a great deal more of the Antarctic continent than had ever been seen before, was Ellsworth's unique Northrup seaplane, the *Polar Star,* equipped with wing flaps enabling it to land on the water at a speed of only 50 miles an hour. It could take off from water in a much shorter distance than that over which Al Cheesman and I had risked our necks in 1929.

It was a fine partnership we had, Lincoln Ellsworth and I, and together, using our own ship and the Northrup plane, with a 2,000-

mile range—about twice what Ben Eielson and I could attempt in our Lockheed-Vega—we did fine work on a bigger scale than was possible for me before. The star of the individual explorer operating with minimal equipment had set, and the day was dawning of the big expedition, financed by huge sums of money, with a supply line and trained men stretching from the frontier of the unknown all the way back to the sources of supply at home. In this period of transition, Ellsworth and I formed a kind of link between the old-school type of expedition and the new.

One experience during these years, not in the Antarctic, that left an unforgettable memory with me was crossing the Atlantic with Eckener once again, and with my wife, this time aboard the mighty *Hindenburg*. Her maiden voyage to America took place in May of 1936. As we drank champagne at her tables, slept comfortably at night in her berths, and admired the beauty of the New York skyline from her windows as we approached it, little did we dream that scarcely one year later she would come crashing down at Lakehurst in a searing hydrogen blast that marked the end of the airship era. When that tragedy did take place in 1937, I could not help thinking back to my carefree hours aboard her, and to the freak chance that had kept me from being aboard the R-38 when she had crashed in England sixteen years before.

The adventure that gripped my attention and energies most vitally at this time, however, began on August 15, 1937, when I was urgently asked by long-distance telephone to appear as quickly as possible at the Soviet Embassy in Washington. The Ambassador, Alexander Troyanovsky, was absent from the city, but his counselor and chargé d'affaires, Constantin Oumansky, was anxious to see me. I found Oumansky to be a short, dark-haired, intense man, with a precise command of idiomatic English. He told me without mincing words that his government was appealing to me to lead a search expedition in the Arctic for Sigismund Levanevsky and his five comrades, already two days overdue in Fairbanks from an over-the-Pole flight originating in Moscow. Oumansky had previously got in touch with Stefansson, at that time president of the Explorers Club in New York, and Stef had recommended me for the job. The Russians were searching on the European side of the Arctic; would I do the same from the Alaska side? Without hesitation, I agreed.

Levanevsky's ill-fated flight, starting August 12 from Schelkov Aerodrome near Moscow, followed by some weeks the brilliant success of two earlier Soviet flights from Moscow to the United States—both in single-engine planes. Pilot Chkalov and two crewmen first flew 5,200 miles over the Pole to Vancouver, Washington in mid-June. Then two weeks later, Pilot Gromov went all the way from Moscow to San Jacinto, California, setting a new nonstop record of 6,262 miles. These two, incidentally were the only trans-Arctic flights on record since Ben Eielson and I had made our big hop nine years earlier.

Levanevsky, sometimes called "the Soviet Lindbergh," had set out with five comrades in a huge, four-engine transport plane with a blue metal body and red wings. The Russians were testing it for a proposed trans-Arctic passenger route, and polar enthusiasts the world over were watching the experiment with keen interest. Levanevsky had radioed that he was passing over the Pole at 5:53 P.M. on August 13, and was later some 300 miles on the Alaskan side when his last complete message was received:

Message No. 19. Motor 34. Flying heavily
against 100-kilometer wind, losing altitude
from 6,000 meters to 4,300 meters.

When decoded, "motor 34" meant trouble with an engine, but operators receiving Levanevsky's transmissions never heard what the trouble was. Shortly after, a tantalizing fragment came in:

48—3,400.

Decoded, this meant, "We are going to land in. . . ." No one could tell if this meant the plane was going to land in a few minutes or in a few hours. But we knew by now that somewhere out there in the Arctic wastes he had come down. Whether he and his crew were alive on the ice awaiting help or had gone to the bottom of the sea, no man could tell.

A search was begun at once. Robert Randall, a pilot of the

Mackenzie River Air Service, started a flight along the Alaskan coast on August 14, landing and questioning every group of Eskimos he saw. Only one group, on Barter Island, off Alaska, reported a clue. These Eskimos had heard what they thought to be the roar of an outboard motor. They could see no sign of a boat, however, and as the noise lasted only a few minutes they paid no further attention to it. Following this report several American and Russian fliers searched the Alaskan mountains from the air, but without result.

There was only one type of plane in my opinion suitable for this search—a long-range flying boat. We discovered that such a boat was in New York, a Consolidated PBY type, with twin engines. It had recently been fitted out for an expedition to tropical New Guinea by Richard Archbold, a fellow-member of the Explorers Club with Stefansson and me. When asked for his craft in this life-and-death matter, Archbold generously consented, and arrangements were quickly made between Archbold and the Soviet Embassy for me to take over that plane.

Two of my companions on Antarctic expeditions immediately responded to my invitation to come along as pilots. They were Air Commodore Herbert Hollick-Kenyon of Toronto, who had flown across Antarctica with Ellsworth, and my old friend Al Cheesman. The two other members of our crew were Gerald Brown, an Australian, our engineer, and Ray Booth, a United States Navy veteran, our radio operator. I acted as navigator.

On August 17, we headed north. Crossing the bleak wastes of northern Canada, we flew over the little-known, low bush country toward the mouth of the Coppermine River, which empties into Coronation Gulf on the Arctic Ocean. This country is north of the spruce tree line, low and rugged and profusely studded with crystal clear lakes. We landed on one of them at nightfall, camped out for the night, and at daybreak were off again, cooking our breakfast on a primus stove in the rear cabin of the plane while in flight. After several hours flying above and below the clouds, we reached the village of Coppermine, a Hudson's Bay Company post about 90 miles north of the Arctic Circle.

Here we were able to purchase some supplies from the Hud-

son's Bay trader. The most treasured item I obtained was ten
pounds of dried caribou meat, which my friend Ole Andreasen
brought to me from his scanty supply. Andreasen had been with
Stefansson on the 1913–1915 expedition, and seeing him and his
Eskimo wife once more was like old times for me. We had both
found that dried caribou meat is most satisfying for chewing on
the trail. Some men prefer tobacco, but caribou meat is much
more sustaining.

The tanks of our machine carried 1,760 gallons of gasoline,
enough for 3,000 miles of flight, but we decided to load ten extra drums in the cabin of the plane, giving us 500 miles additional range. By August 22, four days after we had acquired the
plane in New York, we were ready to set out on our search over
the Arctic area. And truly this was to be history repeated, for
our first few hundred miles lay over the same area that Stefansson,
Natkusiak, myself and the others had crawled over at a snail's
pace long, long before.

Climbing above the clouds which blanketed Melville and Banks
Islands, we ran into what perhaps was the most dangerous experience we had throughout our search. Our Eskimo helpers had
filled the spare gasoline drums right up to the brim. When we
reached an altitude of 10,000 feet, the reduced air pressure caused
the gasoline to expand, and when I came astern from the navigator's cabin after two hours in the air, I found the rear cabin
floor covered 2 inches deep with gasoline. It was really miraculous
that the fumes had not already caused an explosion.

Hastily closing the cabin doors, which shut off the pilot's and
engineer's compartments, I sopped up the gasoline with old rags
and strung the rags from the ventilators at the rear of the plane.
After working for two hours, I finally had the gasoline evaporated.

We flew northwestward from Prince Patrick Island for 130
miles, but saw only a few patches of ice here and there. All else
was blanketed in fog and cloud. The ice we saw was much broken,
and the leads of open water were filled with fragments. Landing by any type of plane would have been dangerous. Mounting cloud banks finally forced us to return. We were out all night,

but nights are not dark at that time of year. During the flight we called Levanevsky by radio every half-hour and listened for his signals thirty minutes of the hour, but heard no sound from him.

In the evening of the next day, we set out again and landed in open water near Cape Russell, on Melville Island, to transfer fuel from our spare drums to the wing tanks. We continued on until we reached latitude 82 degrees north and longitude 147 west. At first, I was asked to search only as far as 82 degrees north, 148 degrees west, because Soviet fliers, working from Rudolph Island on the Siberian side and from Point Barrow on the west were to search other areas. Later I was asked to search as far north as 88 degrees north and between longitude 90 degrees and 153 degrees west.

Soon after we turned back, Coppermine radioed that ceiling there was zero, so we landed at Walker Inlet on the southeast side of Prince Patrick Island, to await clear weather. That day we had flown fifteen hours. The next day a snow storm detained us at anchor until late in the afternoon, and we finally flew back to Coppermine through the clouds, mostly depending on instruments.

The difficulties encountered with the weather during our first two flights pointed to the need for some sort of weather forecast, so as to prevent a great deal of useless flying. To reach the area where Levanevsky was last heard from we had to fly out 1,000 miles. It would have been useless to continue flying back and forth up to that area if we could not be reasonably sure the area itself was clear.

We radioed to the Soviet Embassy in Washington requesting further meteorological cooperation, and received immediate response. Not only the governments of the United States, Canada, and Russia but the meteorological bureaus of all other countries bordering the Arctic Ocean agreed to furnish reports having a bearing on Arctic conditions. Edward M. Vernon of the United States Weather Bureau was sent to Fairbanks to assist Michael V. Beliakov, the Soviet meteorologist, in correlating all the data and issuing to us a thirty-six-hour forecast of weather conditions over the whole of the polar area.

This was, I believe, the first time there had been such international cooperation in forecasting weather over the Arctic regions. We found that throughout our search the forecasts given by Beliakov, Vernon, and later by Mr. Thompson of the United States Weather Bureau, were remarkably accurate. What is more, we received extremely valuable information from the floating scientific station under Dr. Ivan Papanin, which the Russians had set up near the Pole—another of my dreams of long before carried out in practice. We also had reports from Spitsbergen, Greenland, Franz Josef Land, the New Siberian Islands, and Wrangel Island.

During these days of searching there were five of us in the plane, all keeping a keen look-out whenever conditions were favorable. I spent most of my time in the navigator's cockpit in the nose, wearing four-power spectacle binoculars. If any dark object or anything suspicious was observed, I would use a higher powered set for closer inspection. If we sighted the missing men, we had food, fuel, and a radio ready to drop to them by parachute. Then, if possible, I would have landed and picked them up at once, for they might be carried far away on the drifting ice before a rescue ship could reach the point where they were first seen.

Navigation over the ice proved difficult because of the erratic behavior of our four compasses, also due to frequent clouds and varying winds. Sometimes the compasses would set up a swinging motion, and when we took readings each would give a different one, sometimes differing as much as 40 degrees. This was due partly to the nearness of the North Magnetic Pole, which was only about 600 miles away.

We soon used up the Royal Canadian Air Force gasoline supply that had been deposited at Coppermine for just such an emergency as this, and switched our base to Aklavik, some 600 miles west of Coppermine. But I found it was not really suitable for an expeditionary base, so I decided to remain only long enough to fill our fuel tanks and then fly on west to Barter Island, where the Eskimos had heard what might have been the motor of Levanevsky's plane. We landed there on September 2 in rain and fog, a fog that continued for the next five days. At last we received a forecast of fair weather to the north, so we flew out through fairly stormy conditions for the first several hundred miles, before coming to clear weather in which we could observe the ice.

North of 82 degrees we began our intensive search and zigzagged back and forth over the area, moving northward as we did so. Our radio was in constant service, sending messages for Levanevsky or listening for an answer to our signals. But none was heard. Finally, with darkness, closing in, we turned back. The season for using flying boats was fast drawing to a close. At night, a thin skin of ice would form on the surface of the water. Ice and sleet would pile up on the wings and fuselage and remain fast even when the plane was at anchor.

We returned to Barter Island, but not until September 17 were we able to get away on our next flight north. Even then we had to take off in a howling gale, with snow and sleet obscuring all vision at a distance greater than 200 yards. We flew through these conditions almost 400 miles before coming to the clear weather—near 75 degrees—predicted by our meteorologists. This was an example of the accuracy and competency of the weather men. They had said we would find bad weather up to latitude 74 degrees. Within 20 miles of where they indicated, we flew from the snowstorm into sunshine. We continued flying to the north of 86 degrees, in alternately clear and cloudy weather, but finally thick clouds and ice on our wings forced us to turn back again.

With winter coming on, and a freeze-up likely at any time, it was too late to attempt any further flights with the flying boat, so we flew her back to New York. In all, we had covered more than 13,000 miles over the Arctic Ocean, constantly sending signals and listening for any sign from Levanevsky and his companions, but without result. Despite our discouragement, I realized from the first few days that I had never traveled with a more cheery crew.

The Soviet Embassy in Washington, still anxious to continue the search for the missing fliers as soon as winter conditions should permit it, bought for me the single-engine Bellanca flown by Dick

Merrill across the Atlantic and back in May, 1937, on the good-will flight for the coronation of King George VI. This plane was considerably smaller than our flying boat, and carried only two men at a time on long flights. But we put skis on her at Edmonton, and she was well adapted for our purposes because of her long cruising range.

Allan Dyne, engineer from the Canadian Airways, and W.R. Wilson, radio engineer of the Canadian Marconi Company, were engaged to replace Booth and Brown who could no longer continue with us. It was decided to continue our search right on through the Arctic winter, by the aid of moonlight. The moonlight in the Arctic, reflected by the snow and with the air free of dust, easily permits the reading of a newspaper. Furthermore, in the months of December, January, and February, the full moon in the Arctic circles continuously above the horizon for twenty-four hours a day for about five consecutive days a month.

After a long wait for sufficient snow to permit flying on skis, we reached Aklavik on November 23. This time we had brought along two long-wave radio direction-finding outfits to aid us in fixing our position while in flight. One we set up on the ice in the middle of the river opposite Aklavik, in the Canadian Arctic, and the other on the Alaskan coast, at Point Barrow, 600 miles to the west, at the most northerly point under the United States flag. Each station also was equipped to send and receive messages by short wave.

Barrow is the informal "capital" of Arctic Alaska, and since 1928, when Ben Eielson and I flew from there across the Arctic of Spitsbergen, the village had grown considerably. Barrow's leading citizen was still Charley Brower, called the "king of the Arctic." At Barrow we were able to complete our outfits of fur clothing, each man being supplied with two fur coats, two pairs of fur trousers, fur boots, socks, and mittens—all made to our measure by the Eskimo women.

While we were at Barrow, Al Cheesman heard by radio that he had been reelected alderman of his home town, Port Arthur, Ontario. He was required to swear a statement of acceptance of his office, and this he did before Charley Brower's son, the most northerly notary in North America. But later it developed that a newly elected alderman must attend the first meeting of the board. This, of course, he could not do, so a special act had to be passed by the Canadian Parliament to legalize his election.

We had hoped to be able to make our first winter flight during the December full-moon period, but this passed with continuous clouds and bad flying conditions. We spent a jolly Christmas, with the celebration lasting several days, each white family at Barrow entertaining the others in turn, so everyone had five or six Christmas dinners! Much snow fell, but we did not experience a single real blizzard during this unusual Arctice winter.

By January 12, 1938, the snow drifts at Point Barrow were so high that to take off with a maximum load would have been dangerous. So we decided to return to Aklavik, where the river ice would provide a smooth field. Then we found that the accumulation of salty hoarfrost had formed a solid coating of ice both inside and outside our plane. It was only with great difficulty that we were able to remove this ice, by tapping with hammers.

On January 16, with the moon at the full, the weather was forecast as clear, north as far as 80 degrees, with scattered clouds farther north. It was 44 degrees below zero when we started our moonlight flight. While we were warming up, our engines, belching fire from the two exhausts, made the machine look like a huge dragon. In fact, the hot air from the engines set up a fog that soon enveloped the whole village of Aklavik and it was necessary to taxi 2 miles down the river where the wind was across the runway before we could take off.

Snow crystals and high cumulus clouds dimmed the moonlight at the take-off, and we passed through clear and cloudy patches as we flew at altitudes varying from 2,000 to 4,000 feet. The maximum extent of good visibility was about 3 miles on either side of the plane.

Between cloud belts, when the atmosphere was clear, we could see quite well. Pressure ridges distinguished the rough ice from the smooth. The leads of open water—and there were many—

were conspicuous. But the shadows cast by huge lumps of ice, standing out distinctly, could well be mistaken for dark tents or other objects on the ice.

Later, after a long search, we turned back and ran into a hard granular snow that stung our faces as it blew through the open windows. For half an hour, we flew in this snow cloud which obstructed all visibility. The windows were kept open in flight, despite the extreme cold, because otherwise hoarfrost formed on them and prevented us from seeing. Winter flying, therefore, proved to have its own disadvantages.

Later in the winter we searched the northern Alaskan mountains. On March 3, we flew westward over the Richardson, Brooks and Endicott Mountains to 153 west longitude, then back, following the mountain range to Herschel Island, near the mouth of the Mackenzie, and back again to the Colville River, before returning to Aklavik. In all, we flew 1,300 miles east and west along the mountains in one day, without seeing a sign of the missing plane.

The next day the visibility was again perfect, so we flew on short northern and southern courses, covering the mountain ranges from Aklavik to longitude 152 west. We also made two long flights over the foothills, and southward over the mountains, covering a distance of 1,800 miles, and landed at the village of Old Crow, on the Porcupine River, to load some fuel cached there for us. Old Crow is reputed to be the coldest spot in Canada. It was 40 below the night we spent there.

These flights convinced us that the Russians had not crashed in the mountains, for the peaks were fairly clear of snow, and we felt we would have seen the wreckage had it been there.

Later in the month, we swept far out to sea, northward over the floes, but found nothing. In fact, we were impressed by how active the sea had been and how many leads and pools had already formed in it. We were hoping to make several more over-water flights before the season for using skis would end late in March, but upon our return from the last long flight, I received a telegram from Ambassador Troyanovsky of the U.S.S.R., informing me that the Soviet Government had decided to terminate further search from the Alaskan and Canadian coasts.

We flew to New York, arriving March 25. We were disappointed in not having succeeded in our mission. But our flights had proved the adequacy of standard aircraft for Arctic operation. Since August 19, 1937, we had actually spent 284 hours, 35 minutes in the air, covering approximately 44,400 miles. Of that mileage, some 34,000 miles had been flown north of the Arctic Circle.

Allowing for clear vision only 5 miles on either side of the plane, and only 50 per cent of our flying time in clear weather, we had actually observed about 170,000 square miles of the Arctic Ocean. Much of the area we had covered in winter, a season when it had never been seen before, and navigating by moonlight was also something new to the world of aeronautics. We had found that clear moonlight flight is not only possible but safe—whereas flight under a clouded moon is as difficult and dangerous as flying in and over clouds elsewhere.

Our efforts, instigated and supported financially by the U.S.S.R. government, and generously assisted by Vilhjalmur Stefansson and other members of the Explorers Club of New York, could not have been carried out without the cooperation of the governments of the United States, Canada, Norway, Sweden, and Denmark. For all of them furnished weather reports that helped Messrs. Beliakov, Vernon, and Thompson, the meteorologists at Fairbanks, to give us the excellent forecasts of conditions in the Arctic area. Neither could we have carried out our plans without the generous cooperation of the Canadian Airways, the Mackenzie Air Service, the Ethyl Corporation, and many private individuals, far too numerous to mention.

Indeed, as this last adventure in the Arctic drew to a close, and afterward, as I journey to Moscow to receive the official thanks for my work from Commissar Litvinov and other officials of the Soviet Government, I realized how many of my hopes and dreams of my early years had somehow touched me in the search for Levanevsky. I had flown thousands of miles—not in a rickety crate but in sturdy, powerful planes. We had not had one crash, but had flown for months in perfect safety.

Never had we been out of touch with the rest of the world, because our short-wave radio had kept us in contact with every development in the search at all times. We had not flown by guesswork into unknown weather conditions, because the meteorological resources of several governments were at our disposal hourly, and their science enabled us to save many precious hours and avoid needless risks.

In demonstrating the utility of international cooperation in mastering the secrets of nature for our purpose—a crew of two Australians, two Canadians, and an American, searching for six lost Russians—I like to think that we also demonstrated something of the fraternal spirit that binds together, across the barriers of nationalism, men of science and adventure throughout the world.

For to what higher goal, after all, can man aspire?

Hubert once told Mrs. Lowell Thomas that I didn't know the difference between the South Pole and the North Pole. I forgave him, and I don't think he really meant it, but it is fair to say that he didn't marry me because of my geographical knowledge.

Whenever someone asks me how I happened to meet Hubert, my mind goes back to a June day in 1928. I was on Broadway then— an Australian actress making good in the New York theater— when I received an invitation to take part in welcoming ceremonies for a couple of prominent aviators named Wilkins and Eielson.

When I asked my attorney why anyone would want me to meet these men, and what had they done, he inquired gently if I ever read the front page of the *New York Times*. He went on to say that Wilkins was an Australian explorer who had just made the first flight from Alaska to Europe, via the Arctic Ocean, and that I had been asked to welcome him because I was a fellow Australian. If I didn't want to, he said, there were doubtless other Australian girls around who would seize the opportunity.

I agreed to go with some misgivings, got up at the atrocious hour of 5 A.M., made a cup of tea, and dashed off to the Battery, where the *Macom*, a harbor tug, was waiting in the fresh morning air to which we of the theater are not accustomed. We went out to the *Stavangerfjord* and I went aboard with the Australian Consul, who gave me flowers to hand to Wilkins. I had been told all this was in the interest of Australian-American relations, but when the big moment came, the hero paid hardly any attention to me. Wilkins smiled, took my flowers, and, when the Consul mentioned casually

285

that I was an Australian too, said yes, he met them all over the world.

Mayor Jimmy Walker was reported late getting to City Hall for the official reception, so we cruised around the harbor in the press boat to kill time. A photographer suggested that Sir Hubert have his picture taken with me. When Wilkins' quiet manner caused the photographer to think he didn't care for the idea, he blurted out, "Come on, Aussie, 'ave your pitcher tyken!" Another Australian! We all laughed and the ice was broken.

After the ceremony at City Hall we proceeded by motorcade to the old Waldorf at Thirty-fourth Street. I was about to leave, when the Consul asked me to say good-by to the explorer. Sir Hubert said he was sorry I was not staying for lunch, and he had an official dinner that night or he would like me to dine with him. Without thinking how it might sound, I suggested that he telephone me at midnight. Hubert smiled faintly and asked what my number was. I hadn't mentioned that I was an actress and was rarely home before midnight, but someone lost no time in telling the explorer. Whatever the intention may have been in that, the information increased his interest, apparently. I learned later he had much musical and some theatrical knowledge, as well as some earlier ambition in those lines.

I wasn't sure he would telephone, but with the thought that he might, I went home after the theater, changed from my theater clothes, and sat waiting with some orchids I had bought for myself. On the stroke of twelve the Australian explorer called on the Australian actress. My famous compatriot whisked me off to the St. Regis, where we did what the song said—danced till three in the morning. He was a good dancer, too. I mentioned it, which pleased him, and I wondered when he had had time for the lighter side of life with all his adventures. Surely not in the Balkan War, I suggested, nor in the Arctic, the Great War, or the Antarctic. He beamed and seemed pleased to think I had found out this much about him. In reply he said he had brushed up by taking a lesson between the time he telephoned and the time he called for me.

After a few days in New York, Hubert left with Ben Eielson,

his pilot, for a lecture tour and a conference with the Lockheed
Aircraft officials. When he returned I was in another play, which
he saw and must have liked, because he invited me to supper—
and proposed to me. I said "Yes," and two days later saw him off
for Montevideo and the Antarctic.

Soon after I met him, Hubert gave me a copy of *Undiscovered
Australia,* his book about his explorations among the aborigines
in 1923–1925. He wrote on the flyleaf, "To a discovered Australian,
the lovely Suzanne, with love, GHW."

In reading what he had written, and in talking to him, I began
to feel that my explorer had a kind of insight into the future. In
fact, this was a little frightening at times. If he was that good, I
wanted him to let me know why he ought not to stay in New York
and "discover" me some more. He had no fear of the future, and
reassured me of that. "We'll still be married in thirty years," he
said. It turned out to be twenty-nine, but I won't quibble.

It was a short courtship, a longer engagement, and an enduring
marriage, all in spite of necessary career separations. I knew I'd
never be able to keep up with this man, but luckily this was not
required of me. But I did follow his movements on the map and
had mail from all over the world—all of which meant quite a
geography lesson, from an expert geographer.

Once I tried to break our engagement, but he wouldn't listen.
It happened when an old illness, rheumatic fever, attacked me.
Hubert had just returned from the Antarctic and gone to Friedrichshafen, Germany, when I was stricken. I sent word saying
that I might be a burden to him, and that the marriage should be
called off. The *Graf Zeppelin* had just broken down too, so Hubert
came back and saw me through my illness. We were married in
Cleveland—as you have already read—the day after he stepped
off the *Graf* after its round-the-world flight in 1929. Why Cleveland? Well, he wanted to see the National Air Races and he also
needed to pick up a tractor for his next expedition. Before a month
was out, he was off to the Antarctic. And so it went for thirty years
—hello, good-by, and hello again. But before the last good-by there
were many adventures and happy times.

Our honeymoon, delayed by Hubert's trip to the Antarctic,

turned out to be quite an adventure. We were all set to sail on the *Europa* with Bernard Shaw as our traveling companion, when at the last moment William Randolph Hearst called us and asked if we would write up the *Graf's* flight to Germany. Bernard Shaw forgave us our decision, and off we flew, each with one hastily packed suitcase.

It was a pleasant journey through a sort of fairyland up there above the ocean, where big steamers looked like toys in an enormous bathtub. Near the end of the journey, as we were passing over the Rhone Valley, a freak storm hit us and the airship went down like an elevator. Only a minute before, I had said to Dr. Hugo Eckener over coffee that there hadn't been any excitement. Suddenly, I was thrown across the room, followed by cream pitchers, coffee cups, and assorted tableware.

There were no atheists stepping down onto the ground that day in Friedrichshafen. After prayers of thanksgiving for a "safe" landing I went off to finish writing my version of the flight. But Hubert wouldn't let me send it. He said that nobody would ever fly in airships again if they read it. That was the only time he was ever angry with me!

Lincoln Ellsworth was on hand to meet us and take us to his castle in Lenzburg, Switzerland, for part of our honeymoon. I was eager to continue on the next day, but two young Germans had a home-made airplane and wanted Hubert to fly in it. He thought he'd rather like to try it, too. I insisted on going up with him. If anything went wrong I wanted to be with him. Early widowhood in a foreign country did not appeal to me.

We had six very happy weeks at Lenzburg, mountain climbing and taking long walks. In the wonderful air, I began to get my health back. Once, feeling energetic, I went off for a hike in the forest and was as lost as any explorer's wife has a right to be. They sent out a search party and found me at three in the morning. My husband took it all in his usual good humor, but I had fun with him years later when he got lost in Atlanta. He went into the wrong hotel and when the key didn't fit he sent for the manager to ask why they had changed his lock. The manager was already on his way, on complaint from a lady tenant who looked over the transom and said a sinister bearded man was trying to break into her room at midnight.

It was in Switzerland that I first heard of the *Nautilus*. Hubert sprang this on me when we made the return trip down from beautiful Mount Pilatus. I thought he seemed excited on the way up in the funicular, and no wonder with that view. But actually his mind was far away at the moment, and his eyes were seeing the ice and snow of the top of the world, not the white-capped mountains around us. It was evident I would have to accustom myself to sudden surprises and constant fear of what the future might hold for him, and me. Back home, our house in New York became like an engine room, with strange machinery and blueprints littered about the place, and Hubert would go to Connecticut for two or three days at a time to work with Simon Lake. Even though I never learned much about valves, double hulls, and the rest of it, my vocabulary could not help but grow. As the explorer's wife, I made quite an impression on outsiders when I referred casually to Hubert's "fathometer," and I soon found "oceanographical" to be another effective bit of conversational shrapnel.

In some of his leisure moments Hubert went down to see a sculptor friend of ours in Greenwich Village, Antonio Salemme. Antonio had always admired my husband's achievements and his simplicity of manner. The best way to talk with him, he thought, would be to do a head of him. So he invited Hubert to sit while he sculptured him, and tried to find what an explorer was like and what prompted one to take so many chances.

When Antonio asked Hubert if he was afraid he might never return from the unknown icy north, Wilkins merely smiled and said he was always afraid, but it was part of the business. Then his features resumed the characteristic calm that Salemme caught in the handsome bust he made. It can be seen now at the Mystic Seaport Museum, near New London, Connecticut. I like to go up and look at it occasionally. It seems so lifelike.

Nothing and nobody could hold this man down. He had a restless urge to move and act. Since I could not change this, I accepted it.

If my husband was away a lot of the time, there was a great compensation that brings me pleasure still. His letters! How wonderful they were. I have them from all over the world, and when he was unable to send letters, he sent cables and short-wave messages. They served to keep our romance alive and to let me know that he was glad he always had a home to come back to, if he "got back." He conditioned me to the possibility that he might not. I was supposed to accept it with perfect *sang-froid*. Hubert was indifferent to the thought of death. This was hardly conducive to a feeling of security on my part, and since he never "retired" from his active life, even in the later years when he was engaged in research projects for the United States Government, I spent much of my time in a state of suspense.

Probably because of his meticulous care in planning, and his indifference to what might happen to him personally if anything outside his own calculations went wrong, Hubert managed to survive all sorts of hazards. It was always a happy time for me when it was my turn to say "hello" and see him for a while till the next good-by. But the stories he casually narrated in between times made me dread the next departure more than ever.

It was only through the press that I learned that in June, 1940, while flying as a passenger with some French officers getting out of Paris a few hours ahead of the approaching Germans, he had been shot down by a Nazi fighter. When he got back that time, I put my foot down with some firmness.

Poor health prevented me sometimes from even seeing him off from his last civilized point of departure, whether it might be Norway or New Zealand. Also there were journeys I was to have made with him, such as the one to Rome in 1932 after General Balbo and the Italians had flown the Atlantic, and to Moscow in 1938, after he had flown the Arctic for months in search of Levanevsky and his party. I urged him to go alone to receive the honors those governments would accord him. The King of Italy sent me a friendly letter and a cigarette case. After Hubert's return from Moscow, when I asked him what it was like, he said in some ways it was rather better than 1923 when he was working there for the Quakers, during the famine. That now there was lots of caviar and vodka, but far too many photographs of Stalin. In fact, Stalin had sent me one that he fancied of himself, bordered in red linen. Since I felt that I had not helped in the search for the Russian fliers and didn't deserve the autographed picture at all, I used it as a marker in a book on how to invest in the stock market.

Even so, I believe I shared more trips with Hubert than I had to miss. For one thing, we went to Europe nearly every year, which gave me a chance to bask in the pleasure of being his wife, sitting at the captain's table, and everywhere meeting all sorts of fascinating personalities. Since Hubert couldn't stay still for long, we knocked about the Mediterranean together, and I saw what for me was a new part of the world. In Algeria, telling me the story of his abduction, he waved his hand casually. "It happened over that way." To Hubert, who had seen and done so much, the desert episode seemed far away and long ago.

Although my husband never took me on an expedition, in retrospect my life seems to have been one continuous travelogue. It's just that I never went to the North or South Pole, or to the jungle, or into the desert, with him. But he did take me to life's heights.

One exciting adventure we shared was the maiden voyage of the *Hindenburg*. This was several years after our flight aboard the *Graf*. On the older ship, we had traveled in the gondola; on the improved *Hindenburg*, we were right inside the "bag." There was a shower bath too, which I was the first to use—quite an event for that time. On the flight to New York they had me sing "I'm in the Mood for Love." It went out on the air and all over the world. So you see I had two unimportant "firsts," that broadcast from a Zeppelin and the shower in the sky. Hubert said he liked the song, but thought it a long way to go just for a shower! They let Hubert have a go at the controls. He knew his way around airships. But when a storm came up, I lost my enthusiasm and said never again. A year later, 1937, we were in London for the Coronation, trying to keep warm, feeding shillings into a

miserable gas heater, when Hubert told me that matters might
be worse for us—that the *Hindenburg* had just exploded at Lakehurst, one of the great tragedies of that period.

I returned to New York from Australia in 1939, before Hubert
returned from a trip to South Africa, and I had a surprise for him.
There was an old abandoned farm for sale that I'd heard of, miles
away from everything and everywhere, in a part of Pennsylvania
that resembled his home in Australia. I went up and bought it
after one look. Woodchucks and field mice were having a field
day in what was to become the living room. Windows didn't
exist, and you could see sunlight through the roof. But it was a
house on a hill and there was lots of water all around. It would
be an ideal place to store all of his treasures, books, odds and
ends of exploring equipment, and the Lord knows what else.

On his return Hubert took one look, nodded approval, and
went out and bought a station wagon; bright, new, and lovely. It
still goes after twenty-one years, and I'll never part with it.

We managed to get there on one of those sultry afternoons,
climbing the hill in the wagon comfortably, till we arrived at
our "private park," as we called it. He said nothing for a while,
but walked about with that funny grin of his. At the back of the
house I saw him inspecting a big blacksnake with intense interest.
If I'd seen that the first time I was there I'd have moved right
into the Plaza and never budged. He said calmly it was a good
thing, as there'd be no rattlers to look out for. *Rattlers* in Pennsylvania! It turns out there are quite a few, but not on our hill.

When he had looked around and satisfied himself, we engineered
a cup of tea, and sat there laughing like two dinkum Aussies over
a camp fire. That's about all there was to do for the moment. But
I saw that he was as content as he was amused, and was planning.
"It will cost about four thousand to fix it up," he said, "and it's
worth it." I was glad he was pleased, as there were perfectly nice
homes to be had that would have cost less, and no remodeling.

Though Hubert enjoyed roving, he liked coming home to the
house on the hill that we now called Walhalla, after the town in
which I was born in Australia. It was his private joke that, though

he was now an American resident, he was still in the "Common-wealth," since Pennsylvania was one of the four states enjoying that status.

Soon after his return from an extensive tour of the Far East in 1941, the phone began to ring constantly. What do you think about this? a voice would ask, or what's your idea about that? Finally I asked one such voice why, if they valued his opinion so much, they didn't stop picking his brains and give him a job instead. There was a pause and a hush, then the words, "That's not a bad idea." A week later Hubert was in Washington as a consultant with the Military Planning Division. When I asked him what he was up to he answered my question with another. "Can you keep a secret?" I nodded. "So can I." I never asked him anything again that might compromise him.

He was listed at various times as a liaison officer, expert, con-sultant, and various other things. Probably the title he cared for most was that of geographer. He never questioned his right to it, though I never heard him boast of it, either. He didn't think he was infallible, but on the contrary was fond of that office joke about "experts" being people who avoided small errors but rushed forward to make big ones. Since he was one of the few non-American citizens in the employ of the United States in wartime, he took every precaution not to make a mistake and no doubt saved others from making some. If so, he never talked of it or criticized anyone.

Anyone who knew him well will agree that he could be spartan, laconic, and—silent. Thanks to his hearing aid, which he wore in later years and which he would turn off if he was bored or felt he was hearing more than was good for his welfare, he could be totally deaf. This often had some funny results, as when he would hear vowel sounds but not get the sense at first of what was said. I once asked what he'd like for dinner, and his reply was that on the contrary he looked fatter than ever because of the Army food and not enough exercise. This, after telling me he'd been on a 50-mile snowshoe hike with a platoon of young men whom he'd raced back to the barracks. He won.

We were to have gone to live in Washington when it appeared his work would keep him there. But the crowded conditions, the fact that he was away from there in the field as much as he would be from New York, the fact that two men were fired because they had talkative wives, and that there were too many cocktail parties, your attendance at which might cause gossip and your absence from which might cause resentment, made him change his mind. And it was still a comfortable drive from Manhattan to the farm, which we could manage with gas rationing. We were there as often as circumstances permitted, where he would write lengthy reports, edit film, and keep his hand in generally with do-it-yourself projects. Our friend Winston Ross helped like a beaver on Hubert's painting and plumbing projects, and in time the house began to look more and more like a home, and the war might have been on another planet. We had kerosene lamps, music, and absolute peace. Hubert loved to play the little organ he had had on the *Nautilus*. It gave out an eerie sound in the country stillness.

Suddenly one night, Hubert told me that Mrs. Ross, who was visiting us with her son Winston, would die in two weeks. She complained of feeling tired, but I thought nothing of his remark, which he delivered like a weather bulletin, matter-of-factly. A week later she was in the hospital. We visited her there, and Hubert spoke a few words aside to her while I was with Winston. We never found out what passed between them, but I know she was very much at peace when Hubert left. She was home in a week to play her beloved Steinway for one last time, then died fifteen days after he had made his prophecy.

Hubert wrote Winston a letter that gives a clue to his own feelings about the great adventure we all must face:

> You have no doubt had a few trying days and I hope by now you're settling down to the inevitable. We seldom realize how much we would miss someone until they are gone. But the memory of your devotion to your mother you may cherish always. Parting for the moment is sad, but I believe the passing on from

this world to the next is—to the individual concerned—more pleasing than they expected, and although the immediate time is trying for those concerned, time will temper that.

I liked that letter then, and I like it now. I wish a letter like that had come to me when it was his turn. The tragic news came to me abruptly on a dismal winter morning, December 1, 1958. I had talked to him by phone on November 30, a few hours before it happened. He was in Natick, Massachusetts, doing work for the Quartermaster Research and Development Command. We talked about the Sunday *Herald Tribune,* which had an important section on Australia, and Hubert told me he would be home before Christmas.

There are those who will argue that a man never dies before his time. I disagree. Surely the world might have made use of a Keats or a Shelley a little longer. And Hubert, for his part, had lots of important work left to do.

Although he may have been disappointed that his old *Nautilus* never reached the North Pole, the success of the nuclear *Nautilus* was, for him, a final vindication—mixed with the regret that he wasn't younger. But he had had a full life; three score and ten packed with action and great achievement. He died seventy years young, with a slight smile on his lips.

Though he had a ready wit, I will always remember him for his spirituality, a quality that guided him through his life. It was evident when he prefaced his book *Flying the Arctic* with the words from Hebrews 11:1: "Now faith is the substance of things hoped for, the evidence of things not seen."

Perhaps the prayer he wrote for himself is his own best epitaph:

My Father, I beseech support in my desire to worship,
To enjoy privilege without abuse,
To have liberty without license,
To have power and refuse to use it for self-aggrandizement,
So that the experience of living will lead me and my fellows
To greater spiritual reality.

On December 4, at Framingham, Massachusetts, the Armed Services made Hubert's farewell a memorable occasion. My sadness later turned to pride when Commander James Calvert, in the nuclear submarine *Skate*, took his ashes to the North Pole, and scattered them there on March 17, 1959. Hubert had always been a free man and I wanted him free now. I recalled his words that an explorer is happy to be buried where he had his life. He never would have presumed to seek this honor for himself. But he would have liked it. And he got it, thanks to Colonel Eddie Eagan and his old friends of the Circumnavigators Club, and to Admiral F.B. Warder of the United States Navy. I shall always feel poor in my thanks.

Hubert, I might add, had more than a touch of the poet. He liked to read aloud. This is one he liked, and so do I, since it seems to express all the qualities that I loved the most in him.

> Not twice may any stand by the same stream,
> Not twice possess the years that hasten on;
> Something there was we looked on, loved, 'tis gone
> Or stays but as the shadow of a dream.
>
> Hands that we touched clasp ours no more, and eyes
> That shone for us as stars withdrew their light;
> Voices beloved pass out into the night;
> The gift of yesterday, today denies.
>
> Yet must we hold it for a deeper truth,
> Nothing that is, but only that which seems
> Shall find its dwelling in the place of dreams;
> The soul's possession is eternal youth.
>
> Swift flows the stream, but in it as it flows
> The same unchanging stars are mirrored bright.
> Swift fly the years, but heedless of their flight
> The touch of time, nor love nor friendship knows.

About the Author

Born in Woodington, Ohio, in 1892, the son of a colonel in the Army Medical Corps, Lowell Thomas was educated at the University of Northern Indiana, the University of Denver, and Princeton. Having tried his hand as a gold miner and cowpuncher, he began his writing career as a newspaper reporter and editor. For two years, 1912–14, he was a member of the faculty at Chicago Kent College of Law; the following two years, at Princeton University, a graduate student in Constitutional Law, and an English instructor. In World War I he was attached as a correspondent with all the Allied Armies, was the first newsman to report the German Revolution of 1918, and President Wilson appointed him chief of a civilian mission to prepare a historical record of the war. After writing his tremendously successful books about T. E. Lawrence and Count Luckner, *The First World Flight*, and others, he began, in 1930, his career as radio news commentator; in no time his voice and personality made him a national institution. For nearly twenty years he also was the voice of Fox Movietone, and scores of full-length films. Also, in 1939, he was the first commentator with a news program on TV. During World War II he broadcast from Europe, China, India, the Philippines, and Iwo Jima. He has been on some twelve expeditions since World War II. The first of these, in 1949, was the historic journey he and his son made to Tibet. He also brought Cinerama out of the laboratory, and in so doing started the entire "wide-screen era" in motion pictures. Today, he balances the talents of author, commentator, world traveler, and motion-picture producer.